Cartographies of Madrid

HISPANIC ISSUES • VOLUME 43

Cartographies of Madrid:
Contesting Urban Space
at the Crossroads of the
Global South and Global North

Silvia Bermúdez and Anthony L. Geist

EDITORS

Vanderbilt University Press

NASHVILLE, TENNESSEE

2019

The editors gratefully acknowledge assistance
from the College of Liberal Arts and the
Department of Spanish and Portuguese Studies
at the University of Minnesota and from the
Department of Spanish and Portuguese
at the University of Iowa.

*A complete list of volumes in the
Hispanic Issues series follows the index.*

Library of Congress Cataloging-in-Publication Data
LC control number 2017060915
LC classification number DP357 C287 2018
Dewey classificatin number 946/.41—dc23
LC record available at *lccn.loc.gov/2017060915*

ISBN 978-0-8265-2214-6 (hardcover)
ISBN 978-0-8265-2215-3 (paperback)
ISBN 978-0-8265-2216-0 (ebook)

Contents

◆ INTRODUCTION

Madrid as a Capital of the Global South and the Global North: Mapping Competing Cartographies and Spatial Resistance

Silvia Bermúdez and Anthony L. Geist

This volume investigates the ways that capital—political, cultural, and economic—has been both exalted and challenged in Madrid, Spain's capital city, from the decades preceding the end of the Franco dictatorship (1939–1975) to the present. One of our goals is to evaluate the complex and contradictory ways in which Madrid serves as the political, economic, and cultural capital of the Global South, understood as "a concept-metaphor that reterritorializes global space in the interests of repossession by the dispossessed" (Sparke 117). At the same time, we examine how the city functions as a "northern" metropolis within the circuit of the Global North and its pockets of extreme wealth, neoliberal policies, and the impulse of globally connected financial institutions (Trefzer, Jackson, McKee, and Dellinger 1–15). We also understand the city as *lived experience*, where urban space is defined by "human beings in constant flux creating places for work and idleness" (Ugarte "Madrid," 95) and by the argument advanced in Joan Ramon Resina's reading of Martín Santos's *Tiempo de silencio* (1961) that "[i]f Madrid conveys the essence of national life, it does so not through the grandiloquence of power but in the recesses of private life" (74).

It is within these parameters that the lived experience of becoming a *madrileño* was exalted, and then mocked, in a particularly successful subgenre of Spanish cinema of the 1960s, that of *paleto* movies, "comedies of backward rural immigrants in the city" (Richardson, *Postmodern "Paletos"* 21). Madrid as a conflicted lived experience will be at also at the heart of the writings and publications of many of the artists and intellectuals who began to arrive from

Equatorial Guinea in the 1960s as well. First in pockets, to either further their education or to become members of the clergy, and then massively in exile, as a result of Francisco Macías Nguema's brutal dictatorship (1968–1979) immediately after Equatorial Guinea gained independence from Spain on October 12, 1968, and the even more violent regime of his successor, Teodoro Obiang Nguema (1979-present) (see among others; Ndongo-Bidyogo, *Historia y tragedia*; Liniger-Goumaz; Bolekia Boleká; Martin-Márquez; Lewis; Ugarte, *Africans in Europe*). The arrival of exiled Equatoguineans prefigures that of other 1970s political exiles from South America and those from migrant newcomers from Sub-Saharan Africa since the 1980s (de Vicente 1993). It is in light of these and other migratory developments—from the Maghreb, from the Caribbean, and other parts of the globe later—that we contend that, in the time frame we are evaluating, from the late 1960s to 2017, internal and external migrations transformed Madrid into one of the capitals of the Global South (see, among others, Marcu 2011 for Romanian immigration to Madrid; Cassain 2016 for Argentinean immigration to nation's capital).

In assessing internal urban migration, *paleto* movies such as *La ciudad no es para mí* (The city is not for me, 1965) and *Abuelo "made in Spain"* (Grandfather "made in Spain," 1969), both directed by Pedro Lazaga (1918–1979), underscored that the massive movement from mostly rural areas of Andalusia, Castile, Aragon, and Extremadura to the city was an important factor in the mapping and shaping of Madrid's cityscapes. The rural-to-urban migrations were driven first by the economic promises of the stabilization plan (1959), followed by further development plans set in motion by the Opus Dei technocrats who began to dominate Franco's political machine in the last decades of his regime. These plans effectively accelerated industrialization, hastening the integration of the nation into a global economy led by the United States. Three forms of capital—international investments, tourist spending, and remittances from Spaniards working abroad—"poured in during the 1960s and early 1970s" (Richardson, *Constructing Spain* 9; see also Powell 25). This economic growth during "the years of plenty" (1959–1974) attested to the fact that, in that period, "*Spaniards had not become simply capitalists. Spaniards had become urban*" (Richardson, *Constructing Spain* 10, our emphasis). Poised at the intersection where "capitalists" and "urban" meet, 1960s and mid-1970s Madrid foreshadows the city's transformation into a capital of the Global North at the turn of the twenty-first century during massive speculative urbanization. Between 1996 and 2007, for instance, Spanish property prices tripled in comparison to those of the United Kingdom (Knight).

Madrid's transformation into a capital of the Global South requires consideration, among other processes discussed later in this Introduction, of the complex historical events connecting Spain to some of its former colonies when, first, exiled Equatoguineans and then thousands of Argentinean and Chileans, all fleeing from violent dictatorships, began to arrive to Madrid and other Spanish cities. Massive transnational migration increased in the 1980s when Spain officially joined what was then known as the European Economic Community (EEC) on January 1986, a few months after having signed and enacted, on July 1985, one of the toughest immigration laws in all of Europe at that time: the "Ley Orgánica sobre derechos y libertades de los extranjeros en España" (Organic Law of Rights and Liberties of Foreigners in Spain). Two Equatoguinean authors, residing in Madrid for decades now, Francisco Zamora Loboch (1948) and Donato Ndongo-Bidyogo (1950), offer powerful instances of Madrid as lived experience while advancing postcolonial responses to the restrictive effects of the 1985 law, to racism, and to fetishization, in works such as Zamora Loboch's poem "El prisionero de la Gran Vía" (The prisoner of Gran Via)—first published in Donato Ndongo's 1984 *Antología de la literatura guineana*—and Ndongo-Bidyogo's authoritative *El metro* (2007), providing "not only an antidote to the apparent silence of immigrant voices in the mainstream of Spanish thought but also an interrogation of [the] very notion of authenticity [presented by Spanish news media and other outlets]" (Ugarte, *Africans in Europe* 77).[1]

Before all of this transpired, however, urbanization processes had the Franco regime using space as a weapon in the aftermath of the Civil War. On the one hand, this further humiliated the defeated—as in the towering basilica of the Valle de los Caídos (Valley of the Fallen) a few kilometers from El Escorial—attesting to the literal and metaphorical will for empire building (Crumbaugh). On the other, the nation's landscape of ruins was exploited to honor the victors with monuments and statues erected throughout Spain, featuring effigies of the dictator, as ruler supreme, populating countless churches and plazas. By the time the economic promises of the years of plenty materialized, the nation's capital, now more than ever the forceful center of political, cultural, and economic power, had already been remodeled, rebuilt, and renamed as part of the ideological reconstruction that drove Francoism. Avenues, boulevards, parks, and city streets posted names such Avenida del Generalísimo (Generalissimo Avenue, currently Paseo de la Castellana) and Avenida José Antonio Primo de Rivera (today Gran Vía, returning to its original name), to mention two of the many fascist figures who came to define Madrid with their names. A caveat is in order in regard to "ideological reconstruction" since, contrary to what is usually assumed, the dictatorship's ideas about a national regeneration, "akin to those of

Italian Fascism, were gradually abandoned, and anti-communism remained the only unifying sentiment" (Alonso de Val 58).[2] A testament to this particular literal and symbolic reconstruction is found in the buildings of the Nuevos Ministerios (New Ministries), whose construction began during the Second Republic in 1933 with a design by architect Secundino Zuazo Ugalde (1887–1971), taking inspiration from none other than El Escorial. The Civil War halted the construction, and Zuazo, fleeing persecution, went into exile in France. The Nuevos Ministerios were completed in the immediate postwar years, in 1942, by a group of architects loyal to the Franco regime. They eliminated and changed important aspects of the original design, beginning with the replacement of brick by granite in its construction.

Corroborating Joan Ramon Resina's reading of Madrid as a palimpsest, the Nuevos Ministerios and their integration into the business complex, AZCA (Asociación Mixta de Compensación de la Manzana A de la Zona Comercial de la Avenida del Generalísimo [Mixed Compensation Association of Block A of the Commercial Zone of Generalissimo Avenue]), tell one chapter of Madrid's intricate urban history over the past eighty years. The reference to Generalissimo Avenue reflects that it was part of the 1946 Plan General de Ordenación Urbana de Madrid (General Urban Plan of Madrid), while the site was marketed in 2016 as "the financial center of the capital of Spain" ("Azca: La zona de negocios").[3] The Nuevos Ministerios and Azca emblematize how capitalism generates a particular experience of the city where, as David Harvey argues, "[t]he social spaces of distraction and display [become] as vital to urban culture as the spaces of working and living," and where "[s]ocial competition with respect to life-style and command over space [becomes] more and more important within the mass culture of urbanization, sometimes even masking the role of community in processes of class reproduction" (234). In his concluding essay, Edward Baker contextualizes Madrid's asymmetries as state capital and city within a broader historical framework that begins in 1561, when Philip II moved the court from Toledo to Madrid, and looks at its present and future in the figure of Manuela Carmena (1944), Madrid's mayor since June 2015.

The ten essays included in this volume trace the intersections drawn and redrawn in Spain's capital city not only by capital but also, more importantly, by the "myth of an endless flow of capital" (Labrador Méndez 274). Understanding Madrid in the context of this myth helps us discuss the diverse and often contradictory mappings by which the Global South and the Global North "coexist in the same geographic space," since our understanding of these two paradigms subverts notions that identify them "as interdependent yet geographically separate" (Trefzer, Jackson, McKee, and Dellinger 4). With regard to the articulations of the mythology of "an endless flow of capital," we argue that one such myth was established during the economic boom period (1959–1974) set in motion by the development plans mentioned above. A massive rural exodus moved 3.8 million people to the cities between 1951 and 1970 (Schubert 210). This economic success saw Madrid's population grow by two million inhabitants between 1960 and 1975 (Riquer i Permanyer 263). *Cartographies of Madrid: Contesting Urban Space at the Crossroads of the Global South and Global North* constitutes a natural continuation of the groundbreaking study edited by Edward Baker and Malcolm Compitello, *Madrid, de* Fortunata *a la M-40: Un siglo de cultura urbana* (2003) (Madrid, from *Fortunata* to the M-40: a century of urban culture), in which *Fortunata* refers to the narrative treatment of Madrid in Benito Pérez Galdos's canonical novel *Fortunata y Jacinta* (*Fortunata and Jacinta*) (1887), and the M-40 to the circular beltway that rings Madrid with some of the heaviest traffic in the country. To explore how Madrid delineates two competing cartographies, our volume is organized in three sections: Part 1: "Capitalizing on Visual and Literary Cultures and Challenging Urban Exclusion"; Part 2: "Sites of Memory"; and Part 3: "Madrid as Lived Experience."

We begin in the 1960s by calling attention to the already mentioned film *La ciudad no es para mí*, directed by Lazaga, written by Fernando Lázaro Carreter (1923–2004), and starring famed comedic actor Paco Martínez Soria (1902–1982) in the central role, and where we are ironically presented with an incessantly prosperous city that, while appearing to enjoy an "endless flow of capital," also shows an inability to cope with such uneven expansion and growth.[4] Indeed, from the opening shots of *La ciudad no es para mí*, when the audience finds itself positioned in the driver's seat of a car speeding through Madrid's cityscape, an agitated voice-over offers the following data for the sequence of rapidly changing images:

Madrid, capital de España. 2,647,253 habitantes. Crecimiento vegetativo 129 personas cada día; población flotante, 360,580 personas. 472,527 vehículos; 110,853 baches y socavones. Un nacimiento cada 45 segundos. Dos bodas y media por hora. Y una defunción cada minuto y medio; y bancos, muchos bancos. . . . Y supermercados, muchísimos supermercados. Y casas, casas en construcción, montañas de casas en construcción. Y farmacias, toneladas de farmacias. Y zona azul, kilómetros de zona azul; y multas, demasiadas multas. Esta es una ciudad donde todo hay que hacerlo muy de prisa.[5]

(Madrid, capital of Spain. 2,647,253 inhabitants. Growth, 129 inhabitants per day; floating population, 360,580. 472,527 vehicles; 110,853 potholes. One birth every

45 seconds. Two and a half weddings every hour. And one death every minute and a half. And banks, lots of banks. . . . And supermarkets, lots and lots of supermarkets. And houses, houses under construction, mountains of houses under construction. And pharmacies, tons of pharmacies. And blue zone, kilometers of blue zone; and parking tickets, too many parking tickets. This is a city where everything's got to be done in a hurry.)

The obsession with "doing things in hurry" underscored in this charting of 1960s Madrid foreshadows that of the 1970s, when, after the death of the dictator in 1975, the capital city, along with the entire Spanish nation, moved rapidly to complete the transition to democracy. If spatial anxieties were already at work by 1973, when, having been hit by the global recession of that time, the Spanish economy came to standstill, political and social anxiety also came to define the years of the Transition.

The pace of change was dizzying: in 1977, Spaniards lived through the first democratic elections since 1936, then the enactment of the 1978 Constitution, the failed military coup of February 23, 1981 (23-F), and the electoral victory of Felipe González's Spanish Socialist Workers' Party (PSOE) in the 1982 general elections. In response to the deluge of transformative historical events, much of the younger generations of madrileños and madrileñas "decided to commit themselves to fashion, the visual and graphic arts, and to new wave pop and hard rock" during the Movida years (Bermúdez 9).[6] In the opening essay to the section "Capitalizing on Visual and Literary Cultures and Challenging Urban Exclusion," Anthony L. Geist addresses this particular cultural scene by mapping how Madriz—a magazine published between January 1984 and February 1987, funded by the Youth Council of the Madrid city government under Madrid's favorite mayor, Enrique Tierno Galván, whose administration lasted ten years (1976–1986)—reflected and constructed the image of Spain's capital as Europe's hippest postmodern city of the late twentieth century. It was in the 1980s, then, that cultural productions such as Madriz articulated and circulated the image of the city as a capital of the Global North, a hotbed of fashion and award-winning designs within what Guillem Martínez calls "la Cultura de la Transición" (Culture of the Transition)—which, by failing to question the neoliberal approach promoted by the technocrats of late Francoism and by agreeing to consensus and a Pact of Silence (consenso, Pacto de Silencio), ended-up fostering consumerism, individualism, and depoliticization (2012). It is within these neoliberal paradigms of the 1980s that the Global South legally materializes within "the emergence of new logics of expulsion" (Sassen) with the enactment of the 1985 Immigration Law during Felipe González's first administration (1982–1986).

Our cartographies invite you to also remember that the PSOE's arrival to power in 1982 meant the implementation of widespread changes that comprehensively reshaped the nation.[7] One such focal innovation in Madrid's cityscape was the renovation of the Atocha train station—site of the March 11, 2004 train bombings, over which the Monument of Tribute to the Victims of 11-M has stood since 2007.[8] In her incisive contribution in the section "Sites of Memory," Jill Robbins brings the issue of capital to bear on the emotionally charged spatial responses to the bombings by calling attention to how working-class neighborhoods—stations along the Atocha line also affected by the bombs, such as Santa Eugenia and El Pozo del Tío Raimundo—voiced their sorrow while reclaiming a place in the discourses on the traumatic event.

It is not irrelevant that El Pozo del Tío Raimundo is a neighborhood that was home to immigrant workers since, as already stated, internal and external migrations are central to our understanding of Madrid as one of the capitals of the Global South. We contend that the enactment of the 1985 Immigration Law was one of the most significant markers of Spain's transformation into a capital of the Global South. By making a tough position on immigration relevant to Spain's acceptance into the European Economic Community (EEC)—known since the 1993 ratification of the Maastricht Treaty as the European Union (EU)—Felipe González's PSOE inadvertently inscribed Spain within the Global South. In so doing, he placed the capital city at the center of engagement with the marginalized populations of the world, "with those alternately bypassed by capital flows, the 'new wretched of the earth,' in Mike Davis's phrase, or recruited into modes of labor over which the workers retain no organizational control and for wages which exclude them from the practices of consumption through which social and (increasingly) civic entitlements are secured" (Cherniavsky 77). The June 1985 signing of the treaty to join the then ECC, making Spain part of the Global North, was a driving force behind the PSOE-led Congress's passage, only a month later, in July 1985 of what has become known as the "Ley de Extranjería" (Immigration Law) (Bermúdez 11). Along with Portugal, Spain joined the ECC on January 1, 1986, during Felipe González's second term as prime minister (1986–1989).

The Global North is also present in how capital flows were at work in the rampant speculation that assailed the city of Madrid in newly democratic Spain. What was transpiring with Lavapiés in the Embajadores neighborhood—the collusion of the financial and construction sectors with the nation's legal and political systems to redraw spatial relations to enrich a few—prompted young protestors known as *okupas* to combat the city's market-oriented production of housing with the rallying cry of "Kontra la Especulación, Okupación" (Against Speculation, [Squatters'] Occupation).[9] We argue that it is from an understanding of the city as lived experience, and within the premises of the Global South, that the *okupas* deployed spatial resistance to combat the spatial logic of neoliberalization, of Madrid as capital of the Global North. Spatial resistance is also at work in the grassroots organizations that had thousands upon thousands of women traveling, mostly by train, to congregate in Madrid to defend the Abortion Act passed by the Socialist government under José Luis Rodríguez Zapatero (2004–2011). In "Madrid as Lived Experience," Alicia Luna's piece on the 2014 arrival of the Tren de la Libertad in the capital city describes the role played by scores of women filmmakers, screenwriters and camera-women in the documentation of this fundamental victory for Spanish women's rights and feminist groups, women's associations, and all those who supported their cause.

At the intersections where the Global South and the Global North meet, our volume also focuses on the diverse array of grassroots movements originating in Madrid that have arisen since the 1980s and 1990s in opposition to capital's drive to reconfigure urban space for profit and name-branding to favor the few instead of the many. In the twenty-first century, one such contestatory instance can be found in the October 2008 response of the neighborhood group Asamblea Ciudadana del Barrio de Universidad (ACiBU; Citizens' Assembly of the Universidad Neighborhood) to the gentrification processes launched a year earlier in a private initiative known as the TriBall project that sought to transform the Ballesta Triangle—bordered by the streets Gran Vía, Fuencarral, and Corredera Baja de San Pablo—in the lower southeastern corner of the Universidad neighborhood, also known as Maravillas neighborhood, one of the six that constitute the Centro district. The ACiBU's campaign underscored community over branding by asserting "Maravillas, Somos un Barrio, Mucho Más que una Marca" (Maravillas, We Are a Neighborhood, Much More than a Brand) (Vilaseca 12–19).

In the section of *Cartographies of Madrid* titled "Capitalizing on Visual and Literary Cultures and Challenging Urban Exclusion," both Malcolm Compitello and Jonathan Snyder offer incisive analyses of the insurgent "acts of citizenship" (Isin 367; Janoschka 101–10) arising from the 15-M/*indignados* movements which, starting with the occupation of the Puerta del Sol in May 2011, articulated a new political response to the post-political city. Eli Evans and Susan Larson, in their respective readings of Juan José Millás's 2007 novel *El mundo* (The world) and Elvira Navarro's 2014 *La trabajadora* (The female worker), also turn their attention to the contestation of capital in all shapes and forms within the paradigms born out of the 15-M movements. In connection with these four essays, we underscore how a particular spatial location in Madrid, the Puerta del Sol, the symbolic heart of the Spanish state as the Kilómetro Cero (Kilometer Zero), the point of departure of the Spanish radial road and highway system, further cements Madrid as a capital of the Global South and the Global North simultaneously. On the one hand, in 2011 the Puerta del Sol and Kilometer Zero also became ground zero for the 15-M and *indignados* protests. On the other hand, and as per the contract signed between the regional government of Madrid and Vodafone—the British multinational telecommunications company—the Sol metro station, whose entrance is right at the square, was branded Vodafone Sol for the duration of the advertising deal (2013–2016)—a bargain, considering that the government of Madrid received just three million euros over three years. Very much a Global North enterprise in its appropriation of the local—and the political and cultural significance of the 15-M movements of 2011 that resemanticized the Puerta del Sol—by a global corporation at a bargain price, the deal reveals the complex negotiation dynamics that place Spain's city capital at the crossroads of the Global South and North.

All of these processes present Madrid as an emblematic case study for assessing not only the shifting nature of the Global North but also the contestatory practices that define the Global South, as several distinct implosions of capital have given rise to diverse grassroots movements in Madrid throughout the past decades: the *okupas* in the 1990s, the *indignados* and the May 15 movement (known as 15-M) in 2011. Contestation is also in place in the challenge to the two-party political system presented by the emergence of the new party Podemos (We Can) in early 2014.[10] Podemos was one of the forces behind the successful run of the coalition Ahora Madrid (Now Madrid) in the Madrid municipal elections of June 2015, suffering a setback in the June 2016 runoff for the inconclusive December 2015 general elections. Rosa M. Tristán's commentary, the closing essay in the "Madrid as Lived Experience" section, employs her journalistic expertise to analyse these elections. In his contribution to the section "Sites of Memory" Scott Boehm assesses the difficulties encountered by the Madrid city government that won the 2015 municipal elections in attempting to implement the 2007 Law of Historical Memory. The effort to execute Article 15, which mandates the removal of all public symbols that glorify the 1936 military coup, the Spanish Civil War, and repression under the dictatorship, has met with much resistance from conservative circles and, most vehemently, from the Partido Popular. It is in the interstices of these complex crossings that, having established Madrid as a capital of the Global North, we further delineate, in the section below, some of the practices and historical events that transformed Madrid from an urban milieu into a capital of the Global South in the span of six decades.

Madrid's Journey to Capital of the Global South through Migration and the Reappropiation of Public Space

To outline this journey we focus on two groups of transnational migrant new-comers, both with postcolonial ties to the capital city, arriving in the 1950s and the 1960s, respectively. In the first case we have the temporary presence of Cuban exiles—in transition to the United States—during the thawing of relations between the Franco regime and the United States that began with the bill signed by President Truman in September 1950 appropriating 62.5 million dollars for aid to Spain. It culminated with President Dwight D. Eisenhower's visit to the Spanish capital in 1959, during which the two generals, Franco and Eisenhower toured the city together.[11] In the second case, we have the presence of Equato-guinean exiles beginning in the mid-sixties. Both attest to migration's impact on the profound economic and social changes that were transforming Madrid into a modern city.

At the intersection of migration and the mobilization of social forces, Madrid has become one of the capitals of the Global South, which, as Alfred J. López declares in the preface launching the journal *The Global South* in 2007, "[is] a place that is less a place (or even an alignment of/among places), than a condition, and perhaps an orientation" (v). The notions of "condition" and "orientation" are already suggested in Arif Dirlik's 1996 reflections explaining how the "Global South" surfaced as an offshoot of the category of the "Third World," specifically as a north–south distinction that has gradually taken over from the earlier division of the globe into three worlds—so long as we remember that the references to north and south are not merely to concrete geographical locations, but are instead metaphorical: north denoting the pathways of transnational capital, and south the marginalized populations of the world, regardless of their actual location (31).

Moreover, and to differentiate the Global South from postcolonial and colonial discourse studies, Alfred J. López further explains that the metaphorical reference that is the Global South "is best glimpsed at those moments where globalization as a hegemonic discourse stumbles, where the latter experiences a crisis or setback" (3). At the time of the publication of the first issue of *The Global South* in 2007, examples of such setbacks included the 1997–98 Asian,

Russian, and Brazilian economic crises; the 1998–2002 Argentine Great Depression; the end of the United States market boom in 2000; the terrorist attack on the World Trade Center on September 11, 2001; and the implosion of Enron in 2001 resulting from massive scams born out of individual and collective greed in an environment of capitalist euphoria and corporate arrogance. Little did the journal know then that an even more devastating global setback loomed on the horizon with the 2008–2009 global economic meltdown that in the United States took the form of a banking and housing collapse that almost destroyed the economic system.[12] In the case of Spain, the nation lived under what it was called "la crisis" from 2008 to 2017, a financial downturn that took almost a decade to overcome and that made Spain, and in particular its capital, Madrid, the place and space where globalization "experience[d] a crisis or setback" (3). We first turn our attention to how, in the 1980s, Madrid was imagined and promoted as Europe's youth capital, the center of fashion, music, and culture, a metropolis of the Global North foreshadowing its role as a locus point for capital investment—until the crash of the property bubble—between 1996 and 2007. We then examine how the crisis was experienced at the individual and social levels by calling attention to the 15-M phenomenon and its commitment to reappropriating and resignifying public space and politics (Moreno-Caballud).

Anthony L. Geist's essay opens the section "Capitalizing on Visual and Literary Cultures and Challenging Urban Exclusion," underlining the ways Madrid was redrawn as Europe's youth capital in *Madriz*, a comic book art magazine sponsored by the Concejalía de la Juventud (Youth Council) of the Madrid city government. He maps out the role played by this form of cultural production, an important vehicle for expression for La Movida Madrileña, Spain's youth movement that made Madrid the cultural capital of Europe and the continent's hippest city for a brief period in the mid-1980s. *Madriz* gave expression to the Movida in *tebeos*, comics drawn by many young artists, many of whom would go on to become well known in their field. It played a key role in the identity formation of post-Franco Spain by depicting the new street culture in graphical form, giving back an image of the new Spaniards. *Madriz* not only reflected an emerging identity but also, in a complex dialectic, helped create and shape that identity as well.

To address the marginalization of populations and those excluded from the flow of capital, Malcolm Compitello argues that the events of 2011 brought people to the streets in Madrid who coalesced around a common desire to protest the abuses of what David Harvey in *Rebel Cities* has labeled "feral capitalism" (115–65). This experience made evident in Spain, as it had in other countries, both the power and the limits of popular resistance. A geometrically expanding body of scholarship highlights the role of cultural production in these acts of resistance known as the 15-M and the *indignados* and what parts of them eventually morphed into. Compitello's essay provides a contextualization of the recent past in relationship to earlier acts of resistance—such as the *okupas* movement—and the evolution of the urban process in Madrid. As such, it underscores the acutely important role of cultural creation in acts of resistance to capital's attempts to remake space, and by extension social relationships, in its own image and for its own benefit.

In his reflections, Jonathan Snyder calls attention to how the 15-M mass demonstrations reappropriated and resignified space (Sampedro and Sánchez, 2011) to accommodate the protesters standing *within* and *in opposition to* the existing capital flows and regulatory policies of the city. Although the protesters' reshaping of the city may be precarious, forever on the shore of its own disappearance, to paraphrase Jacques Rancière (39), what persists when demonstrators no longer occupy the square are the oppositional practices of protesters who *read* their common subjugation critically and, in the process, make the sources of domination *legible* as a collective circumstance, with material consequences. Snyder argues that protesters read and denounce the processes of gentrification and privatization in the urban landscape, the rhetoric on austerity circulating in the media by government officials and policy makers, and the precarious conditions of work-life in everyday experience, among other discourses. He revisits Ross Chambers's scholarship on narrative opposition in *Room for Maneuver* (1991) to examine the knowledges and practices of reading—or an "oppositional literacy"—by 15-M protesters in Madrid, capable of articulating desirable change.

The narrative treatment of Madrid is assessed by both Eli Evans and Susan Larson who focus, respectively, on novels by Juan José Millás and Elvira Navarro, both cited above, as bookends to the pre- and post-moments of the May 15 movements. In his analysis of Millás's *El mundo* (2007), Evans argues that the novel can be read as both anticipating the looming crisis of (the) Spanish capital and hinting, by way of a narrative closure atypical of Millás's work, at one potential response to that crisis, as a jumping-off point for proposing a utopian municipal politics as an effective counterforce to the excesses and inequities of urban neoliberalization in Madrid. Evans makes the case that Madrid is uniquely suited to such a politics for two reasons: first, because despite the well-documented failures of his administration, the myth of Enrique Tierno Galván (the "old professor"), himself an avowed utopian, provides the rhetorical and symbolic material from which to construct a contemporary utopian politics; and second, because what Joan Ramon Resina describes as Madrid's "irregular origin" (including the fact that, because it was not really a city before it became a capital, as a city it is not historically indexed to any particular identity) provides the rhetorical and symbolic material with which to safeguard a renewed local utopianism against the exclusionary temptations to which such politics too often succumb. Noting the conspicuous echoes of the "old professor" in Madrid's current mayor, Manuela Carmena, Eli Evans concludes with a call to recuperate not just the colorful man-of-the-people personality of Tierno Galván but also the political will to—borrowing the turn of phrase employed by the Tierno Galván administration to describe the primary objective of its 1985 Plan General de Ordenación Urbana—"acabar Madrid" (finish [building] Madrid).

The section closes with Larson's reading of Elvira Navarro's *La trabajadora* and her argument that this novel directly confronts the human cost of austerity measures in Spain by addressing the indignation and frustration experienced by those whose life plans have been destroyed by economic instability and labor precariousness. Specific attention is paid to the predominance of references to garbage, trash, waste, and detritus of all kinds in works of urban social criticism. In these works, garbage and recycling appear as recurring themes but also function at a conceptual level and propose an aesthetic all their own. *La trabajadora* is a direct response to the material conditions of the city and serves as a prime example of art that envisions the reuse and repurposing of refuse within the urban space that it occupies. It is a novel that suggests that there are viable alternatives to the accumulation strategy of debt-driven financial capital, or at least that we human beings can inhabit the cracks and abandoned areas left behind by what has been experienced as a failure of the neoliberal project by many of Madrid's inhabitants.

"Sites of Memory," the second section of this volume, brings to the fore Madrid's cityscape—its streets, avenues, squares, and monuments—and the historical and emotional impact that inheres in them. It is within these coordinates that Jill Robbins evaluates official as well as grassroots responses to the March 11, 2004, terrorist attacks at the Atocha train station to expose the distance that separates official sites of cultural heritage from the memory sites of the working class, all of them erected along the metro line affected by the bombs. By focusing on the responses of the working class, Robbins underscores how capital also impacted the affective relationship people wanted to establish with their memories and in memory of those they lost. For his part, Scott Boehm investigates the memory traces of the Spanish Civil War and the Franco dictatorship on the cityscape of Madrid in the context of the first attempt by a Madrid city government to implement the 2007 Law of Historical Memory. Article 15 of that law calls for the removal of public symbols that glorify the 1936 military coup, the

Spanish Civil War, and repression under the dictatorship. Shortly after the historic 2015 municipal elections brought Ahora Madrid (Now Madrid) to power in Madrid, the municipal team announced its intention to comply with the law, as it had clearly articulated in its campaign platform, a decision that provoked widespread opposition within conservative sectors of Madrid and outright hostility from the Partido Popular. This chapter explores the initial phase of what has become an ongoing controversy with no end in sight, taking it as a critical moment of cultural rupture that has the potential to transform the city and reshape the underlying values that organize public space in Madrid. The desire to establish a more communal conception of urban space and politics is consistent with the *municipalista* roots of several prominent members of Ahora Madrid, a sentiment widely shared by the new city government. As this essay illustrates, however, while such a political ethos has emerged in Madrid since the May 25, 2015 elections, it continues to face significant resistance from the dominant ideology of the Transition, one of the major forces that has shaped the Madrid cityscape into what it is today.

The last section, "Madrid as Lived Experience," brings together the personal account of journalist Rosa M. Tristán and that of award-winning screenwriter and filmmaker Alicia Luna, who furthers the connection between the private and public spheres in her personal commentary on the collaborative project that filmed the documentary *Yo decido. El Tren de la Libertad.* Rosa Tristán's piece offers a detailed account of the momentous occasion of the Madrid municipal elections of June 2015. Taking on the radical significance of the election of the emeritus judge of the Spanish Supreme Court Manuela Carmena (1944–) as mayor of Madrid in June 2015, the section closes with Edward Baker's incisive "Historical Perspectives: From Madrid as *Villa y Corte* to *After Carmena, What?*" bringing *Cartographies of Madrid* full circle by tracing with remarkable clarity the historical context within which the events analyzed in the ten essays that comprise this volume must be inscribed for the fullest understanding. Beginning with the late 1960s and the internal migrations that have reshaped Madrid up to the present day, the contributions necessarily focus on contemporary concerns and events: from the migratory processes that delineated Madrid as a capital of the Global South to the cultural articulations of Transition-era and post-crisis Madrid to the 15-M and the *indignados'* occupation of the capital's iconic Puerta del Sol; from the aesthetics of garbage and the inscription and reinscription of public and private monuments to the making of a documentary by a collective of women filmmakers and a detailed account of the decisive Madrid municipal elections of May 2015. Yet they all acquire a fuller meaning and impact when read through the historical lens that Baker outlines in his contribution.

The relationship between city and state, *villa y corte*, has been fraught since Phillip II made Madrid Spain's capital in the sixteenth century. This struggle has involved the mapping and remapping of public space and redefining the symbolic center of the city from the Plaza Mayor to the Puerta de Sol. Understanding the asymmetry of this relationship through Baker's historical analysis casts a new light on the contestation of urban space that has turned Kilometer Zero into ground zero. This spot is not just the hub from which all the major national highways radiate to the periphery; it is also a crossroads of the Global North and Global South. The true nature of Madrid lies not in one or the other of those trajectories, but precisely in the interstices of their complex crossing.

No one can foresee the future, but it is our hope that the essays in *Cartographies of Madrid* will help those interested in the different mappings of the capital—political, social, and cultural—better understand how Madrid has come to be what it is in the second decade of the twenty-first century and what its configurations may look like in the years to come.

NOTES

1. Ndongo-Bidyogo was first sent by his family to Valencia in 1965 to complete his secondary education. In the 1970s he moved to Madrid, serving many years as the director of the residence hall Nuestra Señora de África near the Universidad Complutense de Madrid. The author's hopeful return to Equatorial Guinea in 1985 as director of the Hispano-Guinean Cultural Center in Malabo was crushed when he was forced to leave his country under duress, definitely returning to Spain in 1994 (Ugarte, *Africans in Europe* 59-60). Zamora Loboch left Equatorial Guinea to pursue a college degree in the metropolis in the early 1970s, and since then resides in Madrid. The poem "Prisionero de la Gran Vía," first published in 1984 in the *Antología de la literatura guineana*, is referenced here to Zamora Loboch's 2008 *Desde El Viyil y otras crónicas* 39 (From El Viyil and other chronicles). Las Hijas del Sol, the Equatoguinean aunt and niece duo of Paloma Loribó and Piruchi Apo, fled their nation sometime after representing Equatorial Guinea in the 1992 Seville Expo. Residing in Madrid, in 1995 they released their debut album, *Sibèba*, sung entirely in Bubi except for one song in Spanish, "Tirso de Molina," a rendition of "A ba'ele" (The foreigners), in reference to the Metro station named after the famed Baroque playwright. Las Hijas del Sol's songs "offer a gendered understanding of the social process of migration and show the manners in which ethnicity, class, and gender intersect" (Bermúdez 112).
2. The symbolic importance of monuments in the development of a national architec-

ture in consonance with the objectives and ideals of the Franco regime was high-lighted in the "Manifiesto de Madrid" published immediately after the end of the Civil War. The proposed model was El Escorial.

3. Madrid's Web Oficial de Turismo (Official Tourism Web) briefly narrates the architectural history of the AZCA grouping in the section titled "Azca: La zona de negocios," after unabashedly promoting the location as a shoppers' paradise: "Considerado el centro financiero de la capital de España, Azca agrupa a algunos de los más importantes edificios y rascacielos de Madrid y reúne una actividad profesional y comercial de un alto ritmo diario. Restaurantes y cafeterías, tiendas de moda y complementos, así como centros comerciales marcan la vida de este complejo" (Considered the financial center of the capital of Spain, Azca comprises some of Madrid's most important buildings and skyscrapers, which house bustling professional and commercial activity. Restaurants and cafés, boutiques offering clothing and accessories, and shopping centers define the life of this complex.)

4. According to Jorge Pérez, the film "attracted more than 4 million spectators to the movie theaters (4,296,281), and generated 440,348.38 €" (22, note 12).

5. Paid parking areas throughout the city are often bordered by blue stripes and are therefore known as "blue zones."

6. For more on La Movida, see, among others, Pérez-Sánchez (2007) and Nichols and Song (2014).

7. The transition to democracy included a much-decried Pact of Silence (Pacto de Silencio)—which will be at the heart of the demands of those calling for justice for the Republican side, as enacted in the Law of Historical Memory, and the assault on the Parliament on February 23, 1981 (23 F), by Lieutenant-Colonel Antonio Tejero.

8. Tragedy also struck the area near the Atocha train station in what is now known as the 1977 Massacre of Atocha that took place on January 24, 1977, in the midst of the Transición. The attack was carried out by the Alianza Apostólica Anticomunista (The Apostolic Anticommunist Alliance, also identified as AAA or Triple A) against the law offices of members of Comisiones Obreras (CCOO, the Workers' Commissions trade union), located at 55 Atocha Street. The attack left five dead and four injured.

9. Embajadores is part of Madrid's District 1, Centro and is one of the 128 *barrios* (neighborhoods) that constitute the capital city of Madrid. The administrative division has the city divided into 21 *distritos* (districts), which are further subdivided into the 128 neighborhoods. The *barrio* Maravillas is also part of District 1, Centro, officially identified as Universidad, but also known as Malasaña. For its part Aluche, central to the novel *La trabajadora*, and Madrid's most populous and most diverse neighborhood belongs to the Latina district and is named after the creek, a tributary of the Manzanares River that used to run through it.

10. To fulfill an election promise, the conservative Partido Popular (Popular Party [PP]) proposed tightening the existing laws by making abortion illegal except in the case of rape or when there was risk to the mother's physical and mental health. The massive protests held in cities across the nation and Europe, which brought thousands of

women and their supporters to Madrid via the Tren de la Libertad, forced the resignation of Justice Minister Alberto Ruiz-Gallardón.

11. Central to the Eisenhower visit was the Pact of Madrid, signed in 1953 shortly after the Concordat with the Vatican. Three separate but interdependent agreements constitute the Pact, stipulating mutual defense, military aid to Spain, and the construction of United States bases in Spanish territory.

12. The US banking collapse has received much filmic and literary attention; see, among others, Chris Smith's documentary *Collapse* (2009); Andrew Ross Sorkin's book *Too Big to Fail: The Inside Story of How Wall Street and Washington Fought to Save the Financial System and Themselves*, published in 2009 and adapted as a movie by HBO Films (2011), directed by Curtis Hanson; and Charles Ferguson's documentary *Inside Job* (2010). In the case of Spain, we have, among others, the foreshadowing 2002 film *Los lunes al sol* (Mondays in the sun), directed by Fernando León de Aranoa; *Vidas pequeñas* (2010) (Downsized lives), directed by Enrique Gabriel; and *Cinco metros cuadrados* (2011) (Five square meters), directed by Max Lemcke. Among the documentaries are *Indignados* (2011), written and directed by Antoni Verdaguer; *Mercados de futuro* (2011) (Future markets), directed by Mercedes Álvarez and written by Arturo Redín and Álvarez; and *En tierra extraña* (2014) (In a foreign land), written and directed by Icíar Bollaín.

WORKS CITED

Alonso del Val, Miguel. "Spanish Architecture 1939–1958: Continuity and Diversity." *Architectural Association School of Architecture* 17 (1989): 58–63. Print.

"Azca: la zona de negocios." *esmadrid.com*. N.d. Web. 12 Sept. 2016.

Bermúdez, Silvia. *Rocking the Boat: Migration and Race in Contemporary Spanish Music*. Toronto: University of Toronto Press, 2018. Print.

Bolekia Boleká, Justo. *Aproximación a la historia de Guinea Ecuatorial*. Salamanca: Amarú, 2003. Print.

Cassain, Laura. "Migration Trajectories and Return Processes: An Exploration of Multi-generational Family Experiences between Spain and Argentina." *Transnational Social Review* 6:1-2 (2016): 41-59. Print.

Chambers, Ross. *Room for Maneuver: Reading (the) Oppositional (in) Narrative*. Chicago: University of Chicago Press, 1991. Print.

Cherniavsky, Eva. "The Romance of the Subaltern in the Twilight of Citizenship." *The Global South*. 1.1–2 (2007): 75–83. Print.

Crumbaugh, Justin. "Afterlife and Bare Life: The Valley of the Fallen as a Paradigm of Government." *Journal of Spanish Cultural Studies* 12.4 (2011): 419–38. Print.

de Riquer i Permanyer, Borja. "Social and Economic Change in a Climate of Political Immobilism." *Spanish Cultural Studies: An Introduction*. Eds. Helen Graham and Jo Labanyi. Oxford and New York: Oxford University Press, 1995. 259-70. Print.

de Vicente, Juan. "Los inmigrantes negroafricanos en la CAM." *Inmigrantes extranjeros en Madrid*. Coordinator Carlos Giménez Romero. Madrid: Comunidad de Madrid, 1993. 251–336. Print.

Dirlik, Arif. "The Global in the Local." *Global/Local: Cultural Production and the Transnational Imagination*. Eds. Rob Wilson and Wimal Dissanayake. Durham, NC: Duke University Press, 1996. 21–45. Print.

Harvey, David. *The Urban Experience*. Baltimore: John Hopkins University Press, 1989. Print.

_____. *Rebel Cities: From the Right to the City to the Urban Revolution*. London: Verso, 2012. Print.

Isin, Engin F. "Theorizing Acts of Citizenship." *Acts of Citizenship*. Eds. Engin F. Isin and Greg M. Nielsen. London: Zed Books, 2008. 15–43. Print.

Janoschka, Michael. "Politics, Citizenship and Disobedience in the City of Crisis: A Critical Analysis of Contemporary Housing Struggles in Madrid." *Journal of the Geographical Society of Berlin* 146.2–3 (2015): 100–112. Print.

Knight, Laurence. "Spanish Economy: What Is to Blame for Its Problems?" *BBC.com*. 18 May 2012. Web. 14 Jan. 2017.

Labrador Méndez, Germán. "Regarding the Spain of Others: Sociopolitical Framing of New Literatures/Cultures in Democratic Spain." *New Spain, New Literatures*. Eds. Luis Martín-Estudillo and Nicholas Spadaccini. Hispanic Issues 37. Nashville: Vanderbilt University Press, 2010. 261–76. Print.

Lewis, Marvin A. *An Introduction to the Literature of Equatorial Guinea: Between Colonialism and Dictatorship*. Columbia, MO: Missouri University, 2007. Print.

Linigier-Goumaz, Max. *Small is Not Always Beautiful: The Story of Equatorial Guinea*. Trans. John Wood. Towota, N.J.: Barnes and Noble, 1989. Print.

López, Alfred J. "Introduction: The (Post)global South." *The Global South* 1.1 (2007): 1–11. Print.

_____. "Preface and Acknowledgements." *The Global South* 1.1 (2007): v–vi. Print.

Marcu, Silvia. "Romanian Migration to the Community of Madrid (Spain): Patterns of Mobility and Return." *International Journal of Population Research* (2011): 1-13. http://dx.doi.org/10.1155/2011/258646.

Martin-Márquez, Susan. *Disorientations: Spanish Colonialism in Africa and the Performance of Identity*. New Haven, CT: Yale University Press, 2008. Print.

Martínez, Guillem, ed. *CT o la Cultura de la Transición: Crítica a 35 años de cultura española*. Barcelona: Debolsillo, 2012. Print.

Moreno-Caballud, Luis. *Cultures of Anyone: Studies on Cultural Democratization in the Spanish Neoliberal Crisis*. Liverpool: Liverpool University Press, 2015. Print.

Ndongo-Bidyogo, Donato. *Historia y tragedia de Guinea Ecuatorial*. Madrid: Cambio 16, 1977. Print.

_____. *Antología de la literatura guineana*. Madrid: Editora Nacional, 1984. Print.

_____. *El metro*. Barcelona: El Cobre. 2007. Print.

Nichols, William J., and H. Rosi Song. *Toward a Cultural Archive of La Movida: Back to the Future*. Madison, NJ: Fairleigh Dickinson University Press, 2014. Print.

Pérez, Jorge. "'¡Hay que motorizarse!': Mobility, Modernity, and National Identity in Pedro Lazaga's *Sor Citroen*." *Arizona Journal of Hispanic Cultural Studies* 11 (2007): 7–24. Print.

Pérez-Sánchez, Gema. *Queer Transitions in Contemporary Spanish Culture: From Franco to La Movida*. Albany: State University of New York Press, 2007. Print.

Powell, Charles. *España en democracia, 1975–2000*. Barcelona: Plaza & Janes, 2001. Print.

Resina, Joan Ramon. "Madrid's Palimpsest: Reading the Capital against the Grain." *Iberian Cities*. Ed. Joan Ramon Resina. Hispanic Issues 24. New York: Routledge, 2001. 56–92. Print.

Rancière, Jacques. *Dissensus: On Politics and Aesthetics*. Trans. and ed. Steven Corcoran. London: Continuum, 2010. Print.

Richardson, Nathan E. *Constructing Spain: The Re-imagination of Space and Place in Fiction and Film, 1953–2003*. Lewisburg, PA: Bucknell University Press, 2012. Print.

_____. *Postmodern "Paletos": Immigration, Democracy, and Globalization in Spanish Narrative and Film, 1950–2000*. Lewisburg, PA: Bucknell University Press, 2002. Print.

Sampedro Blanco, Víctor F., and José Manuel Sánchez Duarte. "La Red era la plaza." Ciberdemocracia. 2011. Web. 14 July 2014.

Sassen, Saskia. *Expulsion: Brutality and Complexity in the Global Economy*. Cambridge, MA: Harvard University Press, 2014. Print.

Schubert, Adrian. *A Social History of Modern Spain*. London: Unwin Hyman, 1990. Print.

Sparke, Matthew. "Everywhere but Always Somewhere: Critical Geographies of the Global South." *The Global South* 1.1–2 (2007): 117–26. Print.

Trefzer, Annette, Jeffrey T. Jackson, Kathryn McKee, and Kirsten Dellinger. "Introduction: The Global South and/in the Global North: Interdisciplinary Investigations." *The Global South* 8.2 (2014): 1–15. Print.

Ugarte, Michael. "Madrid: From 'Años de Hambre' to Years of Desire." *Iberian Cities*. Ed. Joan Ramon Resina. Hispanic Issues 24. New York: Routledge, 2001. 93–121. Print.

_____. *Africans in Europe: The Culture of Exile and Emigration from Equatorial Guinea to Spain*. Urbana and Chicago: University of Illinois Press, 2010.

Vilaseca, Stephen Luis. "The TriBall Case: 'Okupación Creativa ¡Ya!' vs. Okupa Hacktivismo." *Arizona Journal of Hispanic Cultural Studies* 14 (2010): 11–30. Print.

Zamora Loboch, Francisco. "El prisionero de la Gran Vía." *Desde El Viyil y otras crónicas*. Madrid: SIAL Ediciones, 2008. 39. Print.

PART I

*Capitalizing on Visual and Literary Cultures,
and Challenging Urban Exclusion*

FIGURE 1 Javier de Juan,
advertising poster for *Madriz* (1983).

CHAPTER 1

"*Madriz* es mucho Madrid": The Capital Role of Graphic Arts in Identity Formation

Anthony L. Geist

Looking back from today, a decade and a half into the twenty-first century, when Spain is mired in the worst economic crisis since the 1930s, with official unemployment figures standing around 25 percent and half the population between the ages of 18 and 35 never having held their first job, when young Spaniards by the thousands are leaving the country in search of work . . . looking back from today, it is hard to remember or imagine that a scant 30 years ago the country experienced a cultural explosion. I think it's not by chance that this extraordinary cultural production coincided with an unprecedented economic boom under Felipe González's regime.

The Movida Madrileña, Spain's youth movement that made Madrid the cultural capital of Europe and its hippest city for a brief period in the mid-1980s, took place less than a decade after the death of Francisco Franco and that country's return to democracy in the wake of his thirty-seven-year dictatorship. It can be argued that Franco, the longest-lasting fascist dictator from the 1930s in Europe, had outlived his time. Beginning in the 1960s, with the influx of tourism and tourist dollars, Spain's economy became increasingly service oriented. Industrialists, traditionally among the regime's strongest supporters, began pressuring for greater political liberalization because they wanted access to the European Common Market.

At the same time, the European and American youth culture of sex, drugs, and rock and roll began to erode Spain's cultural isolation. The presence of *suecas*[1] on the Mediterranean beaches had a profound effect, not just on Spanish men but on Spanish women as well. One example is the "guerra de los bikinis" (war of the bikinis) that took place in Zaragoza in 1970, which Agustín Sánchez Vidal recounts in *Sol y sombra*. On that occasion a policeman ordered a woman to cover her bikini-clad body at a public pool. The next day hundreds of women appeared in bikinis, and the municipal ordinance was changed.

Contemporary historian Santos Juliá has remarked on the sudden transformation of Spanish society following the death of the dictator. A friend wrote me from Madrid at the time that the first and most visible change was the appearance in newsstands, from one day to the next, of "revistas de culo y teta" (magazines featuring naked women).

Spain went from being a pre-democratic, pre-industrial, and only partially modern country to a democratic, postindustrial, postmodern nation virtually overnight. By postmodern I don't mean a particular cultural style or constellation of styles, or the so-called "end of Ideology" trumpeted by Fukuyama and George H. W. Bush in the wake of the collapse of the Soviet Union. Rather, as Jameson (310) characterizes it, we can understand postmodernism as a "cultural dominant" that is neither monolithic nor hegemonic. It is the space where the contradictions of late capitalism (what Ernest Mandel identifies as the "third stage") are played out. In this regard, it is different from what Lyotard calls the "postmodern condition," distinguished by a crisis of knowledge. In a sense, postmodernism consists of the theorization of its own conditions of possibility in the enumeration of epistemological shifts and changes. Modernism also theorized the new, with the hope of giving birth to new worlds. But postmodernism registers the breaks, the unrelenting changes in systems of representation.

According to Jameson, the adjective *modern* gives rise to three nouns, closely related but clearly delimited: *modernism*, *modernization*, and *modernity*. *Modernization* refers to the particular stage of technological and industrial development of capitalist societies in the first decades of the twentieth century, while modernism is its cultural and aesthetic inflection. Modernity, then, is the awareness of the relationship between the first two terms, and their unequal development, the fact of which is more significant than any specific content. And it is precisely the distance between these two extremes that opens the space of modernity.

If you will allow me an analogy, just as Russia was the last place Marx would have predicted the Communist revolution to break out, Spain seemed an unlikely venue for the explosion of pomo culture that was the Movida. It can be argued that Spain's move from premodern to postmodern in the last decades of the twentieth century is key to identity formation—personal, generational, urban, national, cultural, aesthetic, and ideological—and recalls Habermas's concept of modernity as an incomplete project. The articulation of this recuperation of the project of modernity is particularly complex and fascinating in the realm of culture, both "high" and "low" (including the interrogation of this very binary).

The Spanish Civil War and its brutal aftermath sundered the country's project of modernity. Franco's control of the state apparatuses of production and reproduction during the nearly four decades of the dictatorship not only set the parameters of official discourse but also determined to a large extent the discourse of the opposition. This was as true in the realm of culture as it was in politics.

Juan Goytisolo refers to Franco as the "Monstrous Father of all Spaniards," a father who had to be killed. In many senses Franco *was* the metanarrative for 40 years, emitting, producing, and reproducing a master narrative. The end of the dictatorship and the return to democracy also meant the end of that narrative and created a vacuum of cultural power, rendering both official and oppositional discourses virtually meaningless. The response was a proliferation of different, often contradictory and competing, cultural expressions in music, literature, the arts, and popular culture vying to fill that vacuum. This unprecedented freedom of discourse was simultaneously dizzying and productive on the one hand and confusing on the other.

One of the most fascinating and productive phenomena to arise in the interstices of the complex crossing of these different cultural responses was the Movida. This bar and music scene was centered around the Plaza Dos de Mayo and the Plaza Santa Ana/Barrio de las Letras in Madrid, and brought together *posmodernos* and *punquis*, hippies and yuppies, squatters and students in a heady mix fueled by music, alcohol and sex, drugs and rock and roll. The soundtrack of the Movida was Alaska y los Pegamoides, Radio Futura, and later Joaquín Sabina. The scene found expression in cinema in the early films of Almodóvar (think of *Pepi, Luci, Bom y otras chicas del montón*). In the vortex of these different forces a new, postmodern discourse emerged.

Few cultural artifacts capture the look and feel of the explosion of culture released from the bonds of the dictatorship that was the Movida better than *Madriz*, a magazine devoted to comics and sponsored by the Youth Council of the Madrid city government under the leadership of El Viejo Profesor (the old professor), Mayor Enrique Tierno Galván (Fig. 1). *Madriz* published thirty-three issues between January 1984 and February 1987 and gave expression to the Movida in *tebeos*, or comics, drawn by a number of young artists, many of whom would later go on to become well known in the field.

In a nation struggling with the legacy of Antonio Machado's Two Spains ("Españolito que vienes / al mundo te guarde Dios. / Una de las dos Españas /

ha de helarte el corazón" [Little Spaniard coming / to the world, God save you. / One of the two Spains / will freeze your heart]), I particularly like the cartoon by OPS (Andrés Rábago, better known today as El Roto) depicting Heraclitus going home (Fig. 2). You will recall that the Greek philosopher believed that the world is in constant flux. This drawing alludes to his assertion that you cannot set foot in the same river twice. Not only is the cartoon funny—Heraclitus looks down at the river as he crosses the bridge and finally flees when he realizes it's different from one moment to the next—but we can also take it as a metaphor for the profound changes taking place in Spanish society. *Madriz* played a key role in the identity formation of post-Franco Spain by depicting graphically the new street culture, sending back an image of the new Spaniards who rejected both of the old Spains.

The comic book art published in *Madriz* is part, consciously or not, of a larger project to recover lost or never-fulfilled modernity. But it is modernity revisited from postmodernity, or modernism literally redrawn from a postmodern sensibility and aesthetic. *Madriz* was aware of its postmodern condition. In an introductory note to the second issue, the philosopher Ludolfo Paramio puts it this way:

> A mi edad, por supuesto, no me pretendo posmoderno cuando me consta haber fracasado históricamente—como este país, dicho sea con perdón—en el intento de llegar a ser moderno. Pero creo que podríamos pasarlo mejor en este clima de fragmentación y múltiples referencias que en el viejo y asfixiante monoteísmo cultural que reinaba, en el poder y en la oposición, durante los recientes años de prehistoria. Hemos renunciado a la totalización y a la trascendencia. A cambio, podremos leer buenos tebeos y oír la música que nos guste. A ver si dura. (3)

> (At my age, of course, I don't pretend to be postmodern when I am aware of having failed historically—like this country, I'm sorry to say—in the attempt to become modern. But I believe we can have more fun in this climate of fragmentation and multiple references than in the old, asphyxiating cultural monotheism that reigned, in those in power and in the opposition, during the recent years of prehistory. We have given up on totalization and transcendence. On the other hand, we can read good comics and listen to the music we like. Let's see if it lasts.)

Look, for instance, at the "Poema del suburbio" (Fig. 3). It begins with a stanza from a tango written by El Negro Celedonio, a poet and singer from turn-

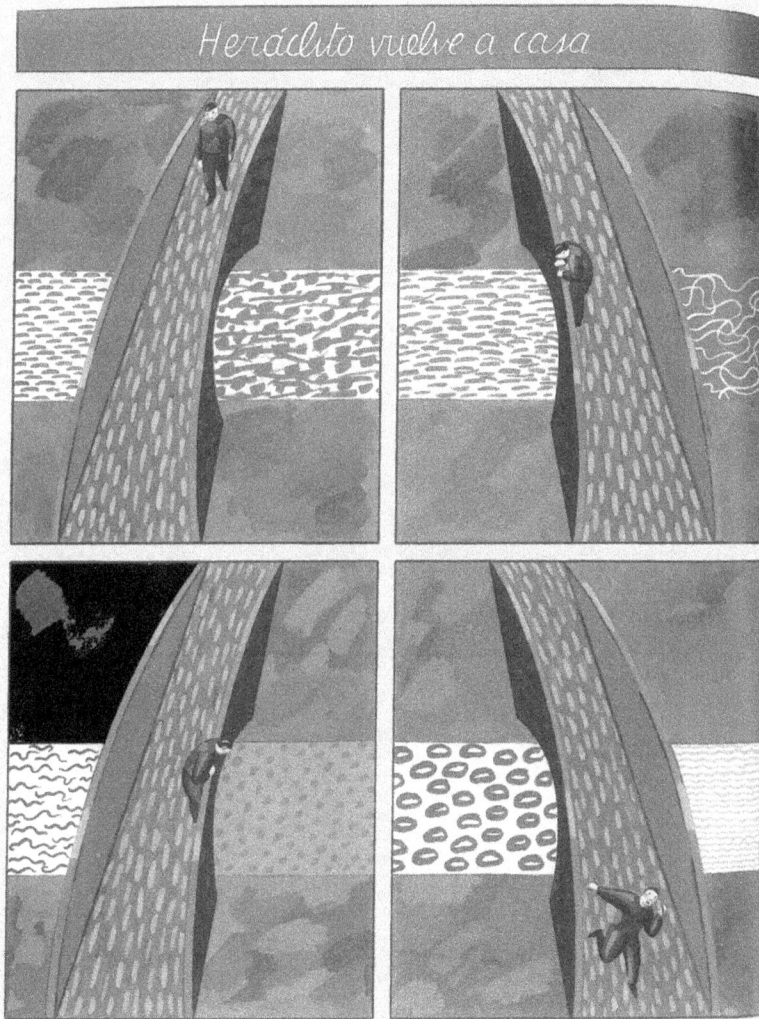

FIGURE 2 OPS, "Heraclitus goes home."
Madriz 18–19 (July–Aug. 1985): 82.

of-the-century Buenos Aires: "Yo no le canto al perfumado nardo / ni al conste-
lado azul del firmamento, / Yo busco en el suburbio sentimiento. / Pa' cantarle
a una flor, le canto al cardo" (38) (I do not sing to the perfumed spikenard / nor
to the blue constellation of the firmament, / I look for feeling in the bohemian
quarter. / If I want to sing to a flower, I'll sing to the thistle).

If we understand *suburbio* in the *porteño* sense of *barrio bajo*, home to bo-

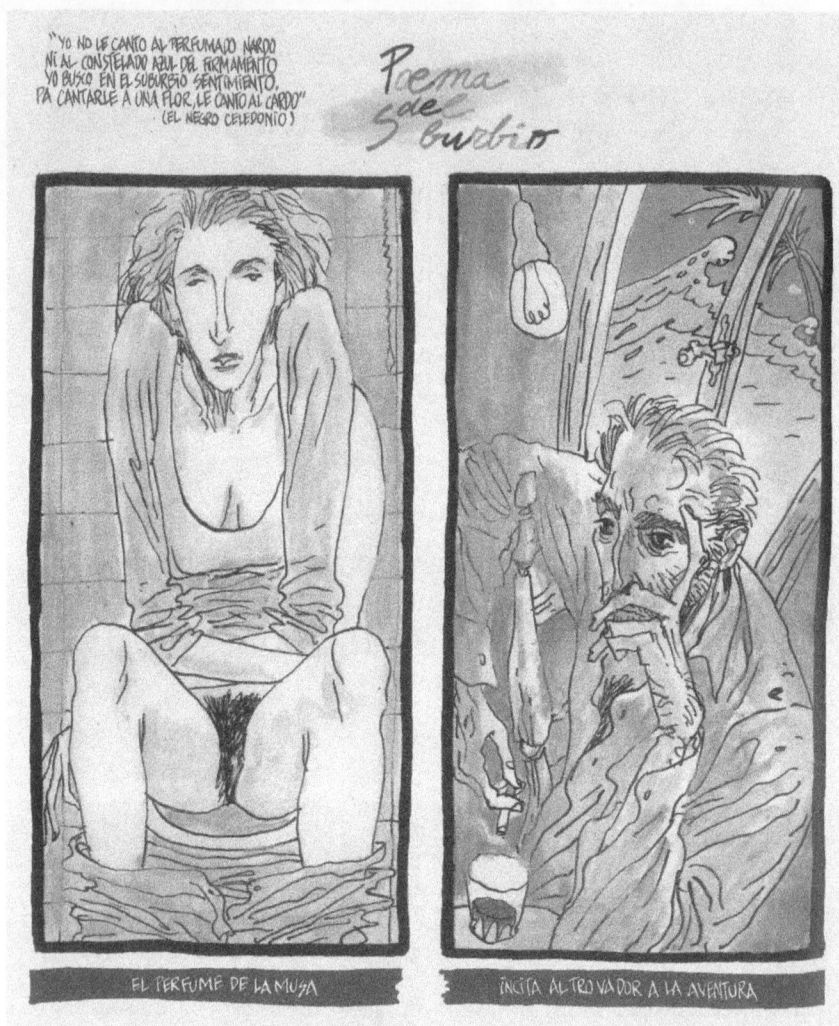

FIGURE 3 F. del Barrio, "Poem of the Bohemian Quarter."
Madriz 27 (May 1986): 38.

hemians, poets, artists, and their groupies, this gives us a context to read the drawing. In the panel on the left we see a woman on the toilet, with an inscription beneath: "El perfume de la Musa" (The perfume of the Muse). On the right a poet sits, dreaming of tropical seas, also with an inscription: "Incita al trovador a la aventura" (Incites the troubadour to adventure). The juxtaposition of two seemingly unrelated portraits are linked ironically by the syntax of the captions, which echo the tango lyrics and between them frame the drawing conceptually.

Throughout its three-year run, numerous artists reinscribe a number of different themes and topics, from the rescripting of Greek mythology that we see in Javier de Juan's "Mitología para todos" (Mythology for everyone), in which Apollo, dressed in flamenco garb, approaches Vulcan's forge, where the workers are wearing the classic Spanish overalls, the *mono azul*. Either Apollo has come, the text tells us, to talk about a girl they're both pursuing on Mt. Olympus, or Jupiter has sent him to complain about the multicolored lightning bolts Vulcan is forging (48–49). Other comics also revisit Spanish history in the legendary figure of the *bandido* Luis Candelas or in the Dos de Mayo, the popular revolt against the French on May 2, 1808; only one vignette in the entire collection addresses the Spanish Civil War, and the Franco years are notable for their absence. In a postmodern pastiche, literature is often woven into the comics, from Lorca to Pessoa, the *Carmina Burana* to Edgar Allen Poe and Borges, including even a seventeenth-century Japanese haiku (Jordi Girben, 44–45).

In a complex dialectical two-step, *Madriz* both mirrors an emerging image of postdictatorial Spain and simultaneously helps create and shape that identity as well. Simply put: "This is what we look like, and this is what we should look like," creating and projecting ideal images to aspire to. Look, for example, at Javier de Juan's "Pequeño compendio de gentes vistas en la inauguración de una feria de arte, o sea 'Arco 84'" (Fig. 4) (Little compendium of people seen at the opening of an art fair—that is, "Arco 84"). They range from a "Neomoderno de camisa hagüallana (o como sea)" (Neomodern wearing a Hawaiian shirt [or whatever]) to "Pálidas y sofisticadas niñas de negro (glamur) (de estas había muchas)" (Pale and sophisticated girls dressed in black [glamour] [there were a lot of them]) and other types: "Matahembras en plan chulín" (Ladykillers strutting their stuff), "y señoras" (and ladies), "y embajadores" (and ambassadors), and finally "Punkos ingleses y transvanguardias italianos y esto es todo" (English punks and Italian transvanguards and that's all). In a kind of postmodern sleight of hand, the sequence—Uno, Dos, Tres, Cuatro (One, Two, Three, Four)—suggests a narrative structure. Yet the narration itself is not sequential; it goes nowhere. It simply ends: "y eso es todo" (and that's all). The crowd that LPO depicts at the Barón Rojo heavy metal concert in the centerfold, called "Zentrales," gives a vibrant representation of the Movida youth, in black leather jackets and with long hair (18–19).

The poster for the Semana de la Juventud (Youth Week) offers a perfect, if idealized, vision of a *posmoderno*, every detail bespeaking youth and hipness, from the broad-shouldered overcoat, the swept-back hair, and the cigarette

FIGURE 4   Javier de Juan, "Little Compendium of People
Seen at the Opening of an Art Fair—That Is, 'Arco 84.'"
Madriz 3 (Mar. 1984): 12–13.

MATAHEMBRAS EN PLAN CHULÓN

Y SEÑORAS

Y EMBAJADORES

Y PVNKOS INGLESES Y TRANSVANGVARDIAS ITALIANOS
Y ESTO ES TODO.

perched in his lips to his stance, one foot cocked against the wall. He owns the street. Who wouldn't want to look like that? (Fig. 5) Examples abound in a diversity of styles and narrative contexts in every issue, but the figures depicted in Martín's "Modern Shit" amply and humorously represent the diverse *tipos* who populate Movida Madrid (13).

Finally, the image illustrating an essay on underground rock (which incidentally refers to an article *Rolling Stone* published on the Movida) is quite eloquent. Of particular interest is the quote from Alaska, one of the leading voices of the Movida music scene. She says: "La música sin moda es una mierda. A mí no me interesa la música como música. Me interesa como moda, revistas, leerla, tocarla, por todo lo que lleva alrededor. No me interesa un grupo sin imagen." (Diego A. Manrique 127) (Music without style is a piece of shit. Music as music doesn't interest me. It interests me a style, magazines, reading it, touching it, everything that surrounds it. A group without an image doesn't interest me).

Certainly the Movida is most readily identifiable through fashion. That's how we distinguish between pomos and punks: through their external signs of identity, as we've seen in the preceding portraits. On the one hand, the emphasis on the exterior speaks to a postmodern aesthetic of superficiality; the essence *is* the surface, in much the same way that in modernism form was content. On the other hand, this is more than just fashion or style. Better yet, fashion and style are the expression of an underlying ideology of the surface. Or, as Coco Chanel puts it, "Fashion is not something that exists in dresses only. Fashion is in the sky, in the street, fashion has to do with ideas, the way we live, what is happening."[2]

All these characters move in and through an urban landscape. Virtually the only nonurban scenes we see are beaches during summer vacation. The city is retraced, Madrid redrawn as postmodern cityscape, itself sometimes the subject, at others a backdrop. Jorge Arranz's drawings of the capital are featured in nearly every issue of *Madriz*. This postmodern cartography maps the major arteries and landmarks of Madrid, from the evolution of the Puerta del Sol to the Paseo del Prado, from the Rastro to the Castellana. I think we can understand this obsessive remapping of Madrid as a reconfiguration and reappropriation of urban space (the *okupa* or squatters' movement was part and parcel of Movida-era Madrid), as a surveying of the terrain from a new perspective on property and ownership. This cartography is less concerned with changing the urban landscape than with resemanticizing it, changing its meanings, rewriting, in Saussurian terms, not the signifier but the signified.

Arranz's "Las cuatro estaciones" depicts Madrid's four iconic train stations

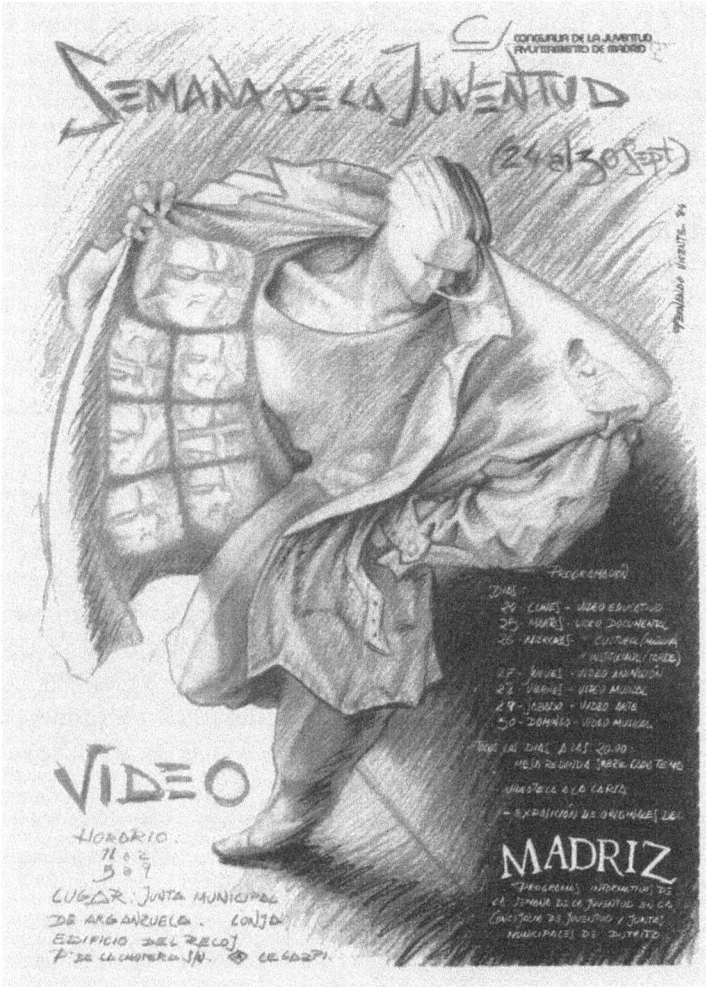

FIGURE 5 Fernando Vicente, "Youth Week."
Madriz 9 (Sept.–Oct. 1984): 31.

(Atocha, Chamartín, Estación del Norte, and Príncipe Pío) as important landmarks that mark the four cardinal points of the Movida Madrileña. Another
reading might understand it to be the appropriation of the very climate of Madrid—the four seasons—in a play on the double meaning of *estación*. I particularly like another drawing by Arranz for its representation of the Malasaña
neighborhood, one of the focal points of the Movida (32–33). He first shows it in

daytime, a lower-middle-class neighborhood, and its transformation by night. In some ways, the uneasy *convivencia* of the Movida hipsters and the working-class residents bespeaks an invasion and transformation of the neighborhood and a contestation of urban space. In other ways, I think, it prefigures the 15-M and *indignados* movements some 30 years later.

The artist OPS captures a darker side of the urban landscape in his "Bestia-rium Matritense" cartoons, also regular features of *Madriz*. He takes everyday objects and imbues them with an ironic, sinister, and funny hidden meaning, as in the "Rude Squid" that preys on unsuspecting housewives as they empty the garbage, or the "Tabernosaurio" depicted in the adjoining panel (14–15).

What are the narratives that weave the urban structures and urban fauna together? They run from love stories to a surprising number of gruesome ur-ban murder tales, with the occasional supernatural force thrown in. They range from images without words that either have no plot or suggest one minimally to full-blown comic strips that tell a story graphically and verbally. In general, they give the impression that image is stronger than narrative. Often they seem to be telling a story yet go nowhere. They simply end, and you might ask, *what's the point?* Well, that's precisely the point. The failure of the master narrative is not replaced with another narrative but with the fragments of one. The final panel in Keko's story "El invitado de René Magritte" (René Magritte's guest), for example, simply states "Este no es un fin" (This is not an end), echoing Magritte's painting *Ceci n'est pas une pipe*. In so doing, it not only interrupts the narrative but ques-tions representation as well.

Nino Velasco's "Las tesis del dibujante de comics" (The theses of a comic book artist) (8–11) is particularly interesting as a reflection on comic book art. The first-person narration begins with the speaker (apparently Velasco himself) cursing realism, declaring that things are not what they seem but how he sees them. From here follows a long, disorderly series of drawings and descriptions that do not follow a strict narrative line but constitute a kind of poetics of the postmodern *tebeo*: "Cabezas pequeñas y cuerpos enormes . . ." (Tiny heads and enormous bodies . . .); "La línea pura es lo más bello . . ." (The pure line is the most beautiful . . .); "Es falaz la simetría" (Symmetry is a fallacy); "Y adoro las viñetas muy confusas . . ." (And I adore very confusing comic strips. . .) "Los guiones no deben entenderse nada" (The scripts should be incomprehensible). All this is punctuated by variants on a bolero that serves as a refrain: "Tuve una novia en Varsovia . . ." (I had a girlfriend in Warsaw).

I find this metacomic particularly interesting for its postulation of a post-modern aesthetic of comic book art. It questions standard representational models, though in the wake of the historical avant-garde this is nothing new.

I think its originality and power lie in the fragmentation of discourse: this *historieta* brings together metanarrative (a reflection on drawing comics) with the lyrics of a bolero, all complicated by the deconstruction of the very process of graphic representation.

An interesting thread of noir runs through many of the different issues of *Madriz*, as in Bellver's "Miserie Negra" (50). These "snapshots," along with a number of more traditional narrative comic strips, reinscribe icons of 1940s and 1950s American film noir and detective novels in a postmodern discourse. In that sense they parallel the boom the *novela negra* (crime novel) experienced in Spain and Latin America in the 1980s and 1990s. I read this revisiting of the genre in both instances as part of the project of recovery of classic modernity that bypassed Spain almost entirely. The gangster and the hard-boiled dick are expressions of an advanced stage of capitalist society, the playing out of its contradictions. Their reinscription in a postmodern graphic narrative strives, consciously or not, to reclaim a culture of modernity never fully achieved in Spain, while at the same time parodying it.

With issue 33, in the winter of 1987, *Madriz* turned the final page on its contestatory adventure. The change in Madrid's city government after the death of Tierno Galván meant less funding for culture in general and for alternative youth culture in particular. The magazine's print run dwindled from 25,000 at its height to 6,000 in the last issues, when distribution was severely curtailed as well. Yet it remained true to its postmodern aesthetic and ideology to the end.

I would like to close by examining LPO's "Cuestiones cruciales de la Posmodernidad" (Vital questions of postmodernity), published in the final issue (38–39) (Fig. 6). Different characters in a swirl of colors and figures utter cryptic statements:

> "Siente el peso de alguna obligación." (He feels the weight of some
> obligation.)
> "¡Ah! ¡Cuántas horas de melancolía, vuelto hacia el limbo!" (Oh! So many
> hours of melancholy, turned toward limbo!)
> "¿Estás rabioso por algún motivo considerable, o es simple rutina?" (Are you
> furious for some major reason, or is this simply routine?)
> "Burp. Créanme: soy un producto de mi tiempo." (Burp. Believe me: I'm a
> product of my time.)

All of which leads to question 1, uttered by the "mente despejada" (clear mind): "Pero, joé, ¿esto es un comic o qué?" (What the fuck? Is this a comic or what?).

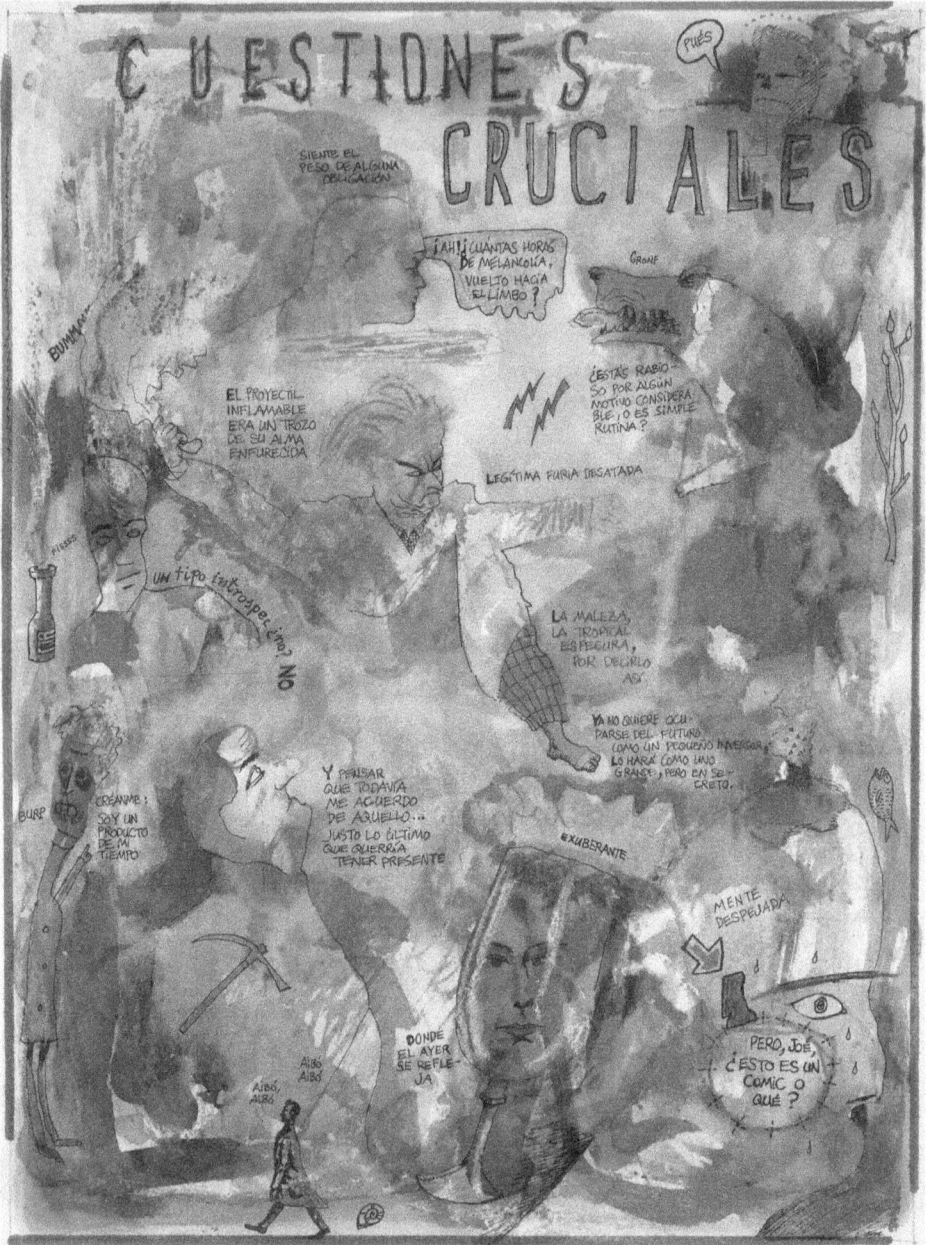

FIGURE 6   LPO, "Crucial Questions about Postmodernity."
Madriz 33 (Winter 1987): 38-39.

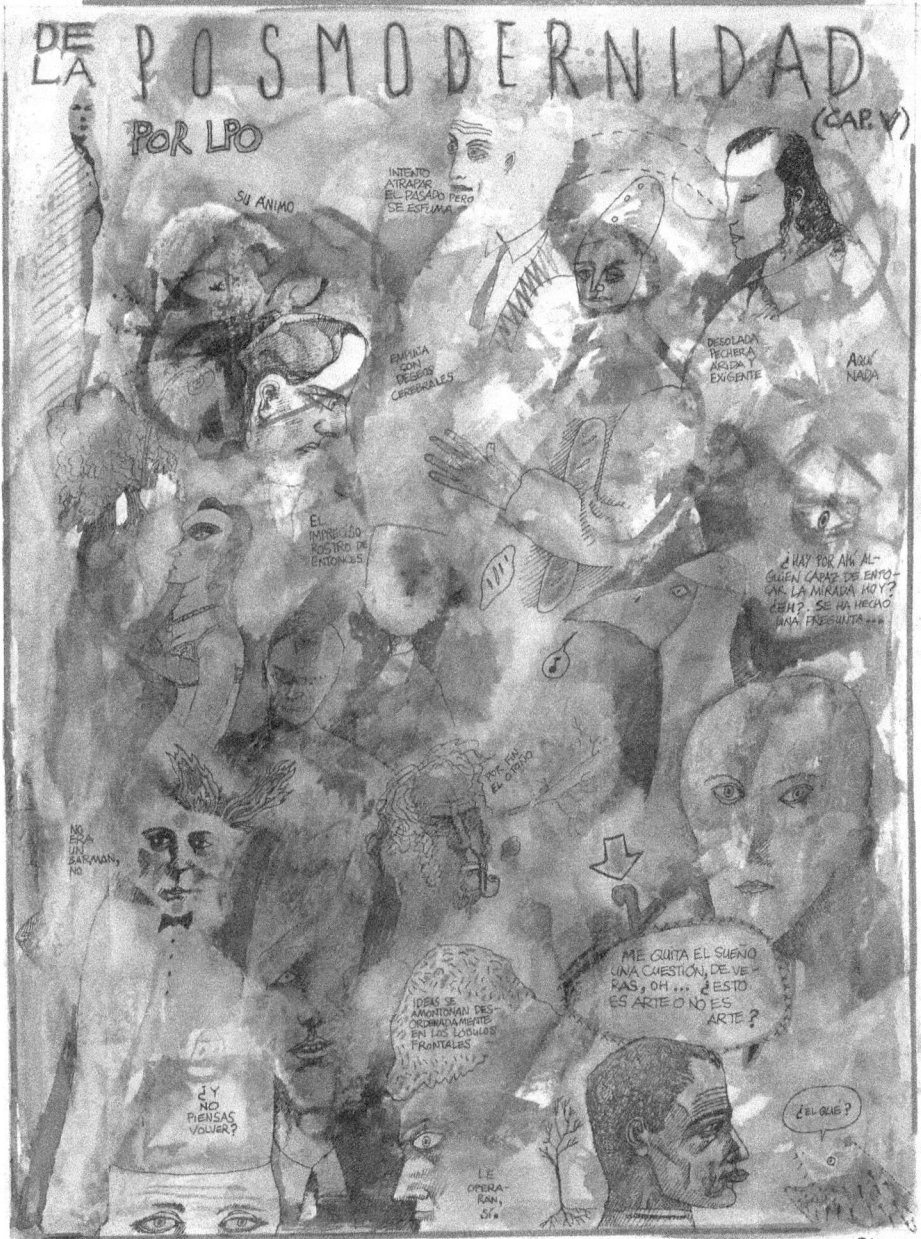

More characters fuel the chaos with other enigmatic comments on the facing page:

> "Intento atrapar el pasado pero se esfuma." (I try to trap the past
>   but it turns to smoke.)
> "El impreciso rostro de entonces." (The imprecise face of that time.)
> "No era un barman, no." (No, he wasn't a bartender.)
> "Ideas se acumulan desordenadamente en los lóbulos frontales."
>   (Ideas accumulate chaotically in the frontal lobes.)

All of which takes us to question 2: "Me quita el sueño una cuestión, de veras, oh. . . . ¿Esto es arte o no es arte?" (I'm losing sleep over a question, truly, oh. . . . Is this art or is it not art?)

I think these two questions pretty well sum up *Madriz's* quest over the course of its intense three-year run.

At the outset of the postmodern adventure of *Madriz*, Ludolfo Paramio posed the question, quoted above, "Let's see if it lasts." It didn't. While the editors of the magazine published three more issues under a different title and without government subvention, it ended. The Movida itself lingered for several years more but by the mid-1990s was a thing of the past. Yet the thirty-three issues of *Madriz* remain today in public and private collections as testament to an extraordinary moment of cultural and social transformation.

NOTES

1. *Suecas*, literally "Swedish women," was a term used to designate all young, attractive Northern European women who flocked to Spanish beaches on vacation.
2. Coco Chanel, "Coco Chanel Biography."

WORKS CITED

Arranz, Jorge. "Las cuatro estaciones." *Madriz* 5 (1984). Print.

Chanel, Coco. "Coco Chanel Biography." Biography Online. Web. 13 Nov. 2016.

De Juan, Javier. "Mitología para todos." *Madriz* 17 (1985). Print.

_____. "Pequeño compendio de gentes vistas en la inauguración de una feria de arte, o sea 'Arco 84.'" Print.

Del Barrio, F. "Poema del suburbio." *Madriz* 27 (1986). Print.

Fukuyama, Francis. "The End of History?" *The National Interest* (Summer 1989): 3–18. Print.

Geist, Anthony L. "An Interview with Juan Goytisolo." *TriQuarterly* 57.2 (1983): 38–48. Print.

Girben, Jordi. "Positives & Negatives, Angles Complementarys [sic]." *Madriz* 15 (1985). Print.

Habermas, Jürgen. "Modernity versus Postmodernity." *New German Critique* 22 (Winter 1981). Print.

Jameson, Fredric. *Postmodernism, or, The Cultural Logic of Late Capitalism*. Durham, NC: Duke University Press, 1991. Print.

LPO. "Cuestiones cruciales de la posmodernidad." *Madriz* 33, 1987. Print.

_____. "Zentrales." *Madriz* 3 (1984). Print.

Javier de Juan, "Pequeño compendio […]." *Madriz* 3 (1984). Print.

Lyotard, Jean-François. *The Postmodern Condition: A Report on Knowledge*. Minneapolis: University of Minnesota Press, 1984. Print.

Mandel, Ernest. *Late Capitalism*. London: New Left Books, 1975. Print.

Manrique, Diego. "Del rollo al bollo (y muchos muertos al hoyo)". *Madriz* 18-19 (1985). Print.

Martín. "Modern Shit." *Madriz* 10 (1984). Print.

OPS. "Tabernosaurio." *Madriz* 3 (1984). Print.

Paramio, Ludolfo. "Terzera." *Madriz* 2 (1984). Print.

Sánchez Vidal, Agustín. *Sol y sombra*. Barcelona: Planeta, 1990. Print.

Velasco, Nino. "Las tesis del dibujante de comics." *Madriz* 22 (1985). Print.

Vicente, Fernando. "Semana de Juventud." *Madriz* 9 (1984). Print.

◆   CHAPTER 2

Rebel Cities: Madrid and the Cultural Contestation of Space

Malcolm Alan Compitello

The events of 2011 that brought people into the streets in Madrid in a common desire to protest the abuses of what David Harvey in *Rebel Cities* has labeled "feral capitalism" (115–65) made clear in Spain, as it had in other countries and would in still more after that date, the power and limits of popular resistance. The geometrically expanding body of scholarship that has begun to appear brings home the importance of the movement and the role of cultural production in these acts of resistance. In so doing, there has been a tendency to highlight the unique nature of what has come to be known as the 15-M, or *indignados*, phenomenon. This essay contextualizes the recent present in relationship to earlier acts of resistance and the evolution of the urban process in Madrid.[1] It thereby underscores the acutely important role of cultural creation in acts of resistance to capital's attempts to remake space, and by extension social relationships, in its own image and for its own benefit.

The pages that follow offer examples of resistance to capitalist accumulation as they have played out over time and space in Madrid and Spain at a variety of scales, as understood by Sallie Marston. David Harvey's fundamental assessment of the nature of the urban in *The Urban Experience*, which underscores the importance of process over product and the tight relationships among space and social and cultural forms, serves as an important point of inflection. It takes as one of its points of departure David Harvey's formulations about the nature of the urban process, also highlighting the importance of cultural representation in this process. It scrutinizes how culture figures into the urban process as described by Harvey when the Scottish geographer argues that it is in the urban context that "firmer connections between the rules of capitalist accumulation and the ferment of social, political and cultural forms can be identified. By so doing, I reiterate that the urban is not a thing but a process and that the process is a particular exemplar of capitalist accumulation in real space and time" (*The Urban Experience*, 247).

Several crucial moments where space and cultural issues are inexorably bound up in reacting to and transforming urban consciousness have been chosen to contextualize the popular uprisings that broke out all over the world in response to political and economic abuse that precipitated the 2007 crisis. The first is the relationship between the *okupa* phenomenon and the establishment of the Casa Encendida cultural center at the end of the 1990s. The second is the 15-M/*indignados* movement as it developed in the Puerta del Sol in Madrid in response to the financial crisis of 2007–2008, how this movement engaged the use of cyberspace, and some of the lessons that can be gleaned from this appropriation in support of their acts of resistance. The intent is to interrogate and align *okupas* and *indignados*, fraught as they are with the tensions that issue from significant social crises, and see them as keywords in understanding resistance as exercised in Spain.

The contextual frame for this paper is the evolution of the urban process in Madrid since the moment when the new democratically elected municipal governments in Spain faced the task of redoing urban planning documents for cities such as Madrid and Barcelona, which were reaching the time frame in which Spain's Ley del Suelo mandated that they be revised (Chamorro González) after the municipal elections of 1979. It builds on the lessons gleaned from Castells (*Ciudad, The Urban Question, Crisis urbana, The City and the Grassroots*) about the role of community groups in resisting speculative urban practices and taking control of neighborhood urban practices during the end of the Franco dictatorship and the *Transición* to democracy that followed it.

Sir Peter Hall's landmark study of the history of urban planning, *Cities of Tomorrow*, points out the consistent history of the unintended consequences of good actions, or perhaps better said, how individual gain has subverted the common good over and over through the efforts of the hidden hand of capital to shape urban space in its image. The anarchist ideals that spurred the origins of the modern planning movement were constantly deflected. This led to results that consistently undid plans or led to plans that eschewed the initial ideals of the planning process.

This has certainly been the case in Spain in the twentieth century and beyond as a number of scholars, including Diéguez Patao, Leira, Carmen, Moneo,

De Terán, and Sambricio, among others, have demonstrated.[2] Madrid's 1985 plan was drawn up with an eye toward guaranteeing the right to the city for all residents—as *Recuperar Madrid* (1982) the *avance* (pre-plan) for the 1985 plan, makes clear—and puts into place a series of urban practices whose intended and unintended consequences make it the last great modernist-inspired urban plan designed to make the city livable for all residents. It is one of the last comprehensive urban planning documents done before urban planning devolved into urban design (Harvey, *The Condition*), with the attendant erosion of state supervision and its replacement by private–public partnerships in which the former had a much stronger say than ever before and special interests (the real estate, construction, and banking sectors) tried to ensure that capital would have its way and continue to shape urban environments in Spain, as elsewhere, in its own image.[3] From the late 1970s forward, urban policy, who controlled it, and whose interests it would serve became one of the principal areas in which battles over the lack of political response to the needs of citizens would play out.

In addition to the works of documentation and direct analysis of specific iterations of urban resistance produced in the wake of the financial crisis of the beginning of the twenty-first century, a number of important urban analysts weighed in on the subject, adjusting their acute sense of the urban process to these popular uprisings. The triangulation of David Harvey's *Rebel Cities*, Manuel Castells's *Networks of Outrage and Hope*, and Andy Merrifield's *The New Urban Question* affords an important point of inflection from which to consider how to evaluate urban resistance in the wake of the financial crisis. A consideration of these three works is acutely important to assessing the importance of the 15-M/*indignados* phenomenon and how it has evolved over time. Because a considerable amount of the work done on this movement relies heavily on Castells's work, triangulating it with Harvey and Merrifield provides a wider and more nuanced frame of reference that explains how and why post–Puerta del Sol events have evolved.

In *The New Urban Question*, Merrifield reiterates a claim he first made in *Metromarxism*, the most important comprehensive study of the relationship between Marxism and the evolution of cities: "[S]ome of the best urban studies has been done by certain Marxists and some of the best Marxism has been done by certain urban theorists" (1). Castells's and Harvey's work certainly proves the accuracy of Merrifield's assertion, whose approachable book represents an important meditation on how to rethink urban studies and resistance in the age of what he calls, in turn, "neo-Haussmannianism" and "parasitic urbanism," and helps explain the points of convergence and divergence with Harvey's and

Castell's proposals. Merrifield's reflections represent a nuanced and thoughtful response to and view of events that help us understand the positions argued by them.

Harvey's work has resided on the cutting edge of critical geography since the 1970s and, along with the contributions of Henri Lefebvre, has set the path this discipline has generally followed. His entire project, as he explained early on, needs be understood as a way of rewriting historical materialism as historical-geographical materialism (Harvey, *Urban* 1–16). As always it is rooted in a progressive vision that sees collective action as the only way to counteract the underlying effects of what he calls "accumulation by dispossession" (137–82), a point of view that Merrifield also embraces. *Rebel Cities* maintains that focus with a thoroughgoing reassessment of capital's pernicious effects on the urban process and concrete advice on how formulate the questions needed to resist feral capitalism and the politics of what Harvey calls the "Party of Wall Street." The first of these is clear.

> The *Indignados* movement in Spain and Greece, the revolutionary impulses in Latin America, the peasant movements in Asia, are all beginning to see through the vast scam that a predatory and feral global capitalism has unleashed on the world. What will it take for the rest of us to see and act upon it? How can we begin all over again? What direction should we take? The answers are not easy. But one thing we do know for certain: we can only get to the right answers by asking the right questions. (157)

Asking the right questions enables one to get beyond the blue smoke of obfuscation thrown up to deflect critical analysis:

> The Party of Wall Street knows all too well that when profound political and economic questions are transformed into cultural issues, they become unanswerable. It regularly calls up a huge range of captive expert opinion, for the most part employed in the think tanks and universities they fund and splattered throughout the media they control, to create controversies out of all matter of issues that simply do not matter, and to propose solutions to questions that do not exist. . . . The one thing that can never be openly debated and discussed is the true nature of the class war they have been ceaselessly and ruthlessly waging (161).

An expanded vision of class and a sensitive reading of the problematic dynamics between the concept of the commons and that of enclosure is also fundamental to Harvey's arguments. A consideration of the importance of scale when assessing the dynamic possibilities of the commons is also crucial. It is even more so today since many critical geographers have backed away from the idea of scale in favor of more Deleuzian, affectively oriented, and other post structural theoretical positions as ways of rethinking the nature of or even the need for a concept of scale.

Networks of Outrage and Hope aligns Castells's work on networks over the last several decades with new forms of social resistance.[4] For Castells, these new oppositional networks are horizontal in nature. By that he means that they are formed and spread democratically in a nonhierarchical fashion. Fundamental for Castells is how these networks appropriate the switching and programming functions inherent in networks of power to seize control of the flows of information. From there he studies an important step: how the democracy of the virtual networks that inspire hope and express outrage as a way of rising up against power end up occupying real spaces (10–11). These new movements combine virtual and real responses to form a new public space, the networked space between the digital space and the urban space which he views as a space of "autonomous communication. Castells explains in some detail how affect creates the two elements, outrage and hope (negative and positive emotions), that help unify and mobilize people around common issues in response to abuse of the network society by oligarchic power structures—especially the state— although he never uses the word "oligarchy." The insistence on the importance of the individual leads to a kind of militant particularism. It is directly tied to the unstated anticommunism that has undergirded Castells's approach since he developed the idea of the network. Individuals, for Castells, make ideology, rather than ideology making the resistance movement. Ultimately, the work of these three theorists leads us to formulate a series of inquiries about the relationships among politics, social movements, and the production and use of space.

Any analysis of the 15-M/*indignados* uprising and how it continues to evolve over time has to take into account the political alternatives and the importance of real and virtual spaces that Castells, Harvey, and Merrifield identify and scrutinize. Crucial here is the relationship between alternative politics and real and virtual revolutions. In discussing what he labeled the end of public space and the effects of the strategies of late capital in transforming it, Don Mitchell observed that the vision of an electronic future as public space is "little more than wishful thinking" (148) since "there has never been a revolution conducted solely in cyberspace" (149). While some of the comments he makes about the issue may seem dated now, his insistence on the primacy of direct physical action in real time and space is important to those who planned, carried out, and transformed the acts of resistance that involved virtual and real uprisings and to those who annualized those decisions and actions. Certainly it is a major fault line for the three theorists discussed above and for a number of the scholars who have studied the 15-M/*indignados* phenomenon, including but not limited to important contributions by Kornetis, La Parra-Pérez, Moreno-Caballud ("La imaginación sostenible," "Desbordamientos culturales," "Cultures of Anyone," "Burbujas culturales," "Cuando cualquiera escribe," *Cultures of Anyone*), and Sampedro and Lobera.[5] Castells's lack of faith in traditional leftist political organizations and his insistence on the important of grassroots, network-based information flows lead him to champion a disaggregated structure of political intervention. Even as he acknowledges the importance of occupying real physical spaces, he eschews the kind of permanent political structure that both Harvey and Merrifield say would be necessary, albeit hard to "scale up" beyond the moment of occupation.

In his chapter on the *indignados* (110–15), Castells looks favorably on the movement's 2011 declaration of a time of reflection and abstention from the 2012 political campaign. He believes this decision to be in accordance with the movement's long view of things—go slow and think things out—and his own recent exploration of a horizontal, rhizomatic view of revolutionary action. Nevertheless, the tactical consequences of that democratically determined strategic decision by the *indignados* were disastrous, leading to the Partido Popular's obtaining an absolute majority that had deleterious economic consequences and vitiated many important aspects of civil society, including the rights to expression and assembly that the *indignados* themselves had fought to preserve and expand.[6] While it is beyond the scope of this contribution to examine the 15-M's role in shaping the post-occupation political landscape in Spain, the role of the *indignados* and others involved in the 15-M and other resistance movements in the formation of political organizations such as Podemos seems to belie Castells's assertion. It certainly indicates that a significant portion of those involved in those direct-action movements eventually saw the need to engage in the political process in some way, albeit without abandoning their desire for grassroots neighborhood-based activism, which became a significant vehicle for alternative politics and resistance to capital and the practices of the major political parties in the years after the initial occupation of the Puerta del Sol. That Podemos's spokesperson, Pablo Iglesias, connected Castells to Podemos's goals may, in fact, have arisen from Castells's suspicion of leftist politics. (See Merrifield, *The New Urban Question*, pp. 11–20, for an explanation of how the erosion of collective consumption sparked this change in Castells's point of view regarding the left.) It may also signal two weak spots in post-15-M politics. The first is assuming that both the PSOE and the PP were equally responsible for causing the crisis, thus erasing important distinctions between left and right. To a great extent, this has been responsible for the logjam in recent Spanish politics since the left-wing parties have been unable to come to a consensus that would allow them to govern nationally after the initial success that Podemos-associated political organizations had in winning the municipal elections in Barcelona and Madrid in 2015.[7]

While there is a considerable amount of blame to go around regarding why this has happened, the current situation to a certain extent arises from what I would call 15-M exceptionalism. In making this assertion, I am fully cognizant that the position of the Zapatero government at the end of its mandate and in response to crisis might lead some to assume that the left and the right were equally responsible for the crisis. That assumption plays into the revisionist thinking about the nature of the transition to democracy that Guillem Martínez and Fernández Savater, among others, have proposed, casting recent political history since the reestablishment of democracy in 1978 as the *cultura de la transición*, or CT.

According to this view, post crisis politics—indeed, even the crisis itself—has been a watershed and to some extent explains why those who went from protesting to joining Podemos and other groups have been somewhat unbending in their ideas. It also explains a certain amount of the unwillingness to connect the 15-M and other movements to a long political trajectory of social, political, and spatial resistance. This point of view is important since it shapes a considerable amount of the important scholarship on the 15-M movement and its repercussions in a variety of fields, as underscored in the work of Abellán Bordallo ("Occupying the #Hotelmadrid"; "De la red a la calle"), Kornetis, Moreno-Caballud, La Parra-Pérez, Abellán, and Sampedro and Lobera. The comments offered here about the nature of this point of view should in no way be construed as a criticism of the acute intellectual acumen and desire for social justice that resides behind these ideas. They have opened the debate over the nature of history and who interprets it to important scrutiny, and fostered a reevaluation of the relationships described by David Harvey in a paper suggestively titled "The Art of Rent" about the pernicious influence of capital on culture, and advocated for a more democratic cultural, social, and political field. In so doing, however, they may have at times engaged in what Lanceros, following Walter Benjamin, referred to as "filosofar con el martillo" (philosophizing with a sledgehammer) in a particularly heated debate several decades ago about the relationship of modernity and postmodernity in Spain during the Transition and after.

Following lines of argumentation suggested by Thomas Kuhn, Michel Foucault, and Walter Benjamin, Lanceros argues that all new forms of thinking are destructive by nature given the hegemoenological implications of the episte-mological break with which new ways of perceiving reality threaten established ones. To make this claim to newness, most intellectual positions must create a "straw man" image of the other and often deploy the aforementioned strategy of "filosofar con el martillo" (141). This is certainly the case with postmodernism, since the definitions of the modern offered by the supporters of the postmodern are certainly reductivist, as Lanceros explains (142).

In the same way, many defenders of the modern misrepresent the positions of postmodern thinkers so as to be better able to launch their attacks on it and defend their own positions. To illustrate his contention about the destructive nature of all thought, Lanceros points out that many of the same arguments of-fered in the modern/postmodern debate are homologous to ones advanced in the debate concerning the Enlightenment (138–39).

The point that Lanceros makes about flattening the arguments of others to create a gap rather than a continuity so as to strengthen one's own argument applies, to some degree, to post crisis thinking in Spain. As such, his comments offer a corrective to the tendency to harden the position of the other that has characterized a number of discursive moves performed by those who subscribe to some or all of the main points proposed by the CT, In general, the latter has to be seen as a corrective to previous visions of the effects of Spain's transition to democracy in the 1970s and of the subsequent thirty years or so of Spain's evolu-tion. This line of thought sees the Transition harden into a kind of monolithic structure that over time saw maintaining its own hegemony as a core objective.

The *Cultura de la Transición* thinking tends to see the 15-M as a fundamen-tal transformation of Spanish political and sociocultural life that can break the hegemony of the regime of 1978 (the year in which the latest Spanish Constitu-tion was adopted). The popular resistance that erupted in 2011 gave voice to a new view of politics with an emphasis on direct democracy and a rejection of the practices of the major political parties, which had been, according to this line of thought, substantially complicit in the abuses that caused the financial crisis and in the post crisis erosion of many of the most important components of civil society in Spain. A fundamental aspect of these new social, cultural, and political formations was the deployment of social media and other technolo-gies, viewed as important components of new democratic forms of assembly and political organization that would belie the view espoused by Don Mitchell discussed above. Affect, as the title of Castells's *Networks of Outrage and Hope* clearly points out, plays an important role in these uprisings, as does the affec-tive turn in cultural criticism.[8]

A number of scholars, while praising the boldness and expansive nature of this point of view, offer a nuanced version of said perspective. Balfour, for example, believes that the idea of a regime of 1978 might be an overreach, while Saum-Pascual questions whether technology that is not readily available to everyone without cost can truly be democratic. Cameron brings up the issue of what the future will bring—"Is the movement a precursor to the systematic overhaul of Spanish parliamentary politics or merely an ephemeral expression of indignation doomed to fade away (4)"—a question now even more important given the Spanish political logjam of 2016. One could add to these the issue of the flattening of political parties during the last 30 years, which looks attractive to some in the light of the present but which does not hold up to scrutiny in terms of performance and accomplishment over time.[9] Aligning Harvey, Merrifield, and Castells provided a view of the power but also the limitations of the commons unless it can be scaled up that the morphing of part of the 15-M energy into political parties such as Podemos, has not been able to contravene.

The understanding of activism and of controlling space is something that the 15-M did well. Its understanding of space as being fundamental to urban resistance has been the subject of a number of important studies. Nofre has done groundbreaking work in this area, as have Abellán Bordallo ("Occupying the #Hotelmadrid"); Amat Montesinos and Ortiz Pérez; and Anonymous, among others. Abellán's "Occupying the #hotelmadrid" represents an important take on the emblematic occupation of the Hotel Madrid after the initial occupation of the Puerta del Sol. It is a nuanced take on the importance of space in direct political struggles.

The authors underscore the importance of occupations for galvanizing public attention and creating a climate of support for contesting what Harvey has called "accumulation by dispossession." In making the case for the importance of the Hotel Madrid occupation associated with the *indignados'* takeover of the Puerta del Sol, they diminish the role of the *okupa* movement in the late 1990s in a way that is not totally congruent with what the *okupas* wanted to accomplish and their role in resistance. Miguel Ángel Martínez and García offer a more nuanced contextualization of the relationship between *okupas* and the 15-M, highlighting the synergies and points of convergence rather than the differences. But their study considers only very recent iterations of the *okupa* phenomenon. To demonstrate the continuity of forms of spatial resistance and be mindful of Marx's admonition to always historicize, the pages that follow explain the *okupas'* crucial role in altering spatial relationships in the Embajadores neighborhood in central Madrid, particularly the area commonly called Lavapiés, and their role in those moments of resistance and confrontation.

The speculation, incipient gentrification, and the mechanics of selling place that overtook Lavapiés from the late 1980s through the election of Ruíz Gallardón as mayor of Madrid in 2003 made it easy to conceive of the area as a volatile urban tinderbox set to explode at any moment.[10] Moreover, the match capable of leading to a true conflagration was gripped tightly in the hands of those whose ultimate goal was to extract the highest possible monopoly rent for their property and restructure a working-class area to incorporate it into a vision of the city center as a cultural pleasure palace. Here, the transformations would suit the aims of the government, the builders, and the financial sector.

What fundamentally changed the dynamics of resistance in Lavapiés and kept the spotlight of public attention trained on the urban struggles there—in ways that those pulling the strings would probably have preferred not be the case—was the efforts of a group of young urban protesters. With their slogan "Kontra la Especulación, Okupación" (Against speculation, occupation), the *okupa* phenomenon took hold dramatically in Lavapiés just as the Partido Popular's rehabilitation plans for the area were scheduled to begin. In essence the young urban protesters had grabbed the match from the hands of capital and threatened to burn down not the neighborhood but the structure of the public/private collusion that was altering spatial relationships in Lavapiés in the interest of capital. The *okupa* phenomenon acted as a kind of social lightning rod that made visible, to use Bourdieu's terminology, the invisible hands of ideological manipulation (288). The youth of the participants and their take on culture and how to appropriate it were and still are fundamental elements of the *okupas'* success.

The *okupa* phenomenon[11] as it developed in Madrid, particularly in Embajadores, the southernmost part of Madrid's District One and just a stone's throw from the Puerta del Sol, played an important role in trying to resist the Partido Popular's systematic undermining of the ideals of Madrid's 1985 plan. The *okupa* phenomenon will act as what Raquel Cartas Martín in an important early study labels an *analizador*, that enables us to see, following Bourdieu, the invisible hands of ideological manipulation.

Over the last decade, a number of important studies have appeared on the history of the *okupa* phenomenon, its "oppositional lineage" and connections to utopian spatial practices of resistance, and its strategies. Cartas Martín, Marina Marinas, Lorenzo Navarette, and others see it as a social movement inexorably bound to problems dealing with youth because of the age of many of those who participated and because the problems facing young people in Spain in the 1980s and 1990s were legion. The ability to marshal and appropriate modern technologies, most especially the Web, in support of their actions is something an older generation of radicals would probably not have been able to accomplish, as Adell Argilés points out. Martínez López (*Okupaciones de viviendas, Viviendas y centros sociales*) and Dieste Hernández, among others, see the *okupas* in a wider social context. Dieste traces the movement's association with radical social conceptions of space such as Debord and the situationists, and Lynch's and Lefebvre's utopian conceptions of spatial relationships. For his part, Martínez López, while not discounting in any way the radical nature of the youth movement with which the *okupas* can naturally be associated, also positions them within the framework of a widening sphere of social movements that took hold in Spain in the 1980s and 1990s. While not affiliated with any particular political party, many of the *okupas* came from the young militants of the radical left, such as Izquierda Unida. They could trace their lineage back to the tenets of anarcho-syndicalism and the previous generations of social protesters woven into the country's social fabric through opposition to the Franco regime and after. Castells persuasively argues that the grassroots approach to urban resistance was crucial at the end of the Francoist period. His ideas on resistance informed the progressive 1985 Plan General de Ordenación Urbana de Madrid (PGOUM; General Plan for Urban Planning for Madrid) for the capital city, which is interesting since he later rejected the politics of many of those who'd taken part in constructing that plan.

This view of urban planning's role was replaced by a wholly top-down decision-making process that remained largely unresponsive to residents' needs under the Partido Popular. Part of the resistance to this sea change in planning practices came together around the efforts of the *okupas*, who offered a much more flexible and supple way to devise solutions to the problems of place. This, of course, is one of the reasons they were criticized by the right and championed by the radical left.

Dieste Hernández makes clear how urban plans tend to be drawn up in such a way as to "recalificar las diferentes partes de la ciudad atendiendo a los principales intereses del urbanismo actual (financiación, seguridad, control, despilfarro del espacio, individualismo, etc.) Sólo responden a la necesidad de mantener los precios del Mercado y que, bajo ningún concepto, ninguna empresa privada y pública están dispuestas a perder" (n.p.) (revalue different parts of the city, attending to the most important interests behind current urbanistic practices [financing, security, control, looting of space, individualism, etc.] All of this is clearly related to the need to maintain market prices for lands that the public and private sectors are totally unwilling to put in jeopardy.)

What made the Labo experiments so important in the late 1990s was that they were providing the types of services and projects that the city government had been unable or unwilling to provide and simultaneously offering criticisms of the renewal plans for Lavapiés and integrative solutions to some of its most pressing problems. The *okupas'* ability to integrate the immigrant community into their plans and actions and provide social and cultural outlets for the youth of the Lavapiés area was crucial at a time when few planners were taking Spain's demographic transformation seriously. Without ever receiving public acknowledgement for their role, the Centro Social Okupado Autogestionado (CSOA; Self-Managed Squatting Social Center), working in conjunction with other socially responsible organizations in Embajadores, was able to alter the dialogue about the renovation of Lavapiés and keep the issue of speculation front and center.

Above all, the *okupas* were able to shift emphasis back to people as decision makers and subjects, not objects, of the decision-making process, and away from cleaning façades and erecting parking structures as a way of confronting spatial transformation in a locale. In making these assertions, I am aware that, in the final analysis, the power of capital was victorious. Holding all the cards and now with more legal power than ever, the state eventually reduced the Labo to a state of exile after four attempts to establish something permanent. The *okupas* were, and still may be, a manifestation of a self-governed, place-centered resistance movement with its roots in the traditions of the anarchist collectives of the first half of the twentieth century and the countercultural movements of the late 1960s. It could be argued that this posture might make a locally based movement like the *okupas* antithetical to the decision-making needs of a complex urban structure such as the megapolis Madrid had become in the 1990s and for dealing with the scale of urban governance and the problems this scale engenders.

David Harvey has insisted on this place-based dilemma for quite some time and discusses it at length in *Rebel Cities* (6788) in relation to the ideas of the commons that were so important to the theory driving the 15-M and the *indignados*. Nevertheless, we need to remember that the *okupas* provided a clear alternative to exclusion-based governance. Moreover, their place-based alternatives were linked to a variety of other movements, as Miguel Martínez López has insisted, that are in their broadest conception antiglobal: antiwar movements, draft resistance, alternative media spaces, ecological alternatives, and important feminist collectives such as the Eskalera Karakola, itself located in Lavapiés (see Marinas Sánchez). I agree with Staeheli, who argues that those resistance movements that are capable of working at a variety of scales will be the ones that have the greatest opportunity for success. The insistence with which the *okupas* from the Labo projects were pursued by governmental administrations is a clear indication of the threat, real or imagined, that their actions were perceived to hold out to the speculative policies practiced in Lavapiés and other parts of Madrid.

What its critics consciously ignore is the confluence of scales of involvement that formed the ideology of the phenomenon and something that the *okupas* were able to manage effectively. On the one hand the movement's politics in Madrid are a direct response to the neoliberal planning and economic policies. Its increased emphasis on CSOA's proposals as a model for *autogestión*, and an alternative politics that connected with other social resistance movements clearly show how the *okupa* phenomenon was in the vanguard of attempts to resist gentrification and speculative urban design.

Culture, as mentioned above, was an important part of the tactics deployed by CSOA in support of its contestatory practices. It would play an important part in a memorable confrontation between the *okupas* of the Laboratorio and more established forms of cultural production. On February 10, 2001, with the support of a number of social agents, the *okupas* entered a printing plant at Amparo 103 close to where it intersects with the Ronda de Valencia, only a short distance from where the skeleton for Nouvel's expansion of the Reina Sofía would soon begin to rise. There at Amparo 103, they established the third iteration of the Laboratorio in Embajadores. One month later, Moreno reported that Caja Madrid planned to invest a substantial amount of money in renovating a building on the Ronda de Valencia 2 as a cultural center.[12] That Neo-mudéjar building stood adjacent to what had recently become Labo III.[13]

This fact was not lost on Moreno and subsequent reporters who traced the development of the Casa Encendida up to and after its official opening in 2002 ("Los Reyes inauguran"). From the beginning, it is obvious how the ideas for the Casa Encendida expropriated the discourse of alterity that characterized the practices of the *okupas* at the various iterations of the Labo. F.S. cites the center's director at the time and former director of the Reina Sofía. The vision that José Girau expounds of what the Casa Encendida wanted to accomplish could also easily have described the *okupas'* cultural offerings. "La solidaridad y el medio ambiente figuran en los objetivos y actividades de La Casa Encendida que, con una vocación pluridisciplinar, está dirigido a todos los públicos" (Social solidarity and protection of the environment are among the objectives of the Casa Encendida, which, with its multidisciplinary vision, it wishes to connect with a wide variety of audiences). F.S. then quotes Girau's assessment of the nature of Casa Encendida's goals "La diversidad de la oferta, con temas abiertos a la contaminación de otras disciplinas y a los mestizajes entre discursos y debates de la culturas y la sociedad contemporáneos, en una visión global y pragmática." (The diversity of cultural offerings all open to interdisciplinary contamination and discursive fusion resulting from debates about the nature of contemporary cultures and societies and all of this examined through a global and pragmatic lens). Girau also highlights the ludic nature of the space "un edificio para perderse y divertirse en Lavapiés" (a building in Lavapiés in which one can enjoy losing oneself). He also points out the nature of the *tienda solidaria* que the center will have which will only sell "artículos de comercio justo" (fair trade items). The nod to commerce stands in sharp contrast to the nature of the *okupas'* connection to capital. Moreno's comments on the nature of the cultural programming envisioned for the center makes this distinction even sharper. "Una de las actividades más ambiciosas de la casa en ciernes consistirá en que jóvenes promesas tengan la oportunidad de dar muestras de su arte a la gente consagrada: 'El cantante podrá ser escuchado por Plácido Domingo, el pintor hablará de su obra con Barceló y el bailarín danzará ante Angel Corella,' aseguran los programadores" (One of the most ambitious of the activities in the works at the center is that promising cultural creators will have the chance to perform for seasoned veterans: "a younger singer will be able to perform for Plácido Domingo, a painter can discuss his work with Barceló, and a dancer can perform for Angel Corella").

This view of culture's relationship to the art of rent was, of course, the antithesis of what the Labo project next door stood for. Padilla writing only a few months after the opening of the Casa Encendida, clearly makes this distinction. The printing plant at Amparo 103, vacant since 1978 and the newly opened renovation of Arbós' Neo-Mudéjar building provided for an interesting clash of alternative cultural spaces. As Padilla reports, these two facilities and the nearby Casino de la Reina offered the Lavapiés area a wide cultural offering absent for many years even if all involved in the area agree that even more offerings were needed. Significantly, the two facilities have clashing administrative styles and organizations. The *okupas*, according to Padilla, criticized the Casa Encendida using exactly the same language they and other members of the Red de Lavapiés had used to criticize the rehabilitation plans for Lavapiés as a kind of a *despotismo ilustrado* (enlightened despotism). In the opinion of Nano, one of the members of the Asamblea that administers Labo III, "Lo que necesita el barrio es un centro donde los vecinos intervengan en la gestión. Por supuesto es mejor que haya algo como la Casa Encendida a que no haya nada, pero no es un centro que tenga canales para participar en su administración, sino que está gestionado por profesionales, lo cual no es criticable éticamente pero tiene limitaciones claras" (What the neighborhood needs is a center where residents participate in

organizing and running it. Of course something like the Casa Encendida is better than nothing, but it is a center that will employ a professional management
team and preclude community involvement in its decision-making processes,
which of course is not open to ethical criticism but does put clear limits on user-
based involvement).

Padilla closes with a prescient observation: "El Laboratorio a buen seguro
será desalojado, dejará de ser el vecino rebelde de La Casa Encendida. Pero con
igual seguridad puede decirse que volverá a haber otra ocupación, porque como
dice su lema El Laboratorio se queda en Lavapiés" (The Laboratory will certainly
be removed and will no longer be the Casa Encendida's rebellious neighbor.
But it is equally certain that there will be another occupation because, as the
organization's motto says, "The Laboratory will remain in Lavapiés"). On June
10, 2003, the police removed the *okupas* from Labo III, what Cózar significantly
called the best-recognized *centro okupado* in the city. Padilla's prediction was
correct. The pull of privatized alternative culture was too great. The speculative
real state value of this particular location made Amparo 103 far too valuable to
be a self-governed site for alternative culture. The old building was torn down
and the vacant site, like so many others in the city's central core, awaits the
perfect development moment to construct a new edifice from which to extract
the highest of monopoly rents when the building housed there could have still
been serving a more useful purpose. Moreover, the Casa Encendida itself could
not endure having the antidote to its partially pseudo alternative culture right
next door. Labo III, like its predecessors and its successor, Labo IV, was out of
place in the new urban order of Lavapiés. Gómez observes that both the Casa
Encendida and the Casino de la Reina project stand with their backs turned to
Lavapiés. What is true physically is also true ideologically. If the place was to be
sold through the mechanics of domesticating alternative culture, as Duncombe,
Frank, and others have documented, then a real alternative could not remain
in such close proximity. The Labo and the Biblio had to be removed. As Gómez
reports, referencing a period beyond the scope of this discussion, the Labo is
now in exile from the space it tried to liberate in the name of resistance and
transform in the name of development rather than growth. What stands in its
place is a somewhat sanitized version of the alternative, showing no signs of the
battle scars that marked it as hegemonic and exiled the resistant.

When Jean Nouvel announced that he wanted his expansion of the Reina
Sofía to connect with the neighborhood in ways that it had not previously done,
he expressed a genuine desire to establish a much more meaningful connection
between the museum expansion and the traditional working-class areas that

bounded it in Arganzuela and Embajadores. Had he opened his eyes to the surrounding neighborhood, he might have seen what truly lay beyond the Reina
Sofía's back door, visible through the glass that wraps the expansion. He might
have been able to delve beyond the simulacra and into the traces of the alternative that might have been, seen Argumosa not as it had evolved to be in 2005—
the most bourgeois street in Lavapiés, as Gómez argues—but as it was when a
building only a stone's throw from the expansion was "okupied" in the late 1980s.
In this way, he could have better understood the effects that his shiny structure
and the gentrification that pulsed from it would have on its surroundings. How
it short-circuited any meaningful relationship with the neighborhood, which
the expansion may have actually doomed to failure, and underscored the power
of capital and what lies behind battles over cultural representation.

The occupation of the Puerta del Sol, which became the more widely based
ongoing *indignados* movement, and the Occupy Wall Street phenomenon and
its rapid expansion to other cities point dramatically to the power of social mobilization. The intensity and breadth of the 15-M/*indignados* revolt obviously
underscore the participants desire to combat predatory capital's noxious effects
on the social fabric, financial stability, the nature of space, and the urban process, as is vividly apparent in the Hotel Madrid example and many others. These
movements focused bright spotlights on issues that were widely disseminated in
strikingly powerful images seen around Spain and the world. Nevertheless, it is
important to understand the historical context here.

Earlier, the *okupas* were the lightning rod, resisting the forces that had made
the urban process in Madrid go seriously wrong, as urban planning ceded to
urban design, and the idea of guaranteeing the right to the city to everyone
was abandoned. The *okupas'* attempt to change the nature of the dialogue, while
unsuccessful, did plant the seeds that allowed subsequent movements begin to
flourish. As more of the city's residents began to understand what was truly
at stake, how badly out of balance the elements of civil society had become,
more and more people from wider segments of the population were willing to
engage in the type of civil disobedience they had rejected when the *okupas* had
previously initiated it. Morever, as Martínez underscores, the *okupas* from Casa-
blanca and Maravillas from a decade after the Labo III disappeared were instrumental in offering the 15-M and *indignados* occupiers tactical and strategic help.
At the same time, the *okupas* gained valuable lessons from the wide variety of
people who planned the initial protest and subsequently decided to remain in
the Puerta del Sol and return on a number of occasions.

Like the *okupas*, the *indignados* were able to marshal technology and cultural representation in support of their activities.[14] A substantial body of work

on culture, cartography, space, and the *indignados* movement has also appeared recently, including work by Moreno Caballud, Díez Cortés and Sequera, Feixa and Nofre, Snyder, Vilaseca, and others.[15] This connection with culture, including virtual representations, was important, as Castells has pointed out better than anyone else. It helped create the virtual networks that "spread the word" and redefined how to do politics, Mitchell's and others' admonitions notwithstanding. These tactics created new venues for political activism and created virtual moments of clarity for those who interacted with them. It is instructive to close with one such example that brings home the importance of the 15-M/*indignados* movement in helping to redefine resistance.

In the runup to what would become the 15-M, a number of groups advocating for change looked for all manner of social media and technology-driven platforms to spread the word through groups including including Toma la Plaza and ¡Democracia Real Ya! The latter, according to Miguel Angel Martínez and Angela González, instigated the plans for the initial occupation of the Puerta del Sol and the subsequent occupation that took place in October of the same year. These plans included using newer forms of social media, as many have documented. What almost nobody has mentioned is the role of a virtual reality program, Second Life, a product of Linden Laboratories, as part of that strategy.[16] Both groups were very active in the Second Life community, promoting the importance of resistance and drumming up support for their efforts.

At the moment when opposition to spatial inequities in Spain were expanding their message through virtual means, the Department of Spanish and Portuguese at the University of Arizona was expanding its presence in Second Life, building its own region called Cibola. The goal involved the University of Arizona's use of the Second Life virtual reality platform as a tool to teach about spatial relationships in the Hispanic world using a portion of the virtual world.

The department's project had several goals that played on aspects of the Second Life space that had been underutilized by academics who were expanding into Second Life. Expanding pedagogical research and investigation about the nature of space was one of them, as was exploring collaborative opportunities and outreach efforts related to the Hispanic and Luso-Brazilian world beyond the confines of the physical space of the University of Arizona. The project's goals also included building on the qualities that distinguish Second Life from other virtual reality platforms, including the ability to facilitate direct visual and voice interaction that is superior to other virtual reality environments available in the distance-learning array of pedagogical possibilities, and serving as our laboratory for looking at urban theory from the perspective of the study of space. Other important project goals were situating Cibola as a site for conducting advanced undergraduate and graduate classes in areas that combine the study of spatial theory, works of the imagination, and the mechanics of the construction of space, and offering opportunities for participants to reflect on the results of their actions by providing a simulated "reality" where they can explore the interventions they have read about in case studies written by critics and theorists.

While exploring ways to pursue these avenues and find material I could incorporate into teaching graduate students how to exploit the benefits of innovative technology in the classroom, I had a chance encounter with some of the participants in Toma la Plaza and ¡Democracia Real Ya! In a series of conversations in Second Life, they explained that the Spanish-oriented site they had been using to promote their activities had closed. When they found out that I had just organized a new site based on virtual creations of real iconic cultural spaces in the Hispanic world, they asked me about the possibility of using Cibola to promote the October 15, 2011 protest in Madrid. They were visiting as many Spanish content regions as possible in Second Life to try to foment support for the October 15 rally. They asked if they could use Cibola as one of their bases of operations; the Department gave them permission on the condition that they visit the class I was teaching and engage in a dialogue with the students about the movement and its strategies and tactics.[17]

Based on what I knew about the *okupas* I had assumed that the ¡Democracia Real Ya! activists wanted to occupy one of the buildings on Cibola and convert it into a CSOA. What they really wanted, however, was to occupy public space as a means to taking it back and using it to disseminate their message about assuring the continued existence of public space against the pull of privatization. For those who participated in the 15-M uprising, public space was the connective tissue that assured the continuation of an open and equal civil discourse and underscored Don Mitchell's crucial assertion that public space must be fought for to stay public.

Moreover, when the owners of Cibola stepped back to think about it, we realized that public space—the spaces between coffeehouses in Madrid, Mexico City, Buenos Aires, and Rio de Janeiro as well as the Palacio de Bellas Artes in Mexico City that were planned as the anchors of the built environment of Cibola—was the connective tissue of the site. In a curious but significant way, the role of public space that Cibola's owners discovered to be so important to social discourse in spatial relationships in Second Life underscores the advantages of this platform over other ones. It is the mobility that Second Life fosters and the social interaction this mobility fosters in and outside of class settings that makes this platform, with all of its baggage, still far superior to any other VR platform.

This is the case precisely because of the real and implied public spaces on which it is based. These spaces, where those who visit spend a great deal of time, have become, just as in the real Hispanic world, the public place of social connection and assembly and, to reiterate what was stated above, a way to ensure equality of access to public and private spaces. These lessons about what is really at stake when one intervenes in the urban process bend what was gleaned from Cibola back from virtual (places) to real spatial issues. This underscores what David Harvey maintains about the dynamic relationship between space and place, the general and the particular, and what Cibola has demonstrated about how to deal with re-creations of real places and the dangers of not doing so. It also underscores the scope and reach of Spanish efforts to resist spatial exclusion and the relationships between the virtual and the real in taking back public spaces in the way that Mitchell advocates. In short, the lessons Cibola's architects learned about spatial protest parallel, as Miguel Angel Martínez and Angela González have pointed out, the symbiotic relationship between the different generations of those using space as a vehicle of resistance to the predatory practices of capital in Spain, demonstrating that, from its inception, the project of the 15-M undermined any attempt to categorize it as exceptional.

Harvey has described the crux of his project as rewriting historical materialism as geographical historical materialism (*Urban* 6), thus connecting space and time as coterminous in any attempt to understand how capitalism evolves and what its effects are. Keeping that in mind helps frame the importance of the moments of confluence and context that this essay has explored. They demonstrate the importance of contesting space as a means of resisting capital and the evolution of the tactics involved that effort. Those tactics may involve a variety of ways of disseminating information and forming all kinds of networks, but in the final analysis several issues are crucial.

To begin, no moment along a historical continuum is explicable without understanding other iterations of the urban process. In addition, historicizing offers a much more accurate assessment than striving, for whatever reason, to erect moments of exceptionalism. Space, moreover, remains fundamental to any acts of urban resistance. Keeping these facts in mind strengthens rather than diminishes the importance of recent revolts against capital; remembering and building on the energy those struggles produced is important if they are to overcome whatever obstacles are put in their path and advance an agenda that would, as Madrid's urban plan of 1985 promised, "garantizar el derecho de la ciudad a todos" (guarantee the right to the city for all).

NOTES

1. There is a wealth of informational sources that contextualize the 15-M/*indigna-dos* phenomenon in the broader scope of how these popular rebellions played out around the world. Good points of departure are Carol Illanes, ed. *En marcha: Ensayos sobre arte, violencia y cuerpo en la manifestacion social*; Schiffrin, Anya and Eamon Kircher-Allen, ed *From Cairo to Wall Street: Voices of the Global Spring*; Paolo Gerbaudo; Byrne, Janet, ed. *The Occupy Handbook*; and *Understanding European Movements: New Social Movements, Global Justice Struggles, Anti-Austerity Protest*. Many of these include pieces that address Spanish resistance movements.

2. González Esteban offers a succinct introduction to the history of urban planning in Madrid and is a good place to start for those who want to see the larger context of recent events.

3. On the 1985 plan, see Compitello, "Designing Madrid" and "A Good Plan Gone Bad" (2012); Larson, "Shifting Modern Identities"; Eduardo Leira, "Una apuesta"; López de Lucio; and the roundtable discussion in *Urbanismo* among the many works of description and analysis of the plan. Special issues of the journal *Urbanismo* 7 (1989) and 13 (1991) are also instructive.

4. Marcuse offers an important interpretation of this turn in Castells's work.

5. The same double issue of *Journal of Spanish Cultural Studies* in which the 2014 article by Moreno-Caballud and those by Kornetis, La Parra Pérez, and Sampedro and Lobera appeared also included commentary on them by Belfour (La Parra-Pérez) Medina (Kornetis), Martín-Estudillo (Sampedro and Lobera), and Saum-Pascual (Moreno-Caballud). Cameron's introductory essay to the volume is also insightful in situating this strain of reasoning about the 15-M and *indignados*. A number of those who participated in the 2012 special issue of *Hispanic Review* (80.4) expressed similar views. In addition to Moreno-Caballud's essay, which introduces the special-issue essays by Benavente, Fernández, Fernández Savater, and Labrador-Méndez, makes similar kinds of arguments. The essay by Martín-Cabrera offers a somewhat different approach that contextualizes the points of view expressed in the other essays.

6. "Las elecciones generals de 2011" offers a comprehensive assessment of that election cycle in Spain. The Anduiza et al. article focuses on the 15-M's effects on the elections and offers a wealth of information about the electoral propensities of those who identified with the 15-M and how all of this affected voting for particular parties. Based on the data they amassed, the authors conclude that the 15-M had little effect on the high rate of abstention in the elections. They do conclude, however, that sympathizing with the 15-M had a significant effect on deciding what parties voters chose.

7. Interestingly, one of the most "popular" explanations of the financial crisis, Saló's *Españistán*, which was turned into a YouTube video that went viral, blames only the right, the financial and construction sectors, and greed, not the left.

8. Tova and Lagham offer an important contextualization of the effects of affect on recent social theory. Anderson and Harrison are also a useful point of reference, and "Cartografías Afectivas—Behind the Openness" offers an important case study of how this plays out in Madrid.

9. Criticism of political practice on the left, it should also be pointed out, is not new even among its supporters. While many now scorn Javier Pradera's political positions, his 1993 essay "Las pasiones del poder. El PSOE tras diez años de gobierno" is an important critical assessment that demonstrates a position, if not a tone, very similar to that of those insisting on the uniqueness of their own position. Martín-Cabrera makes arguments similar to the one I am espousing.

10. This section draws from Compitello, "A Good Plan Gone Bad" and *From the Reina Sofía to Lavapiés: Urban and Cultural Change in Madrid's City Center* (a book-length manuscript nearing completion).

11. The term "phenomenon" has been chosen carefully so as to not suggest a level of generalized organization for the movement that would misrepresent its essentially grassroots nature in Madrid. The slogan the *okupas* developed, "Kada Okupación un Mundo" (Every squat is a world), aptly represents the nature of the movement, in which the *autogestión* of each CSOA was a fundamental aspect of both the process and the result of the act of taking a building.

12. Jiménez's "El Ayuntamiento propone destinar a usos universitarios dos edificios abandonados de Lavapiés" points out that as early as 1997 the city had asked the national government and the Caja Madrid for a donation of two abandoned buildings. While the article does not specify which buildings they are, they appear to be Embajadores 68, site of Labo I, and Ronda de Valencia 2, site of the Casa Encendida, intimating an early connection between *okupas* and the Casa Encendida project.

13. The architect for the renovation, Carlos Manzano, spent 11 million euros in conserving the architectural details of Sebastián Arbós's original 1913 design (F.S).

14. On the *okupas* and technology and media in general, see Alcalde Villacampa and Sádaba Rodríguez and Roig Domínguez.

15. The collective volume *Una mirada transdisciplinar del 15-M* also has an expansive section on spatial politics of the 15-M.

16. What follows synthesizes part of an essay by Malcolm Alan Compitello and Juliana Luna Freire currently under revision.

17. Unfortunately, the lively and enlightening transcript of that session was lost due to server issues. The highlight was the conversation thread that dealt with protesters' unwillingness to commit to engaging in the political process and the objections to that strategy raised by various graduate students from around the Hispanic world who were enrolled in the class.

WORKS CITED

15MP2P. Una mirada transdisciplinar del 15M. Ed. Eunate Serrano. 2014. Web. 15 May 2016.

Abellán Bordallo, Jacobo. "De la red a la calle: El proceso de movilización previo a las manifestaciones del 15-M." *ACME: International E-Journal of Critical Geographies* 14.1 (2015): 10–29. Print.

_____, Jorge Sequera, Michael Janoschka "Occupying the #Hotelmadrid: A Laboratory for Urban Resistance." *Social Movement Studies* 11.3–4 (2012): 320–26. Print.

Adell Argilés, Ramon, and Miguel Martínez López, eds. *¿Dónde están las llaves? El movimiento okupa: Prácticas y contextos sociales*. Madrid: Los Libros de la Catarata, 2004. Print.

_____. "Mani-fiesta-acción: la contestación okupa en la calle (Madrid: 1985–2002)." *¿Dónde están las llaves? El movimiento okupa: prácticas y contextos sociales*. Eds. Ramón Adell Argilés and Miguel Martínez López. Madrid: Los Libros de la Catarata, 2004. 89–113. Print

Amat Montesinos, Xavier, and Samuel Ortiz Pérez. "La ruralidad del 15-M. Iniciativas desde el movimiento agroecológico alicantino." *ACME: An International E-Journal for Critical Geographies* 14.1 (2015): 185–99. Web. 15 May 2016.

Balfour, Sebastian. "'Revueltas lógicas: El ciclo de movilización del 15M y la práctica de la democracia radical' by Pablo La Parra-Pérez." *Journal of Spanish Cultural Studies* 15.1–2 (2014): 59–60. Print.

Benavente, Fran. "Formas de resistencia en el documental español contemporáneo: En busca de los gestos radicales perdidos." *Hispanic Review* 80.4 (2012): 607–30. Print.

Bourdieu, Pierre. *Outline of a Theory of Practice*. Cambridge: Cambridge University Press, 1977. Print.

Byrne, Janet, ed. *The Occupy Handbook*. New York: Back Bay Books, 2012. Print.

Cameron, Bryan. "Spain in Crisis: 15-M and the Culture of Indignation." *Journal of Spanish Cultural Studies* 15.1–2 (2014): 1–11. Print.

Cartas Martín, Raquel, Manuel Ortiz Mateos, Juan Luís de La Rosa Municio. "La Okupación' como analizador." Universidad Complutense de Madrid, 1996. Web. 10 June 2007.

"Cartografías Afectivas—Behind the Openness." VIC Vivero de iniciativas ciudadanas 2015. Web. 15 May 2016.

Castells, Manuel. *The City and the Grassroots*. Berkeley: University of California Press, 1983. Print.

_____. *Ciudad, democracia y socialismo. La experiencia de las asociaciones de vecinos en Madrid*. Madrid: Siglo XXI, 1977. Print.

_____. *Crisis urbana y cambio social*. Madrid: Siglo XXI, 1981. Print.

_____. *Networks of Outrage and Hope: Social Movements in the Internet Age*. Malden, MA: Polity Press, 2012. Print.

_____. *The Urban Question. A Marxist Approach*. Trans. Alan Sheridan. Cambridge, MA: MIT University Press, 1977. Print.

Chamorro González, Jesús María, ed. *Derecho y urbanismo: Principios e instituciones comunes*. Vol. X. Madrid: Consejo General del Poder Judicial, Centro de Documentación Judicial, 2004. Print.

Compitello, Malcolm Alan. "Designing Madrid, 1985–1997." *Cities* 20.6 (2003): 403–11. Print.

_____. "A Good Plan Gone Bad: From Operation Atocha to the Gentrification of Lavapiés." *International Journal of the Constructed Environment* 2.2 (2012): 75–94. Print.

Cózar, Rafael de. "La policía desaloja en Lavapiés el centro 'okupa; más conocido de la capital." *www.elpais.com*. 10 June 2003. Web. 10 July 2004.

De Terán, Fernando. *Historia del urbanismo en España. 3 siglos XIX y XX*. Madrid: Cátedra, 1999. Print.

_____. *Madrid: ciudad-región. Entre la ciudad y el territorio en la segunda mitad del Siglo XX*. Madrid: Comunidad de Madrid, Consejería de Obras Públicas, Urbanismo y Transporte, 1999. Print.

_____. "Notas para la historia del planeamiento de Madrid (de los orígenes a la Ley Especial de 1946)." *Madrid: Cuarenta años de desarrollo urbano 1940–1980*. Vol. 5. Madrid: Ayuntamiento de Madrid, 1981. 37–52. Print.

_____. "Planeamiento metropolitano: la revisión del Plan General de Madrid 1960–1965." *Madrid: Cuarenta años de desarrollo urbano 1940–1980*. Vol. 5. Madrid: Ayuntamiento de Madrid, 1981. 95–100. Print.

Diéguez Patao, Sofía. *Un nuevo orden urbano: "El Gran Madrid" (1939–1951)*. Madrid: Ministerio para las Administraciones Públicas, Ayuntamiento de Madrid, 1991. Print.

Dieste Hernández, Jorge, and Angel Pueyo. "Procesos de regeneración en el espacio urbano por las iniciativas de autogestión y *okupación*." *Scripta Nova. Revista electrónica de geografía y ciencias sociales* 7.146 (2003): 1–11. Web. 5 Aug. 2004.

Díaz Cortés, Fabia, and Jorge Sequera. "Introducción a 'geografías del 15-M, crisis, austeridad y movilización social en España.'" *ACME: International E-Journal of Critical Geographies* 14.1 (2015): 1–9. Print.

Duncombe, Stephen. *Notes from Underground: Zines and the Politics of Alternative Culture*. New York: Verso, 1997. Print.

Ezquiaga Domínguez, José María. "Entre el plan y el proyecto. Las transformaciones del Madrid de los ochenta." *A&V Monografías de Arquitectura y Vivienda* 30 (1991): 4–15. Print.

Feixa, Carles, and Jordi Nofre, eds. *#GeneraciónIndignada: Topías y utopías del 15M*. Lérida: Editorial Milenio, 2013. Print.

_____, José Sánchez García, Joana Soto, and Jordi Nofre. "El cine indignado." *#GeneraciónIndignada: Topías y utopías del 15M*. Eds. Carles Feixa and Jordi Nofre. Lérida: Editorial Milenio, 2013. 191–202. Print.

Fernández, Eva. "Destello paciente de un escape: Notas para una literatura española contemporánea que se fuga." *Hispanic Review* 80.4 (2012): 631–50. Print.

Fernández-Savater, Amador. "El nacimiento de un nuevo poder social." *Hispanic Review* 80.4 (2012): 667–82. Print.

Flesher Fominaya, Cristina, and Laurence Fox, eds. *Understanding European Movements: New Social Movements, Global Justice Struggles, Anti-Austerity Protest*. New York: Routledge, 2013. Print.

Frank, Thomas. *The Conquest of Cool*. Chicago: Chicago University Press, 1997. Print.

F.S. "La Casa Encendida surge en Madrid como un espacio de cultura y solidaridad." *www.elpais.com*. 26 Sept. 2002. Web. 1 Dec. 2003.

Gavira Martín, José, and Carmen Gavira Golpe. *Madrid: Centro y periferia*. Madrid: Biblioteca Nueva, 1999. Print.

Gerbaudo, Paolo. *Tweets and the Streets: Social Media and Contemporary Activism*. London: Pluto Press, 2012. Print.

Gómez, Mayte. "El Barrio de Lavapiés: Laboratorio de interculturalidad." *Dissidences: Hispanic Journal of Theory and Criticism* (2006). Web. 3 Mar. 207.

González Esteban, Carlos. *Madrid: Sinopsis de su evolución urbana*. Madrid: Ediciones La Librería 2001. Print.

Hall, Peter. *Cities of Tomorrow: An Intellectual History of Urban Planning and Design in the Twentieth Century*. Cambridge, MA: Blackwell, 1996. Print.

Harvey, David. "Accumulation by Dispossession." *The New Imperialism*. New York: Oxford University Press, 2003. 137–82. Print.

_____. "The Art of Rent: Globalization and the Commodification of Culture." *Spaces of Capital: Towards a Critical Geography*. New York: Routledge, 2001. 394–411. Print.

_____. *The Condition of Postmodernity*. Cambridge, MA: Blackwell, 1990. Print.

_____. *Consciousness and the Urban Experience: Studies in the History and Theory of Capitalist Urbanization*. Baltimore: Johns Hopkins University Press, 1985. Print.

_____. *Rebel Cities: From the Right to the City to the Urban Revolution*. New York: Verso, 2012. Print.

_____. *The Urban Experience*. Baltimore: Johns Hopkins University Press, 1989. Print.

Illanes, Carol, ed. *En marcha: Ensayos sobre arte, violencia y cuerpo en la manifestación social*. Santiago, Chile: Adrede Editora, 2013. Print.

Kornetis, Kostis. "'Is There a Future in This Past?': Analyzing 15M's Intricate Relation to the Transición." *Journal of Spanish Cultural Studies* 15.1–2 (2014): 83–98. Print.

Labrador Méndez, Germán. "Las vidas subprime: La circulación de historias de vida como tecnología de imaginación política en la crisis española (2007–2012)." *Hispanic Review* 80.4 (2012): 557–82. Print.

Lanceros, Paxti. "Apunte sobre el pensamiento destructivo." *En torno a la posmodernidad*. Barcelona: Anthropos, 1990. 137–59. Print.

La Parra-Pérez, Pablo. "Revueltas lógicas: El ciclo de movilización del 15M y la práctica de la democracia radical." *Journal of Spanish Cultural Studies* 15.1–2 (2014): 39–57. Print.

Larson, Susan. "Shifting Modern Identities in Madrid's Recent Urban Planning, Architecture and Narrative." *Cities* 20.6 (2003): 395–402. Print.

Leira, Eduardo, Gago Dávila, and Jesús Solana. "Madrid: Cuarenta años de crecimiento urbano." *Madrid: Cuarenta años de desarrollo urbano 1940–1980*. Vol. 5. Madrid: Ayuntamiento de Madrid, 1981. 135–63. Print.

Leira, Eduardo. "Una apuesta por la transformación." *Urbanismo* 7 (1989): 8–23. Print.

López de Lucio, Ramón, ed. *Madrid 1979–1999: La transformación de la ciudad en veinte años de ayuntamientos democráticos*. Madrid: EGRAF, 1999. Print.

"Los Reyes Inauguran La Casa Encendida en el tercer centenario de Caja Madrid." *www.elpais.com* 3 Dec. 2002. Web. 10 Aug. 2005.

Marcuse, Peter. "Depoliticizing Globalization: From Neo-Marxism to the Network Society of Manuel Castells." *Understanding the City*. Eds. John Eade and Christopher Mele. Oxford: Blackwell, 2002. 131–58. Print.

Marinas Sánchez, Marina. "Derribando los muros del género: mujer y okupación." *¿Dónde están las llaves? El movimiento okupa: Prácticas y contextos sociales*. Eds. Ramón Adell Argilés and Miguel Martínez López. Madrid: Los Libros de la Catarata, 2004. 205–26. Print.

Marston, Sallie A. "The Social Construction of Scale." *Progress in Human Geography* 24.2 (2000): 219–42. Print.

Martín-Cabrera, Luis. "The Potentiality of the Commons: A Materialist Critique of Cognitive Capitalism from the Cyberbracer@S to the Ley Sinde." *Hispanic Review* 80.4 (2012): 583–606. Print.

Martín-Estudillo, Luis. "The Spanish 15-M Movement: A Consensual Dissent?' by Víctor Sampedro and Josep Lobera." *Journal of Spanish Cultural Studies* 15.1–2 (2014): 81–82. Print.

Martínez, Guillem, ed. *CT o la cultura de la transición. Crítica a 35 años de cultura española*. Madrid: Debolsillo, 2012. Print.

Martínez, Miguel Ángel, and Ángela García. "Ocupar plazas, liberar edificios." *ACME: International E-Journal of Critical Geographies* 14.1 (2015): 158–84. Print.

Martínez López, Miguel. *Okupaciones de viviendas y de centros sociales: Autogestión, contracultura y conflictos urbanos*. Barcelona: Virus, 2002. Print.

_____. "Viviendas y centros sociales en el movimiento de *okupación*: Entre la autogestión doméstica y la reestructuración urbana." *Scripta nova: Revista electrónica de geografía y ciencias sociales* 7.146 (2003): 1–20. Web. 6 July 2005.

Medina, Alberto. "Is There a Future in This Past?: Analyzing 15M's Intricate Relation to the Transición "by Kostis Kornetis." *Journal of Spanish Cultural Studies*. 15 1-2 (2014): 99–100. Print.

Merrifield, Andy. *Metromarxism*. New York: Routledge, 2002. Print.

_____. *The New Urban Question*. New York: Pluto, 2014. Print.

"Mesa redonda: El urbanismo español en la última década." *Urbanismo* 1 (1987): 8–24. Print.

Mitchell, Don. *The Right to the City: Social Justice and the Fight for Public Space.* New York: Guilford, 2003. Print.

Moneo, Rafael. "El desarrollo de Madrid en los años sesenta." *Madrid: Cuarenta años de desarrollo urbano 1940–1980.* Vol. 5. Madrid: Ayuntamiento de Madrid, 1981. 101–12. Print.

———. "Madrid: Los últimos veinticinco años (1940–1965)." *Madrid: Cuarenta años de desarrollo urbano 1940–1980.* Vol. 5. Madrid: Ayuntamiento de Madrid, 1981. 79–94. Print.

Moreno, Susana. "Caja Madrid invertirá 1.200 millones en un centro cultural y educativo." *www.elpais.com.* 21 Mar. 2001. Web. 24 Dec. 2002.

Moreno-Caballud, Luis. "Burbujas culturales y culturas del compartir. Notas sobre producción de subjetividad en torno al 15M." *15MP2P. Una mirada transdisciplinar del 15M.* Eds. Eunate Serrano Antonio Calleja-López, Arnau Monterde, and Javier Toret. 2014. Web. 15 May 2016.

———. "Cuando cualquiera escribe. Procesos democratizadores de la cultura escrita en la crisis de la cultura de la transición española." *Journal of Spanish Cultural Studies* 15.1–2 (2014): 13–36. Print.

———. *Cultures of Anyone: Studies on Cultural Democratization in the Spanish Neoliberal Crisis.* Liverpool: University of Liverpool Press, 2015. Print.

———. "Cultures of Anyone. The Spanish 'Indignado' Movement and Its Contexts." *culturasdecualquiera.wordpress.com.* 21 Oct. 2013. Web. 15 May 2016.

———. "Desbordamientos culturales en torno al 15-M." *Teknokultura. Revista de cultural digital y movimientos sociales* 10.1 (2013): 101–30. Print.

———. "La imaginación sostenible: Culturas y crisis económica en la España actual." *Hispanic Review* 80.4 (2012): 535–56. Print.

Navarette Moreno, Lorenzo. *La autopercepción de los jóvenes okupas en España.* Madrid: Instituto de la Juventud, Ministerio de Trabajo y Asuntos Sociales, 1999. Print.

Nofre, Jordi. "Cartografías de la indignación." *Arachne* 169 (2013). Web. 10 May 2014.

———. "Del pacto social a la imaginación: Geografía(s) de la #spanishrevolution." *#GeneraciónIndignada: Topías y utopías del 15M.* Eds. Carles Feixa and Jordi Nofre. Lérida: Editorial Milenio, 2013. 21–52. Print.

Padilla, Andrés. "Dos focos culturales, pared con pared. El nuevo centro La Casa Encendida y los 'okupas' de El Laboratorio multiplican las propuestas en la misma manzana de Lavapiés." *www.elpais.com.* 3 Jan. 2003. Web. 6 July 2005.

Postill, John. "Democracy in an Age of Viral Reality: A Media Epidemiography of Spain's Indignados Movement." *Ethnography* 0.00 (2013): 1–19. Print.

Pradera, Javier. "Las pasiones del poder. El PSOE tras diez años de gobierno (1982–1992)." *Claves* 26 (1992): 32–42. Print.

Recuperar Madrid. Madrid: Ayuntamiento de Madrid, Oficina Municipal del Plan, 1982. Print.

Sádaba Rodríguez, Igor, and Gustavo Roig Domínguez. "El movimiento de okupación ante las nuevas tecnologías: Okupas en las redes." *¿Dónde están las llaves? El movimiento okupa: Prácticas y contextos sociales*. Eds. Ramón Adell Argilés and Miguel Martínez López. Madrid: Los Libros de la Catarata, 2004. 267–91. Print.

Saló, Aleix. *Españistán*. Barcelona: Editores de Tebeos, 2011. Print.

Sambricio, Carlos. *Madrid: Ciudad-región. De la ciudad ilustrada a la primera mitad del siglo XX*. Madrid: Comunidad de Madrid-Consejería de Obras Públicas, Urbanismo y Transporte, 1999. Print.

Sambricio, Carlos, ed. *Madrid y sus anhelos urbanísticos. Memorias inéditas de Secundino Zuazo, 1919–1940*. Madrid: Nerea, 2003. Print.

____, ed. *El Plan Bidagor 1941–1946. Plan general de ordenación de Madrid*. Madrid: Nerea, 2003. Print.

Sampedro, Víctor, and Josep Lobera. "The Spanish 15-M Movement: A Consensual Dissent?" *Journal of Spanish Cultural Studies* 15.1–2 (2014): 61–80. Print.

Saum-Pascual, Alexandra. "Cuando cualquiera escribe. Procesos democratizadores de la cultura escrita en la crisis de la cultura de la transición española." *Journal of Spanish Cultural Studies* 15.1–2 (2014): 37–38. Print.

Schiffrin, Anya, and Eamon Kircher-Allen, eds. *From Cairo to Wall Street: Voices of the Global Spring*. New York: New Press, 2012. Print.

Snyder, Jonathan. *Poetics of Opposition in Contemporary Spain: Politics and the Work of Urban Culture*. New York: Palgrave Macmillan, 2015. Print.

Staeheli, Lynn A. "Empowering Political Struggle: Spaces and Scales of Resistance." *Political Geography* 13.5 (1994): 387–91. Print.

Villaseca, Stephen Luis. "The 15-M Movement: Formed by and Formative of Counter-mapping and Spatial Activism." *Journal of Spanish Cultural Studies* 15.1–2 (2014): 119-39. Print.

Villacampa, Alcalde. "La batalla de los medios: La definición de la problemática okupa en los medios de comunicación de masas." *¿Dónde están las llaves? El movimiento okupa: Prácticas y contextos sociales*. Eds. Ramón Adell Argilés and Miguel Martínez López. Madrid: Los Libros de la Catarata, 2004. 227–66. Print.

◆   CHAPTER 3

Practices of Oppositional Literacy in the 15-M Movement in Madrid

Jonathan Snyder

> Si no nos dejan soñar, no les dejaremos dormir.
> (If they won't let us dream, we won't let them sleep)
> Protest banner in La Puerta del Sol, 2011

The global financial crisis of 2007–08 has many facets that continue to bear on Spain with regional and local particularities: an urban crisis, a housing crisis, a labor crisis, a state crisis of sovereignty, a political crisis of governance to neoliberal policy aims, an everyday crisis of survival for many, and so on. In times of crisis, the mass demonstrations convened after May 15, 2011, known as the 15-M movement, drew unexpected multitudes of protesters before the local and regional elections. Outrage and the slogan "¡No somos mercancía en manos de políticos y banqueros!" (We're not commodities in the hands of politicians and bankers!) were understood to be the common denominators among protesters, called the *indignadxs*—the angry ones. Demonstrators occupied public plazas and raised self-managed encampments throughout Spanish cities, communicating through social networks, cell phones, and the Web. Mobilizing against the government's austerity measures, rising unemployment, political corruption, and restrictive copyright laws among numerous other reasons, the protesters endured confrontations with the police through passive resistance and the National Election Board's verdict that declared the demonstrations illegal.

By mid-June, protesters in Madrid's Puerta del Sol lifted the encampment voluntarily, for the 15-M movement had transformed into a network of local assemblies and self-organized working groups coordinating sustained actions, which have since garnered supporters across demographics (Sampedro and Lobera). As the primary civilian response to Spain's compounded crises, the 15-M mobilizations have forcefully "irrumpido desde la primavera de 2011 como un actor nuevo en la ciudad" (Observatorio Metropolitano 171) (irrupted as a new actor in the city ever since the spring of 2011). Across Spain to date, these networks have halted forced evictions for homeowners and the deportation of undocumented immigrants, rallied against privatization and cutbacks to public education and health care, and organized debates, textbook exchanges, and neighborhood film screenings, to name a few lines of action. Though unexpected, the events of May 2011 reinvigorated direct democratic participation in public affairs in which, according to Spanish public television (TVE), an estimated 6 to 8.5 million residents in Spain had participated to some degree in a matter of three months ("Más de seis millones").

What persists when demonstrators no longer occupy the square are the oppositional practices of protesters who read their common subjugation critically and, in the process, make the sources of domination legible as a collective circumstance, with material consequences. Reading, it seems, has played an important role in constituting and reconstituting multitudes that mobilize toward change. What are the mechanics of these readings? How are they produced, and what work can they possibly do across different publics? What relationships exist among the ways in which, contextually, these readings are produced with sensible intensity, circulated among other readers, and performed into existence in urban space?

There exists no one material that is read and made readable in these practices of assembly and protest, but an array of singularities bound together by the common circumstances of production across them, in the sinews between them. Protesters read and denounce the processes of gentrification and privatization in the urban landscape, rhetoric on austerity circulating in the media by government officials and policy makers, precarious conditions of everyday work life, economic-political consensuses forged against the interests of the represented, social inequalities recast in media analysis as the personal failings of the poor, and so forth. Madrid's Sol encampment in 2011 formulated multiple responses to the circumstance of the crisis in which, on the one hand, protesters refused to accept their constituent condition as "the represented" by government officials and policy makers making decisions against their interests and without their consent: "¡No a banqueros y políticos!" (No to bankers and politicians!), "¡No pagaremos vuestras crisis!" (We won't pay for your crises!), and so on (Hardt and Negri). These statements generally rebuke austerity measures justified by policy makers and government officials from both the socialist (PSOE) and conservative (PP) parties who, borrowing from the language of 1980s Thatcherism ("There Is No Alternative"), repeatedly denied the existence of any alternative at all.

On the other hand, and related to the above, the language of protest critiqued the growing social exclusions being forged amid the economic down-turn and the dismantling of social welfare protections: "Violencia es cobrar 600 euros" (Violence is earning 600 euros a month), "España, un país de gente sin casa y casas sin gente" (Spain, a country of people without houses and houses without people), and so forth. Banners, slogans, and the language of protest tended to contest official state discourse on neoliberal policies in particular, and the ways these policies shape inequalities and exclusions from public access to an extensive range of issues in general (access to public education, free culture, the right to the city and affordable housing, and so on). They are, in the words of protesters, struggles for "dignity" and "quality of life" (Acampada Indefinida).

These are two interrelated types of critical reading, the former based on re-fusal ("They don't represent us!") and the latter on denouncing how inequalities and exclusions to access are shaped under the rule of capital and the fiscal priori-ties of the European Union. Both are strongly associated with "anger," "outrage," and frustration, notes sociologist Manuel Castells, born of the sense that the ca-pacity for autonomous decision making had been usurped from the population in the Spanish state's management of the crisis (Networks 110–55). Democracy, to cite the words of the first demonstrations, had been "held hostage" by elite political and economic interests in which Spanish residents were compelled to repay the public debt funneled to private enterprise and rescued banks—a de-nouncement depicted in the protesters' chant and gestures "¡Manos arriba! ¡Esto es un atraco!" (Hands up! This is a robbery!). The demands for "Real Democracy Now" captured the popular estrangement from democratic participation aimed at resisting those interests that protected, at great cost to social and labor rights, the economic policies of the European Union, the established party system, and financial and banking capital. In his analysis of the politics of spectatorship, Ángel Luis Lara argues that 15-M may therefore be understood as a rebellion of the public against its constructed role as passive viewers (the "represented") whereby "los públicos ya no se contentan con la recepción de las narraciones y los contenidos culturales, ahora se los reapropian, los reescriben y resignifican" (662) (publics are no longer satisfied with receiving narratives and cultural con-tents; now they reappropriate them, they rewrite and resignify them).

In this light, 15-M's critical readings of the crisis can be understood as ensu-ing from a form of oppositional literacy (that is, knowledges and practices of reading oppositionally) that bear a specific mechanics. First, in their opposi-tional readings, 15-M protesters critique how predominant powers shape the world through which subjects move and then, in assembly, pursue imagined alternatives that mitigate the authoritative effects of power wherever they have a policing or repressive function—a dynamic comparable to oppositional narrative examined in Ross Chambers's *Room for Maneuver*. In certain contexts of storytelling, notes Robert C. Spires, "Chambers argues that oppositional reading consists of seducing the reading subject away from the subject position of narratee into that of interpretive subject" (208). The practices of protest, in the ways I address them, are less concerned with narrative seduction, or the act of being drawn into the story (though they certainly may do so), than they are with the transformative becoming in this movement from addressee to interpretative subject that responds oppositionally to power as addresser (Snyder 69–124). In the practices of the *indignadxs*, the activity of critical reading shifts from the "passive" reception of addressee (the "represented") to an "active" participant as addresser when interpreting the collective sources of perceived domination—indeed, even an active participant in mobilizing for change in opposition to them. That is, Chambers provides some analytical tools that can approach the mechanics of this productive drift in 15-M from the ways in which protesters construct the political as legible material wherever it shapes everyday life, to diminishing the authoritative status of existing powers through oppositional readings and practices that articulate desirable alternatives to, and within, the current conjuncture (Chambers 179).

Oppositional literacy does not presume a body of literature per se, nor is this line of inquiry concerned with perceiving in social movements a form of literary practice that "reading literature" might imply from the privilege of an academic position. Rather, oppositional readings can be, and indeed have been, taught and learned from one another, even mimetically, in the experimental practices of assembly by doing together without the need for formal education (Corsín and Estalella, "Asambleas" 73–88). Reading critically, in this sense, is an activity that is socialized collectively and pays great attention to the cognitive process of analytical thought, on the one hand, as well as to the "contagious" character of emotions/affects that take shape around certain forms of reading, on the other—or, in the words of the youth organization JuventudSinFuturo, "Organiza tu rabia, pero no te olvides de defender la felicidad" (Organize your anger, but don't forget to defend happiness). As Judith Butler has noted similarly regarding demonstrators in Tahrir Square in 2011, the language of protest is indissociable from what performative bodies do, and can prove capable of doing, when assembled in specific spaces and contexts around specific issues ("Bodies in Alliance"); this returns us to the context of reading for the ways in which bodies perform interpretation through action and situate (and are situated by) what they read, say, and do. So, if there is some character to "being drawn into" the narrative, it would possibly start with the plaza, which was a place that invited viewers to read its multiple statements and commentary on the recent aftermath of Spain's crises, and to do so among a growing plurality of readers who also participated in weaving the narrative through statements and actions.

Oppositional Readings as a Collective Practice

In 15-M, the oppositional practices and readings of the crisis by protesters are part and parcel of the urban transformations in the public square. In an action clamoring against the Spanish state's management of the crisis, reported corruption scandals, and so on, the platform Democracia Real Ya! (Real Democracy Now! or DRY) issued an open call for a nationwide demonstration on May 15, 2011, which was seconded by numerous others. The protest #TomaLaCalle (Take the Streets) was to be held "without ideologies" or adherence to a specific political party, one week before the elections for municipalities and autonomous communities in Spain. The demonstration was articulated from a position of refusal itself: removed from any specific ideological banner, party, or labor union, the organizers rejected existing institutionalisms and partisan channels—that is, the refusal to be represented, or at least not in these ways (Hardt and Negri). Therefore, one organizing principle for the first demonstrations was intimately related to the inclusive uses of public space as the locus of demonstration and assembly, which would transform with the practices of protest throughout the consolidation of the Sol encampment.

As Víctor Sampedro and José Manuel Sánchez have noted, these practices of "reappropriating space" for public use were already prevalent in the discursive practices of "reappropriating political discourse" in cyber-culture at that time, whereby the network of virtual protest activities materialized in the public plaza and contributed to garnering support for assembly in urban space (Sampedro and Sánchez, "Del 15-M a la #acampadasol"; "La Red"). The correlation between spatial and discursive reappropriation, to elaborate on Sampedro and Sánchez, resided in the protesters' actions to retake urban space and foster within it a space for deliberative discussion and debate in order to develop proposals to take action. Both forms of reappropriation proved vital to the production of an alternative spatial arrangement made possible by these oppositional practices:

> [T]ras sucesivas reformas, la Plaza del Sol, como tantas otras, era un "no-lugar": un espacio de paso, sin bancos ni árboles, donde conversar o encontrarse resultaba casi imposible. Tomar las plazas no pretendía sólo visibilizar determinadas demandas. Implicaba detenerse y habitar los espacios colonizados por el tráfico y el capital. ("La Red")

(After successive renovations, the Plaza del Sol, like so many others, was a "non-place": a space of transit without benches or trees where it was nearly impossible to meet or talk. Taking the square did not only aim to make certain demands visible. It involved detaining and inhabiting spaces colonized by traffic and capital.)

Describing Sol as a space of transit and commerce alone, or a non-place, the authors make reference to Marc Augé's assessment of the kinds of policed spatial arrangements proliferating in advanced capitalism, dedicated to the priorities of the service industries, transit, entertainment, and the flows of commercial and investment capital over those of public interest and collective use (94). Whereas the historic Puerta del Sol conjures up an image of the bustling, modern *fin-de-siècle* Madrid in the popular imaginary, one century later the square had become largely divested of its public and civilian functions, its sense of place eroded to a commercially homogenous brand of tourism.[1] This historic epicenter would make Sol appear to be a symbolic location for protesters, thus made so in their signifying, collective practices that reappropriated the plaza for direct democratic participation in open debates.

For 15-M demonstrators, the spatial practices of assembly and protest in the urban milieu arose together from the outset in order to articulate desirable change. The reterritorialization of public space and political discourse to which Sampedro and Sánchez refer is one that hinged on the critical activity of refusal: "We're not commodities in the hands of politicians and bankers," "They don't represent us," "We won't pay for your crises," and so forth. Specifically, in space, the language of refusal also pointed to the demonstrators' participation in deliberative democracy and assembly as a struggle for the public, subtracted from the existing channels of popular sovereignty that had failed to represent them: "La lucha está en la calle, no en las urnas" (The struggle is in the streets, not in the ballot boxes). Practiced inseparably in language and space, then, was a refusal to concede a collective right to the city, as the host to inclusive democratic assembly in urban space, against the priorities of capital in everyday life.

To illustrate the authors' claim, one needs only to consider the ways in which the protesters and campers in Madrid's Puerta del Sol had repurposed this space with oppositional readings just five days after May 15. Sol's buildings—under renovation, covered by scaffolding—became motley collages where demonstrators pinned banners on the surfaces of walls, billboards, and facades. Their oppositional readings, which combined language and visual elements, pointed out the responsible parties for the crisis in the protesters' view; made appeals to readers in solidarity; and denounced the deteriorating conditions of life, often in English for a movement aware of its possible international projection:

"Bankers, Robbers, responsible for the crisis," "Working-class families demand a solution for our mortgages," "People of Europe Rise Up!" and so on. Wrapped around one scaffold was a commercial advertisement for L'Oréal shampoo, which demonstrators had cut and added words to in order to form the demand "REAL democracy now!" This reshaping of the commercial billboard, which left nearly the whole of its advertisement intact, stood as an exemplary form of reappropriation among the interpretive activities of the demonstrators with art and posters in which the original material of critique (here, consumer society) was layered with readings for viewers to see in slogans, banners, and calls to solidarity. As the Sol encampment reappropriated language and space together, not only were the multiple responses to political and economic powers captured in protest slogans used to redesign the look and feel of Sol, but they likewise played an integral part in producing this space according to the protesters' aims through resignifying practices.

Concomitant to the reclaiming and rewriting of public space was Sol's generator-powered communication hub of tech teams that worked to distribute information online with growing visibility: to document events, communicate with other camps, broadcast the encampment by live webcam, and issue statements on Twitter, Facebook, Google Maps, and Web sites (Saleh and Pérez). This confluence of the uses of public and virtual space sustained the autonomous, self-managed network of the encampments with growing sophistication and public visibility. By broadcasting itself live online, Sol circumvented the mainstream media through direct communication with potential sympathizers for the demonstrations via alternative media sources online as it transformed the public square in oppositional practice. "Nos hemos enterado todos por Internet" (We all learned about it on the Internet), stated one interviewed protester compelled to join the demonstrations in Sol ("Indignados"). In effect, the intensity of this volume of activity, online and in the square, can be said to be sensed even before it is articulated, as one might say "something is going on in Sol." This uncertain "something" is made perceptible by the buzz of activity surrounding it, thanks in part to the volume of noise generated in these plural critical readings and refusals circulating with growing visibility. Noise, which contributed to the visible irruption of the protests in virtual and physical space, may have been an oppositional technology to mobilize sympathizers in great volume, though it cannot substitute for assembly or for the kinds of critical readings that brought protesters together.

Specifically, this multiplicity of refusals circulating online and in the square had a mechanics to them: they were spoken from the protesters' plural readings of social and political relationships between the technologies of government and the governed ("No to Bankers and Politicians") and what was inseparable from them, the ways in which these predominant power relations shaped inequalities and limitations to access in everyday life—in short, their biopolitical dimension ("Violence is earning 600 euros a month"). They are, in other words, critical readings that articulate political subjectification in great volume and difference, constitutive of a plural multitude. Stated in announcements for demonstrations and the slogans and signs used in them, these heterogeneous responses detected and refused the discursive formations of power in the everyday, even if the statements were not formed through negation alone ("Capitalism: System Error, Reboot"). As Eduardo Romanos and Ángel Luis Lara have noted, the 15-M protest statements, banners, and slogans interpreted and reappropriated the language of power, often with irony, in which oppositional practices can be said to form one part of a transformative process of critical interpretation in plural ways (Romanos, "Humor"; Lara, "Virgil"). Should visitors in Sol have any doubt about the occasional irony of these readings, a black-and-white portrait of SS officer Heinrich Himmler was depicted wearing Mickey Mouse ears with the euro currency symbol at center. The use of metaphor, in this case, took the perceptible source of outrage and domination—confluent economic and political powers—and rendered them visually as a Disneyfied fascist regime under the rule of capital, with the euro as the common currency. This visual troping of power in urban space performed the language of statements refusing subjection to the perceptible source of domination, such as the statement issued later by the Economy Group from Sol that attributed the usurping of popular sovereignty to the Spanish state's complicity with a "dictatorship of the markets": "Elevar a rango constitucional la limitación del déficit público no solamente es un atentado contra la vida de los habitantes de nuestro país . . . , es un golpe de Estado encubierto de los mercados, al que nuestro gobierno se somete de manera voluntaria" (Acampada Sol, "Grupo de Trabajo") (To proclaim a public spending cap on the deficit at a constitutional level is not only an attack on the lives of residents in our country . . . , it is also an underhanded coup by the markets to which our government has submitted itself willingly.)

Although "noise" refers to intelligibility in certain contexts, to not being able to hear or discern what another is saying, in this case the volume of the refusals lends itself instead to being read in multiple ways from different subject positions. In this sense, in practice, the protests' rejection of institutionalisms, parties, and ideological banners for the demonstrations may have played an effective role in mobilizing protesters, due to these messages in their openness to being read. Not only were these institutions often the very object of disenchantment and rejection in the context of Spain's crisis, but the plurality of protest statements also contributed to the multiplicity of readings articulated in relation to common concerns.

Reading and reappropriating from the discourse of power is an oppositional activity that involves critical thought and response to different forms of political subjectification, whether articulated as one's indebtedness to banking institutions on a subprime mortgage, as the conditions of precarity sustained by labor law, or anything else. Perhaps one of the technologies of mobilization, then, was the openness of these statements in their difference from and troping of one another, to be read with difference across segments of the population that found some form of agreement with the content of what they denounce or, as Manuel Castells notes in other social mobilizations, with the emotional attachments formed around the injustices they decried (*Communication Power*). Multiple refusals, in many senses, had an open character to them—in open circulation in physical and virtual circuits, and in open association with others who made likeminded claims. In this light, language, per Judith Butler, is not simply an expression but rather bears the potential to perform what it speaks, and its speakers, into material practice. In circulation via social networks and other circuits, these statements comprised an open field of social contact and relational difference with new and repeated critical readings for other readers—not through accumulation, but through difference in their many enunciations repeated in other contexts: "Lo llaman democracia, pero no lo es" (They call it democracy but it's not), "Más educación, menos corrupción" (More education, less corruption), and so forth. The volume of noise generated by refusal, in other words, may also bear its own "riff," so to speak, in which statements can be read with multiple meanings while readers are invited to join in contributing their own note. "If reading, then, is the mediation by which narrative discourse makes its impact on history," writes Chambers, "this impact depends on the fact . . . that reading is itself a realization of the implications . . . of the phenomenon of mediation," or the oppositional interpretation of power and collective subjugation across plural subject positions (18).

Specifically, regarding the adage that "there is no alternative," those who are called *indignadxs* do not read this official discourse on the crisis literally by any means. As statements in political discourse attempt to legitimize law and policy on austerity, speech acts also become fodder for demonstrators who read critically and oppose the official state discourse on the crisis. The protesters' response, in opposition, is captured in one slogan from the demonstrations, "¡Somos la alternativa!" (We are the alternative!). The assertion by government officials that "there is no alternative" was contested directly by 15-M Sol's open call for proposals on change as the very possibility from which to imagine alternative models of direct democratic participation, constitutionalism, and inclusive social well-being. As Chambers notes, "the very possibility of appropriation" of powerful discursive formations, much like the critical interpretations by protesters in 15-M's speech acts, "is evidence that no meaning can be 'dictated' permanently and that change is therefore always possible" (220).

As the demonstrators in Madrid's Sol encampment transformed the public square into a space of reflection, action, and expression for the movement's plural aims, the protesters' multiple statements—their oppositional readings of the crisis—traveled beyond discontents articulated against government officials and policy makers into practices of collective action, captured in the Sol encampment's banner, "Si no nos dejan soñar, no les dejaremos dormir" (If they won't let us dream, we won't let them sleep). As Raúl Sánchez Cedillo argues, the first mobilizations materialized quickly into what Félix Guattari understood as "una tensión afectiva y cognitiva que, por así decirlo, pone en suspenso, tornándolo susceptible de cambio y mutación enriquecedora, el régimen normal de las funciones de trabajo-vida sometidas a la movilización total" ("El 15-M como insurrección") (an affective and cognitive tension, so to speak, that suspends the normal regime of the functions of work-life subjected to total mobilization, turning it into something susceptible to enriching change and mutation). Deserving greater attention here, the mechanics of this transformation in the practices of protest and informed public debate, shared a critical dynamic in common with the activity of interpretation among participants attempting to address these complex problems through coordinated, self-managed action.

On the relations of power and authority in address, Chambers notes:

> If reading . . . is a technology of the self that is fostered in social formations . . . , we can understand that fact in terms of an apparent paradox. Power depends on that which simultaneously opposes it, that is, on "reading" as a manifestation of mediation. If we need to learn to read—learn, that is, to oppose power in acquiring the techniques of interpretive reading . . . —it is because reading is also, and primarily, a condition of the production of authority, and "power" is a product of the same system as "opposition." Power is not given but a (produced) "effect of power," an allegory read as literal; and it depends therefore on being read, a by-product of that fact being that it is simultaneously vulnerable to oppositional (mis-)reading. And so the "effect of power," when it succeeds, is itself the product of a repression, since it is the inhibition of oppositional (mis-)reading through the ability to "forget" and to cause to "forget" the role of mediation. It is only as a result of that inhibition that the discourse of power comes to seem (to be read as) literal. (251)

Following Chambers, the refusals of protest statements in their many forms negate the assertions made by power, such as those on "No Alternative" by re-instating their mediated character, via interpretation, from these statements' literal address. In this manner, the interpretive character of protest language performs something else in its production of statements, whether by reappro-priation, resignification, ironic troping, or otherwise: it restores the possibility of reading the discourse of power wherever the latter asserts its authority at face value, with "no alternative" but to be read literally. If, for Chambers, this form of oppositional reading rebukes the literal—and, in the practices of 15-M, reading tropes it in multiplicity (sometimes with irony)—then the question of repres-sion in the assertion of authority is one that hinges upon "denying" any room for interpretation—that is, repressing the mediated character of power upon which this authority depends. One might say that dictation, in this light, works to "naturalize" the authority of the power relationship over the addressee in the asserted speech act itself. It is in this way that speech acts can, in part, perform their authority; as Chambers reminds his readers, the activity of critical read-ing and response can likewise always destabilize the "naturalized" character of this authority by pointing out to power that its assertions are necessarily medi-ated within this power dynamic, however imbalanced the strike. Such a power dynamic, in other words, is at the heart of sovereignty, in which the sovereign's right to rule (authority) is dependent on the willingness of his subjects to as-sume that role.

This relational field of indirect address—for protesters, one of reading the discourse and everyday materiality of political subjectification—tends to sug-gest that outrage is not purely an emotional reaction but is necessarily rooted in readerly responses as a basis for action and possible mobilizing potential. The activity of critical reading by protesters comes to light as a necessary condition for understanding how "outrage" and its many forms arise as an affective criti-cal response capable of compelling demonstrators to act, not only from specific social circumstances of economic hardship but also from the multitude's plural readings, for example, of how officials justify the adoption of economic policies that foster disparity. Or of how media analysts attempt to recast citizens as ir-responsible economic decision makers. When taking into account their mobi-lizing potential for action, emotions and affects can take shape around critical responses to events, statements, and surroundings, as much as they are also re-ciprocally shaped by contexts, experiences, and systems of thought that inform interpretation. It is thus that the oppositional practice of reading critically is folded into the so-called *indignación* in the 15-M movement, as is, inseparable from it, its affective potential to compel others to take action from stasis. Affect is the nexus of intensity for action and critical response that are bound together, arising in the same way that someone who views a video of a policeman wielding the force of a truncheon against an unarmed protester recognizes, "That's an injustice" without necessarily passing through the cognitive process to articulate the values or ideals informing this immediate response in the viewer's specific context. Or, far from physical violence enacted on the body, in the same way that someone would hear an analyst on television argue that Spanish residents have lived beyond their economic means irresponsibly ("han vivido por encima de sus posibilidades"), which stirs a critical response without thinking twice: "That's simply not true," and then "What about government officials' appropriation of public funds to benefit their own spheres of influence?" And yet certainly not all viewers will read and respond similarly.

Desiring Change, Mitigating Authority

Demonstrators in Sol held the first few assemblies addressing collective needs and self-management (food provisions and supplies, camp maintenance and monitoring, peer education on protesters' rights, the prohibition of alcohol on site, and so on) at the same time as debates on the movement's initial demands. Labor dedicated to these structural, logistical, and educational matters was, in part, the basis from which Sol could develop sustained actions and demands through a deliberative process. An accessible sign language was employed as a voting system for inclusive, horizontal participation in the popular assemblies (to express agreement, disagreement, a desire to continue to the next topic, and so on), in which administrative roles rotated among volunteers elected by the assembly (moderator, secretary, caller-of-turns, etc.). It is noteworthy that the Madrid neighborhood assemblies modeled after Sol would also designate volunteers to care for the *ambiente*, or atmosphere where the debates took place—distributing water, spray bottles, fans, sunscreen, and so forth—calling attention to the debate as taking place in a hospitable environment.

This arrangement and its attention to care, note Alberto Corsín and Gabriel Estalella, is one element that may contribute to making the assemblies "stick around" through the attachments developed in hospitality toward others:

> Like all experimental forms, however, the assembly and the neighbor share in the problem of duration. It remains unclear and uncertain how to make experiments last. Thus, an organizational problem for the assembly, common to squatting projects at large, is that people are known to come and go, only to eventually disap-

pear forever. "People show up to help, work awhile, then disappear," Keith Gessen noted of Occupy Wall Street. Hence, perhaps, the practice of care: a technique for upholding hospitality under conditions of provisionality and adversity. Hence, too, the importance ascribed to the atmospheric, which performs the role of a political ambulatory. ("What Is a Neighbor?" 14–5)

Thus, care is not exclusively an oppositional practice for demonstrators faced with the task of collectively disengaging violence in a standoff scenario with security forces. As Corsín and Estalella argue, an open disposition to others in hospitality and ambiance may have contributed to the sustainability of the assemblies for the forms of care developed in these practices.[2] Attention to care in the assemblies and protests, as a practice of caring for others, takes shape around the collective project at hand and those participating in it. The sustainability of activism is, in this light, one that partly depends on "the emotional value of protest [as] continually re-experienced . . . to remain emotionally fulfilling to be sustainable" (Brown and Pickerill 30). Or, as Eduardo Romanos notes, the spatial arrangement of the assemblies was an invitation for bystanders to join in:

> One of the novel aspects of the 15-M movement was the way it placed experiments with new forms of democracy in the center of public space. In this way, the movement brought practices of deliberative democracy—previously confined to more or less limited spaces such as social forums, social movement headquarters, peace camps and social centers—out into public squares, where passers-by were invited to join in. ("Collective Learning," 211)

There is something to be said, then, for the openness of the assemblies and this openness to others as part of the critical practices of opposition in 15-M. It is, after all, a disposition that is valued by protesters, named, and reenacted in practice with political implications.

All participants, regardless of citizenship, had a voice and vote in the open-air assemblies, in which long debates favored processual, cognitive synthesis sustained by multiple contributions from a variety of members, rather than an outcome by a given majority alone (Serrano). Yet the question of reaching a "consensus of minimums" would become a point of contention that evolved in different assemblies and their debates on procedure.[3] In this manner, the assemblies' initial operative structure aimed to disable the potential concentration of power or cooptation of interests by specific platforms, partisan politics, or individual participants, which when reenacted in practice contributed over time to defining another element of its self-managed care for the assembly: the defense of inclusive participation against potential concerted interests among participants. The structuring of alternative modes of policing, those developed in order to defend the assemblies from cooptation by specific interests, can be understood as a self-regulatory mechanism aimed at protecting the open inclusiveness of the debates while at the same articulating "social forces grounded in values and not merely organizations or networks" (Eyerman 42).[4] The attitudes and practices of open engagement with others would be defined subsequently in the online 15-M WikiLibro resource as the foundations for conserving the movement's horizontal, inclusive participation: "nonviolence, no-machismo, no-homophobia, no-racism, no-leadership, no-membership" and so on, thereby giving names to a series of common values for engagement already in practice ("Descripción").

Self-managed labor and deliberation were practiced through open engagement with others, among participants familiar with assembly procedures who could teach and learn from one another by doing together, before procedure itself was a matter of consideration. For Gilles Deleuze, these practices constitute acquired habits or routine repetitions subject to change over time as they are practiced. "Repetition is a condition of action before it is a concept of reflection," Deleuze stresses. "We produce something new only on condition that we repeat—once in the mode which constitutes the past, and once more in the present of metamorphosis" (*Difference* 90). As Jon Beasley-Murray takes this observation further in his work *Posthegemony*, repetition in the practice of "habit leads us to the multitude: a social subject that gains power as it contracts new habits, new modes of being in the world whose durability is secured precisely by the fact that they are embodied well beneath consciousness"—that is, folded into action over time, as habit, before these actions are the subject of contemplation (178). Beasley-Murray's argument on the multitude here rings true, for self-managed labor and the open engagement of others were routine practices in the Sol encampment well before they were named, documented, or consciously contemplated for improvement. Stated otherwise, bodies came into contact with others by doing together, and their practices transformed into new habits and ways of doing together in repetition. In this manner, the popular assemblies' guidelines for propositions, deliberation, and consensus would continue to change over time, developing into the movement's multiple lines of self-management and democratic process, compiled today on the Madrid Popular Assembly's Web site ("Metodología asamblearia"). If reading is a social practice, then it should not go unstated that the forms of oppositional literacy outlined here (practices and knowledges of critical reading) have developed from contingent social relations, of being and doing together, and of teaching and learning from one another—or, for Corsín and Estalella, the politics of care in 15-M—that have in common a hospitable disposition to alterity, to others, in these valued procedures for assembly and demonstration.

Oppositional literacy also extends to the self-regulatory mechanisms of social interaction among protesters in assembly. Because the large-scale cohabitation among strangers was not without reported social tensions—and even led to a split among some demonstrators who claimed that the Sol encampment was not synonymous with the 15-M movement—the campers restructured the activist information points and assemblies to include specific working groups on "respect" in defense of the norms of engagement, difference, and dialogue in the popular assemblies.[5] Wherever language, attitudes, or practices were considered disrespectful or exclusionary to participants, the assemblies addressed the issue by generating peer education initiatives in defense of the common values developed in the assemblies (e.g., nonviolence, no-machismo, nondiscrimination, respect). Montserrat Galcerán reports, for example, that some participants were reluctant at first to include feminist committees, skeptical of identity positions as potentially divisive to collective aims; after peer education, however, feminist commissions were successfully incorporated, outlined in Galcerán's proposals and excellent documentation on teaching others (31–36). In electronic communications, attention was drawn to the use of the plural masculine *indignados*, which was replaced by the gender-inclusive *indignad@s* or the non-binary form *indignadxs*. Although the use of inclusive language alone cannot guarantee nondiscrimination, and indeed can give the false appearance of equality, the participants understood forms of communication as being vital to their practices, inextricably bound together—that is, desirable for the movement's aims.

Such a case is evident in the open invitation to a "bike criticism," an event to meet others and discuss common concerns, culminating in a performative parade of cyclists, banners, and flags through the city streets. The public invitation to the "Bici-crítica Trans-mari-bollo-bi-queer-feminista" takes derogatory slurs for LGBTQ identities (trans, mari, bollo) and, in a well-established formula, reappropriates them for the empowerment of the collective by affirming them as their own ("tranny," "fag," "dyke"). It provides an example of what Luis Martín Cabrera calls "queering the commons"—that is, of deconstructing existing forms of oppression, whether racialized, gendered, or sexualized, so that they are prevented from "endangering the very same project of living in common," here, through the oppositional practice of reappropriation as empowerment itself (602–3). In the invitation to the bike criticism, the string of hyphenations tends to exceed naming difference in its many identity constructions of gender and sexuality, in an attempt not to leave anyone out. As it does so, the conjunctions among them replicate one of 15-M's organizing principles in the assemblies through assemblage-work: the desire for inclusiveness, or the hospitable invitation to join the assembly, in the turn to others.

Chambers reminds his readers that desire is a mediated affair, subject to change in the shifting power relations of its circumstance; conversely, desire can beget change (232). Just as these desirable outcomes were articulated regarding, and in critical opposition to, the prevailing structures of power, they likewise partook in imagining the future effects of limitations placed on these powers wherever their relations worked (at present) to repress or police these material possibilities. One needs only recall the protest banner in Sol ("If they won't let us dream, we won't let them sleep") to understand that the demonstrators made this point themselves: the possibility of imagining futures (*soñar*) is articulated directly as one that is perceptibly conditioned by the prevailing structures of power (*si no nos dejan*). This temporal dimension, in relay between the current conjuncture and future actions conceived for the latter's ability to mitigate forms of repression at present (the effect of authority), appears as a mediated space of desires that opens up radically to imagined possibilities. Within it, the articulation of desirable outcomes can be sensed as emancipatory, with affective force, ensuing from "the deflation of desire [that] results from a self-education, of the awareness of the damage done, to ourselves and to others, by the desires that are controlled by power" (Chambers 232).

One year after the first Sol encampment, protesters assembled again to reclaim the public square, collecting and documenting desires for change that were written on notes, categorized by theme, and released for publication in the mainstream press (Comisión de Información; García de Blas). Although any summary of these points risks reductionism, which tends to collapse a series of conjunctions into a general schematic, one can also note a set of organizing principles shaped around these desirable outcomes. In the interstices between conjunctions, one can locate the desirable effects of future actions: to recuperate state decision making in the face of economic and financial interests in a more equitable management and distribution of common resources and wealth; to guarantee egalitarian access to public services, common resources, and public space; and to secure the protection of residents from confluent interests of state powers in concert with external (largely private and financial) institutional arrangements. The alternatives proposed in the popular assemblies, and at once practiced in them, likewise demanded some form of direct democratic participation in the decision-making powers of the state. On the whole, these desirable outcomes and their effects tended to articulate, with oppositionality, the very conditions of political subjectification that had constituted the multitude in its multiplicity of refusals. Nevertheless, there exists a productive drift or becoming that moves beyond the latter to articulate (future) desirable outcomes imagined collectively from the cognitive process of democratic assembly.

It is in this instance that I would like to underscore that the critical practices and knowledges of opposition among demonstrators (their oppositional literacy) have been capable of calling attention to the ways in which power is necessarily mediated, despite and due to authoritative claims that there exists "no alternative." It is what happens in between, however, in the mediated scenario of imagining desirable outcomes capable of mitigating forms of repression, where the authoritative status of power is seemingly displaced, if only momentarily—that is, until it comes to bear again upon subjects in whatever form (an eviction notice, a charge by antiriot forces, the idle time of unemployment, and so on). For Jacques Rancière, the partitioning of this space of mediation is precarious, "always on the shore of its own disappearance," threatened by being subsumed into the very logics, if not powers, that it opposes (39). In 15-M, however, it is also this room for maneuver that has been made to work toward producing desirable changes, which, once articulated in speech, can be conceived of as conscious changes in desire, in a productive movement from the perceived forms of domination to coordinated actions that pursue alternative futures. In this scenario, nevertheless, there is no emancipating line of flight, as Deleuze and Guattari would have it, that escapes repression completely as it mitigates the authoritative status of prevailing powers. Nor does it suppose an ideological fantasy, as it would for Žižek, in which revolutionary change requires the castration of power. Rather, change can be hatched first within the prevailing structures of domination, but it would presume, as Chambers suggests, a plural critical questioning of the ways that desires are shaped by the prevailing relations of power.

In the case of 15-M, this transformation has resided in part in the critical activity of reading and responding with oppositionality, or of identifying and contesting the existing structures of power and the ways they shape the possible (desires for alternatives) and, in turn, condition the real. In other words, the tools of interpretation already known at present, to draw from Chambers's argument, have been able to provide the necessary "room for maneuver" to pursue desired change through collective action, experimentally and somewhat haphazardly. On the other hand, as all power is a paradox, oppositional "relations of power are not in a position of exteriority" to predominant relations decried by protesters (economic, state, and so on), and indeed always risk dissipation or absorption within the logics they oppose, which makes them precarious (Foucault 94).

On May 27, security forces in Barcelona charged and fired rubber bullets to disperse protesters from #acampadabcn in Plaça Catalunya, citing hygienic reasons and the need to clean the plaza in the event of a victory that evening by Barcelona Football Club and ensuing celebrations in the streets. The images of police brutality circulating online outraged and further fueled massive protests across Spain in solidarity with the Barcelona 15-M encampment. Protesters demanded the immediate resignation of Counselor of the Interior Felipe Puig, who insisted that the use of police force was justified. Tens of thousands of protesters joined the *indignadxs* in Madrid and Barcelona, even as the Community of Madrid urged the Ministry of the Interior to clean Sol in the same manner, describing it as a *chabola* (shantytown) with unhygienic conditions. The following day, 15-M hosted the first Popular Assemblies in over forty neighborhood associations in Madrid, which have since taken part in the many "mutations, effects, and convergences" to mobilize protesters since the first demonstrations of May 2011 ("Mapa mental").

*I would like to thank co-editors Silvia Bermúdez and Tony Geist for their feedback on an earlier draft of this essay, and to Edward Baker and the anonymous reviewers at Hispanic Issues for their additional insight.

NOTES

1.   On La Puerta del Sol's historic status as a symbol of modernity in the Madrid popular imaginary and cultural production, see Larson. My thanks to Edward Baker for suggesting this point.
2.   Teaching and learning from one another are contingent on chance encounters and disconnects in mobilizing activities, as observed by Alberto Corsín and Gabriel Estalella. The authors argue that these social practices produce space through action and temporal-spatial relations—or urban rhythms, as Henri Lefebvre understood them. Corsín and Estalella analyze the assembly's activities as a rhythmic arrangement, one that produces social forms of care, as the "assembly is an urban object of care—and an object of urban care" ("What Is a Neighbor?" 3). The construction of time as a spatial arrangement, which the authors view through Lefebvre's rhythmanalysis, is one that shapes and is shaped by the social practices of providing care for others.
3.   For a discussion of consensus in activism and the structuring of an emotional hierarchy within queer activist groups (one that tends to repress "personal" emotions in favor of collective affects), see Wilkinson.
4.   However, the emotional hierarchies that arise from collective assemblies should also be the subject of critical reflection, notes Elanor Wilkinson, given that they can

structure a social consensus of feeling around group decision making, driven by co-operation, and can contribute to over-determining "appropriate" or "inappropriate" emotions for a given group (39). Though I have no evidence of Wilkinson's observation in the case of 15-M, this possibility should not be discarded out of hand.

5.   An independent news source reports on the proceedings of the assembly on May 29, 2011: "Aludieron a importantes problemas de convivencia interna y con los vecinos y comerciantes de la zona y de infraestructura (eléctricos y de alimentación principalmente). Su propuesta fue 'reestructurarse', lo que podría implicar, según explicaron, reducir el campamento y reorganizar los puestos y los grupos de trabajo" ("Última hora") (They alluded to significant internal problems related to living together and to the neighbors and business owners in the area, as well as to infrastructure [electricity and food, primarily]. They proposed "restructuring," which could mean, as they explained, reducing the encampment and reorganizing the information points and working groups).

WORKS CITED

Acampada Indefinida en Sol. 16 May 2011. Web. 10 Aug. 2014. *concentracionsolmadrid. blogspot.com.es/2011_05_01_archive.html*

Acampada Sol. "El Grupo de Trabajo de Economía Sol convoca una asamblea con carácter de urgencia para tratar la reforma constitucional anunciada por el presidente del Gobierno." 23 Aug. 2011. Web. 9 Jan. 2012. *madrid.tomalaplaza.net/2011/08/23/*

Augé, Marc. *Non-Places: Introduction to an Anthropology of Supermodernity*. Trans. John Howe. London: Verso, 1995. Print.

Beasley-Murray, Jon. *Posthegemony: Political Theory and Latin America*. Minneapolis: University of Minnesota Press, 2011. Print.

Brown, Gavin, and Jenny Pickerill. "Space for Emotion in the Spaces of Activism." *Emotion, Space, and Society* 2 (2009): 24–35. Science Direct. Web. 27 Dec. 2012.

Butler, Judith. "Bodies in Alliance and the Politics of the Street." European Institute for Progressive Cultural Policies. Venice. 7 Sept. 2011. Lecture. Web. 9 Jan. 2014. *www.eipcp.net/transversal/1011/butler/en*

Castells, Manuel. *Communication Power*. Oxford: Oxford University Press, 2009. Print.

———. *Networks of Outrage and Hope: Social Movements in the Internet Age*. Cambridge, UK: Polity, 2012. Print.

Chambers, Ross. *Room for Maneuver: Reading (the) Oppositional (in) Narrative*. Chicago: University of Chicago Press, 1991. Print.

Comisión de Información Acampada Sol. "Compilación final de propuestas." 24 Apr. 2012. Web. 17 Sept. 2012. *madrid.tomalaplaza.net*

Corsín Jiménez, Alberto, and Adolfo Estalella. "Asambleas al aire: La arquitectura ambulatoria de una política en suspensión." *Etnografías de la indignación*. Spec. issue of *Revista de Antropología Experimental* 13.4 (2013): 73–88. Web. 12 Mar 2014.

_____. "What Is a Neighbor? Notes on #Occupying the urban relation," *Prototyping*. Sept. 2012. Web. 12 Mar. 2014.

Deleuze, Gilles. *Difference and Repetition*. Trans. Paul Patton. New York: Columbia University Press, 1994. Print.

Deleuze, Gilles, and Félix Guattari. *Anti-Oedipus: Capitalism and Schizophrenia*. Vol. 1. Trans. Robert Hurley, Mark Seem, and Helen R. Lane. Minneapolis: University of Minnesota Press, 1983. Print.

_____. *A Thousand Plateaus: Capitalism and Schizophrenia*. Vol. 2. Trans. Brian Massumi. Minneapolis: University of Minnesota Press, 1987. Print.

"Descripción." WikiLibro 15M.cc. n.d. Web. 17 Sept. 2012. *wiki.15m.cc/wiki/ WikiLibro_15M.cc*

Eyerman, Ron. "How Social Movements Move: Emotions and Social Movements." *Emotions and Social Movements*. Eds. Helena Flam and Debra King. London: Routledge, 2005. 41–56. Print.

Foucault, Michel. *Discipline and Punish: The Birth of the Prison*. Trans. Alan Sheridan. New York: Vintage, 1977. Print.

Galcerán Huguet, Montserrat. "Presencia de los feminismos en la Puerta del Sol madrileña." *Youkali: Revista crítica de las artes y el pensamiento* 12 (Jan. 2012): 31–36. Web. 10 Aug. 2014.

García de Blas, Elsa. "Las 14.700 propuestas de cambio del 15M." *El País*, 11 May 2012. Web. 17 Sept. 2012.

Hardt, Michael, and Antonio Negri. *Declaration*. New York: Argo Navis, 2012. PDF.

"Indignados." *Informe Semanal*. RTVE, Madrid, 21 May 2011. Television. Web. 17 Sept. 2012.

Lara, Ángel Luis. "Virgil Starkwell en la Puerta del Sol: públicos en revuelta, políticas hacia el ser por venir." *Hispanic Review* 80.4 (2012): 651–65. Project Muse. Web. 26 July 2012.

Larson, Susan. *Constructing and Resisting Modernity: Madrid 1900–1936*. Estudios de la Cultura de España, 20. Madrid: Iberoamericana and Vervuert, 2011. Print.

Lefebvre, Henri. *Rhythmanalysis: Space, Time, and Everyday Life*. Trans. Stuart Elden and Gerald Moore. London: Continuum, 2004. Print.

"Mapa mental de mutaciones, proyecciones, alternativas y confluencias 15M." *AutoConsulta Ciudadana*. 2 Mar. 2014. Web. 10 Aug. 2014. *autoconsulta.org/mutaciones.php*

Martín Cabrera, Luis. "The Potentiality of the Commons: A Materialist Critique of Cognitive Capitalism from the Cyberbracer@s to the Ley Sinde." *Hispanic Review* 80.4 (2012): 583–605. Project Muse. Web. 26 July 2012.

"Más de seis millones de españoles han participado en el Movimiento 15M." *Servimedia*. RTVE.es. 6 Aug. 2012. Web. 17 Sept. 2012.

"Metodología asamblearia." Asamblea Popular de Madrid. n.d. Web. 17 Sept. 2012. *madrid.tomalosbarrios.net/metodologia-asamblearia*

Observatorio Metropolitano de Madrid, ed. *Paisajes devastados. Después del ciclo inmobiliario: Impactos regionales y urbanos de la crisis*. Madrid: Traficantes de Sueños, 2013. Print.

Rancière, Jacques. *Dissensus: On Politics and Aesthetics*. Trans. and ed. Steven Corcoran. London: Continuum, 2010. Print.

Romanos, Eduardo. "Collective Learning Processes within Social Movements: Some Insights into the Spanish 15-M/Indignados Movement." *Understanding European Movements: New Social Movements, Global Justice Struggles, Anti-Austerity Protest*. Eds. Cristina Flesher Fominaya and Laurence Cox. London: Routledge, 2013. 203–19. Print.

_____. "Humor in the Streets: The Spanish Indignados." *Humor and Politics in Europe* Spec. issue of *Perspectives on Europe* 43.2 (2013): 15–20. Web. 24 Mar. 2014.

Saleh, Samira, and Carmen Pérez Lanzac. "Un campamento con calles y baños portátiles." *El País*. 19 May 2011. Web. 17 Sept. 2012.

Sampedro, Víctor, and Josep Lobera. "The Spanish 15-M Movement: A Consensual Dissent?" *Journal of Spanish Cultural Studies* 15.1–2 (2014): 1–20. Taylor and Francis Online. Web. 8 Jan. 2015.

Sampedro Blanco, Víctor F., and José Manuel Sánchez Duarte. "La Red era la plaza." *Ciberdemocracia*. 2011. Web. 14 July 2014.

_____. "Del 15M a la #acampadasol: Topologías para un experimento político urbano." Medialab Prado. Madrid. Lecture. Web. 8 July 2011.

Sánchez Cedillo, Raúl. "El 15M como insurrección del cuerpomáquina." *Rebelion.org*. 28 Feb. 2012. Web. 17 Sept. 2012.

Serrano, Eduardo. "El poder de las palabras: Glosario de términos del 15M." *Madrilonia. org*. 2011. Web. 4 Apr. 2013.

Snyder, Jonathan. *Poetics of Opposition in Contemporary Spain: Politics and the Work of Urban Culture*. Hispanic Urban Studies. New York: Palgrave Macmillan, 2015. Print.

Spires, Robert C. *Post-totalitarian Spanish Fiction*. Columbia: University of Missouri Press, 1996. Print.

"Última hora, 30 de mayo: Sigue la Acampada Sol en directo." *LaInformación.com*. 30 May 2011. Web. 10 Aug. 2014.

Wilkinson, Eleanor. "The Emotions Least Relevant to Politics? Questioning Autonomous Activism." *Emotion, Space, and Society* 2 (2009): 36–43. Science Direct. Web. 27 Dec. 2012.

Žižek, Slavoj. *First as Tragedy, Then as Farce*. London: Verso, 2009. Print.

♦　CHAPTER 4

Acabar Madrid: "Future Perfect" Utopianism and the Possibility of Counter-Neoliberal Urbanization in the Spanish Capital

Eli Evans

Back to the Future:
Times of Scarcity in *El mundo's* Madrid

These reflections on the possibility of opening a breach in Madrid between the capital as city and the capital as what Jamie Peck, Nik Theodore, and Neil Brenner described, in their "Neoliberal Urbanism: Models, Moments, Mutations," as a strategic node "in the uneven, crisis-laden advance of neoliberal restructuring projects" (49) that constitute contemporary capitalism's primary mode of survival were provoked by a look back at Juan José Millás's 2007 autobiographical novel *El mundo* from the other side of that crisis on the eve of which it was written, published, and—winning both the Premio Planeta and the Premio Nacional de Narrativa—widely celebrated. For anyone familiar with what I would categorize as Millas's "mature" work, beginning with his 1987 *El desorden de tu nombre*, *El mundo* marked a kind of double departure that demanded such engagement and reengagement, especially after he returned to more established form in subsequent novels.[1]

The first of those departures pertains to setting. While most of Millás's mature novels are set in a kind of postmodern any-city sometimes given the name Madrid, and other times located elsewhere—often a sterile Northern European location—or even nowhere in particular, the opening sections of *El mundo*, assuming a tone at times closer to memoir than to the novel the book purports to be, transpire largely in the intensely specific Madrid of Millás's own childhood: not so much a city as a neighborhood, and one indelibly linked, moreover, to a no less particular and specific psyche: that of the author-narrator himself as a child. Unlike Millás's more typical Madrid, where even literature generates its own "productos secundarios" (*Dos Mujeres* 30) (secondary products), the Madrid of those opening sections of *El mundo* is characterized above all by a lived, embodied experience of economic scarcity. Madrid, recalls Millás's author-narrator, "era un mundo hecho a la mitad: teníamos la mitad del calor que necesitábamos, la mitad de la ropa que necesitábamos, la mitad de la comida y el afecto que necesitábamos para gozar de un desarrollo normal" (15) (was a world halved: we had half the heat we needed, half the clothing we needed, half the food and affection we needed to enjoy normal growth and development). Even more, the scarcity described by the author-narrator as characterizing his and his family's life in Madrid is portrayed, albeit indirectly, as not so much the result as the very real substance of the broken promise of not just abundance but the particular abundance of capitalism: abundance as a by-product of exponential or "compound" growth.[2] At a certain moment early in the novel, for instance, the author-narrator recalls overhearing adult conversations about the family's impending move from his birthplace of Valencia to the capital city. "Madrid," he remembers them saying, "es la capital, un lugar en el que las oportunidades se multiplican" (21) (Madrid is the capital, a place where opportunities multiply).

If the scarcity of the Madrid evoked in the opening section of *El mundo* is thus depicted as the consequence of a failure or absence of a kind of growth described in terms not of addition but of multiplication, however, the restoration or resuscitation of growth as a salve is thematically problematized in the novel. This problematizing is accomplished by way of a character by the name of El Vitaminas, on whom much of the novel's second section focuses its attention. Consider, as an example of this thematization, the following introduction to El Vitaminas with which that second section of the novel, "La calle" (The Street) begins: "Un chico de mi calle tenía una enfermedad del corazón que le impedía ir al colegio. . . . Según mi madre, las personas que sufrían la enfermedad del Vitaminas morían al hacer el desarrollo. Dado su horizonte vital, no valía la pena hacer ninguna inversión en él" (43–44) (A boy who lived on my street had a heart disease that prevented him from going to school. . . . According to my mother, people who had the same disease as El Vitaminas died from growing. Given his survival prospects, it wasn't worth investing in him).

Looking back, the foregoing seems to be only another example of the uncanny accuracy of Oscar Wilde's axiomatic observation that "literature always anticipates life." In "Globalización, neoliberalismo y dinámicas metropolitanas en Madrid," Ricardo Méndez describes Madrid between 1998 and 2008 as an "exponente destacado del intenso crecimiento que experimentó la economía española" (30) (prime example of the intense growth experienced by the Spanish economy). He cites an OCDE report published in 2007 lauding more than eight years of growth at twice the rate of the Eurozone average in the Madrid metropolitan area, and anticipating a continuation of the same (36). As is now well known, of course, that promise of continued growth—one implied in Madrid's exemplary performance in the global urban marketplace during the first eight years of the twenty-first century—was not kept. Growth slowed, and that slowing led to further slowing, and the result was a city marked, like the Madrid of the author-narrator's childhood in *El mundo*, by evaporating opportunity and lived scarcity. By now, the numbers are largely redundant, but a few of those Méndez cites may nonetheless be worth repeating here if only to emphasize the intensity of that scarcity.

> Entre el cuarto trimestre de 2007 y el de 2011, la ocupación en la región metropolitana se redujo en 330 400 trabajadores según la *Encuesta de la Población Activa*, (−10,7%), lo que unido al persistente incremento de la población activa provocó que el volumen de desempleados creciera en 413 900 personas, multiplicando por tres su cifra inicial (de 210 000 a 623 300). De este modo, la tasa de desempleo se elevó del 6,4% al 18,5% en tan solo cuatro años, y se duplicó esta cifra entre los jóvenes menores de 25 años mientras superó también el 25% entre los inmigrantes. (42)

> (Between the fourth quarter of 2007 and that of 2011, employment in the Madrid metropolitan region dropped by 330,400 workers according to the Census of the Working Population (−10.7 percent), which, together with the continued expansion of the working-age population, caused the number of unemployed to increase by a factor of three, to 413,900 people (from 210,000 to 623,000). In this manner, the unemployment rate grew from 6.4 percent to 18.5 percent in only four years, with unemployment twice as high among those under twenty-five years of age and over 25 percent among immigrants.)

Retrospectively, El Vitaminas is no less legible than the Madrid of scarcity that opens *El mundo*. The massive protests that erupted in Madrid's Puerta del Sol in March 2011 and subsequently spread to other parts of Spain were by and large a popular rejection of neoliberalism, which for the purposes of this essay I will define, following David Harvey, as the political project, emerging at the end of the 1970s and beginning of the 1980s, of, on both the state and municipal levels, "facilitat[ing] . . . profitable capital accumulation" (*Brief History* 7) by enlisting public wealth—tax revenue, existing and potential infrastructure, public

land, and so on in the accumulation of private profit, and at the same time rolling back regulatory legislation designed to protect that very commonwealth, as
Hardt and Negri dub it, from such cooptation.[3] Insofar as the neoliberal politics
and policies that were the target of much of the 15-M protesters' ire are precisely
what allow for continued compound accumulation and the circumvention of
the crises that inevitably threaten it, those protests, in their piecemeal outcry
against the cooptation of the commonwealth, problematized renewed growth as
a viable solution to the conditions of scarcity in the midst of which their movement took form.[4]

In contrast to the rather easily interpreted first detour, however, is a second
detour Millás takes, in *El mundo*, from his typical modes of operation, this one
more formal or structural in nature. *El mundo* is structured by parallel plotlines, one pertaining to the composition of the narrative itself, and a second to
the author-narrator's quest for a kind of self-realization or self-actualization, to
achieve that "identity" in search of which he describes himself setting out as a
child, in the psychoanalytically charged moment in which, he recalls, he decided
to "poner caras" (put on faces) in order to no longer resemble his mother (30): a
search that will only be completed if he can free himself of a traumatic past by,
ironically, integrating it into the story he tells himself about himself. Similar to
El mundo, in this regard, is Millás's 2002 *Dos mujeres en Praga* (Two women in
Prague), one of the main plotlines of which pertains to the composition of the
novel's own narrative, which tells the story of the final days of a woman by the
name of Luz Acaso, and the second to the narrator's pursuit of something of the
same sort of self-realization or self-actualization. At the end of *Dos mujeres*, following Luz Acaso's death, the narrator discovers that

> me había convertido en el albacea o ejecutor . . . de aquel curioso testamento
> que dejaba los escasos bienes de Luz Acaso—el piso de Praga y una cuenta de
> ahorro—a Álvaro Abril y a María José. Era evidente que para llevar a cabo ese
> reparto no hacía falta una albacea, pero sí un narrador, un narrador que al contar
> los últimos días de Luz Acaso tuviera, sin comprender por qué, la impresión de
> ordenar su propia vida. (230)

> (I'd become the executor . . . of that strange will in which Luz Acaso left her few
> possessions—the apartment on Praga St. and her savings account—to Álvaro
> Abril and María José. It was clear that to carry out this distribution of assets,
> however, what was needed was not an executor but a narrator, a narrator who in
> recounting the Luz Acaso's final days would, without understanding why, feel as
> though he were putting his own life in order.)

Like the narrator of Beckett's *The Unnamable*, the narrator of *Dos mujeres en Praga* finds himself, at the end of his story, standing on the threshold of his actual story. This recursive structure, which at its end returns the narrative to its own beginnings in an endless narrative loop, is a postmodern trick or tic typical of Millás's mature work.[5] In *El mundo*, however, something radically different occurs. At the end of the novel, in an epilogue possessed of something of a dreamlike quality, the author-narrator describes driving to Valencia (a place characterized early on as his own personal lost paradise [23], with the Madrid of his childhood embodying the "Fall") to throw his dead parents' ashes to the sea. This journey back to the author-narrator's own beginnings is explicitly compared to a journey backward through the interior of the very book whose final episode it will constitute, such that it pertains at one and the same time to both of the parallel plotlines I have described here. The stated objective of these two-returns-in-one to the beginning of the author-narrator's own (within the parameters of the novel) "autobiography"—to "llevar a cabo un acto (desprenderme de los restos de mis padres) que la completaría" (224) (carry out an act [get rid of my parents' remains] that would complete it)—does not itself stand out within the context of Millás's *ouvre*, but their result very much does. Recalling his return from Valencia to Madrid in the closing lines of *El mundo*, Millás's author-narrator states, "No sé en qué momento comencé a ser Juan José Millás, pero sí tuve claro durante el viaje de vuelta . . . que aquel día había comenzado a dejar de serlo" (233) (I don't know in what moment I began to be Juan José Millás but it was clear to me during my return trip . . . that on that day I'd begun to cease to be him). In light of his claim, only a few paragraphs earlier, that "el nombre es una prótesis" (232) (the name is a prosthesis), the disavowal of the name in this all-but-final moment must be read as marking the achievement of that true (and therefore nameless) identity the search for which has constituted one of the novel's two parallel plotlines. This account of self-realization is immediately followed by a brief final paragraph in which the author-narrator recalls that "al llegar a casa estaba un poco triste, como cuando terminas un libro que quizá sea el último" (233) (on returning home I was as bit sad, like when you finish a book that might be your last). In reality, *El mundo* would not be the author Juan José Millás's final book, but this is largely beside the point. According to the terms of its own artifice, that narrative the composition of which constitutes the other of the novel's two parallel plotlines is depicted, at the end, as having been so definitively completed that there is not only no need for the author-narrator to continue writing it (much less start over from the beginning, as in the case of the narrator of *Dos mujeres en Praga*), but also no need for him to continue writing at all: the final word has been had. Thus, the double task the author-narrator assigns himself at the novel's outset—the labor of self-attainment and the work of composing the narrative of that labor—is, when all is said and done, depicted as profoundly achieved. At its end, to put it succinctly, the story is over.

To the Mountaintop: The Case for "Future Perfect" Governance in Madrid

Relative to the sociopolitical context in which Millás, consciously or otherwise, was motivated to take it, how might one read this second detour or departure from his established literary modes? Or, to put it otherwise, how might one interpret, relative to what I address as Millás's staging of a sort of proto-crisis Madrid in *El mundo*, its subsequent staging of its own completion or closure? To begin to venture an answer to that question, I return to neoliberalism and in particular neoliberal urbanization as the redirection of the commonwealth of the city toward the purpose of private accumulation in a moment in which, as Peck, Theodore, and Brenner write, cities—and especially capital cities—"have become strategic targets and proving grounds for an increasingly broad range of neoliberal policy experiments, institutional innovations, and political projects," and as such "incubators for, and generative nodes within, the reproduction of neoliberalism as a 'living' institutional regime" (65). To begin with, it is important to note that neoliberalism and more specifically *neoliberalization*, as the ongoing process of such appropriation, do not just produce crises such as that of 2008, but in fact rely on them as a means to continue to direct and determine policy decisions. Author Naomi Klein has introduced this general concept into the popular imaginary by way of her book *The Shock Doctrine*, in which she depicts crisis—real and cooked up—as creating necessary opportunities for "neoliberal 'restructurings'" (132), and Peck, Theodore, and Brenner describe actual cases of neoliberal urbanization in terms of "a range of crisis-displacing strategies" (64) that not unironically tend to displace crises that have been generated by neoliberalism's own "vulnerability to regulatory crises and market failures" (Peck and Tickell 392) and "the very economic cycles and localized policy failures that it was complicit in creating" (400).

The extent to which the neoliberal facilitation of capital accumulation by the redirection of public wealth into the service of private profitmaking relies on crisis or its specter in order to effectively orchestrate policy making is exemplified in the highly situated the case of Madrid's bid (its third consecutive failed bid, ultimately) for the 2020 Olympics. In 2013, as only one of a multitude of such examples, Alejandro Blanco, president of both the Spanish Olympic Committee and Madrid's 2020 campaign, promised that, in exchange for what he at the time dubbed a rather modest investment of approximately two billion dollars of public money, the Olympic Games "nos ayudarán a salir del bache" (will help us get past this rough patch) by reawakening "la bonanza [que] no ha desaparecido sino que está dormida" (the bonanza that hasn't disappeared but is hibernating).[6] While it is no doubt true that "winning" the 2020 Olympics would have provided some measure of at least temporary relief for Madrid's exploding unemployment problem, it is equally true that, as geographer Christopher Gaffney writes, "sports mega-events" such as the Olympics "function as mechanisms for the implementation of neo-liberal modes of governance within urban contexts" ("Mega-Event City"), systematically redirecting social wealth into the service not of social well-being and social welfare but rather of private profit making, and that the immediate benefits for local populations of such events, in the form of short-term employment and short-lived spikes in economic activity, are exactly that: short-term and short-lived. Writing for *Jacobin* magazine's Web site, Carolyn Prouse examines, along precisely these lines, the specific case of Maracanã soccer stadium in Rio de Janeiro, a piece of infrastructure that is woven deeply into the history and identity of the city and was refurbished in anticipation of the 2016 World Cup and upcoming 2020 Olympic Games. According to Prouse, approximately $598 million dollars in public money—coming from federal, state, and municipal sources—were spent on the stadium upgrade, ultimately resulting in the transformation of "this once-public facility . . . into private space, with all activities now oriented toward making profit for the public–private partnership that currently manages the stadium" ("Jock Doctrine"). If, as Blanco's assertions aver, the urgency of pursuing an Olympic bid is tied to crisis—as a way of reviving local prosperity or, in times of plenty, preventing it from going into hibernation—the reality is that the "white elephant" infrastructure projects and hemorrhaging of public funds that subsidizes them generate enormous quantities of profit while inflicting long-term harm on public well-being and often irreversibly appropriating public wealth.

But the question of how to resist the hegemony of neoliberalism and neoliberalization—of how to not merely identify but pursue alternatives to Thatcher's infamous "no alternative"—remains, as evidenced by both the energy and the clear shortcomings of the uprisings and occupations of 2011, remains very much an open one. Furthermore, any search for an answer must no doubt be located, no less than what Peck, Theodore, and Brenner call the "production" of neoliberal projects, "within distinctive national, regional and local contexts, defined by the legacies of inherited institutional frameworks, policy regimes, regulatory practices and political struggles" (50). Going forward, what I want to suggest is that in inscribing itself within the double horizon of completion and closure that I describe above, *El mundo* can be read as prescient with respect to more than just the imminent economic crisis as it would be lived in a Madrid once more unable to provide for its residents' needs. Rather, I want to argue that a municipal politics similarly inscribed within a utopian horizon of the achievement of the city as a space of shared and collective flourishing may be Madrid's best answer to the aforementioned question.

The first reason I offer for this is more generic than place-specific, and to explain I turn to the terminology of utopianism. Susan McManus, in "Fabricating the Future: Becoming Bloch's Utopians," draws a distinction between what she sees as two "modalities" of utopianism: utopianism as the positing of a kind of "future perfect" on the basis of which to "blueprint or legislate a polity" on the one hand and, on the other, utopianism as a "'fictive' mode of process" that "resists any attempt to reduce the possible to the given" (1). While McManus privileges the latter and lauds it for its "resistan[ce] to legislative modes of politics" (15), I would contend that, precisely because of its tendency to legislate or impose an order—much the way the conclusion of a narrative retrospectively imposes an order on all that precedes it—it is the former, to which category the end of *El mundo* no doubt belongs, that is better suited to challenge the ideological hegemony of neoliberal rationality and in so doing resist the momentum of neoliberalization. My basis for making this assertion lies, on the one hand, in the fact that the self-generated cycle of crisis and response that provides justification and ideological cover for processes of neoliberalization is itself a form of short-termism, and, on the other, in the fact that, as Peck and Tickell write, the processes of neoliberalization themselves propose no "end-state" (383), but only, confronted with the imperative to continuously create new pathways for profit making in order to sustain capitalism's need to maintain itself at a rate of 3 percent compound growth, a constant deferral of the same. Thus, utopianism as a "mode of process" that "resists any attempt to reduce the possible to the given" is, at least formally, perfectly compatible with the ideological underpinnings of neoliberalization. Moreover, as neoliberalization tends to be "brutally effective" (397) in its confrontation with crises and other immediate concerns (for instance, by alleviating high unemployment through deregulations of the labor market that may attract more precarious, lower paying jobs destined to depart for still more favorable terms elsewhere sooner or later, or forging public-private partnerships that in the long run will divert public wealth for private profit but in the short-term may relieve urban degradation), it is always likely to prevail, in the commonsense competition between potential policy programs, over "paths of urban development based . . . on social redistribution, economic rights, or public investment" (394) when that competition is adjudicated from the perspective of an always imperfect present or potentially disastrous near future. By contrast, inasmuch as it provides a representation of an "unequivocally better" future imaginatively "linked to the present by some identifiable narrative" (Levitas 98), the sort of "future perfect" utopianism McManus disavows may be in fact far more likely to open space for a perspective from which the counter-neoliberal paths of urbanization described by Peck and Tickell are not condemned to compete with neoliberal urbanization in its own territory, and the foundation for a very different political rationality: one disposed to reject policies that shift the needle ever more in the direction of private abundance at the cost of public well-being and to embrace policies that foster the conditions for the city's own self-realization as a space of shared and collective flourishing.

The second reason I see the "future perfect" utopianism rehearsed in *El mundo* as pertinent to and perhaps prescient with respect to the case of Madrid, in particular, is that if, as Peck, Theodore, and Brenner write, contemporary processes of neoliberalization and neoliberal urbanization necessarily unfold "within distinctive national, regional, and local contexts defined by the legacies of inherited institutional frameworks, policy regimes, regulatory practices and political struggles" (50), successful "reformist and counter-hegemonic movements" (65), as they dub them, no doubt must do the same; and as it happens, "constitutional" Madrid already boasts a legacy of municipal utopianism of just such a "future perfect."[7] The legacy of the much-mythologized *viejo profesor* (old professor), Enrique Tierno Galván, Madrid's mayor from 1979 to his death in 1986, not only provides a perhaps usefully mythic foundation for a reconstitution of the same, as I will argue going forward, but as well at least partial confirmation of the hypothesis advanced immediately above. Although the actual impact of Tierno's tenure has been deservingly questioned—among others by Michael Ugarte, who in "Madrid: From 'Años de Hambre' to Years of Desire" decries the Tierno administration for failing to institute "a great deal of economic, political, architectural or urbanistic reforms" (105)—here I want to draw attention to what I nonetheless view as a significant tension between the policy making, or at the very least the policy-making aspirations, of that administration and the processes of neoliberal urbanization both in general and as they were specifically advocated by a national PSOE with which the Madrid PSOE, under Tierno, found itself frequently at odds.[8] To begin with, there is what Hamilton Stapell describes as "Tierno Galván's unwavering belief in an egalitarian utopia, which for him symbolized peace, liberty, and equality" (41), and no less his commitment to municipal policy making guided by precisely such a "future perfect" vision of the city. In an interview with *El País* in

1979, one hundred days into his mayoral tenure, Tierno accordingly averred that "[l]o que a mí me mueve y a otros muchos compañeros es que somos hormigas que llevamos nuestro granito a la montaña del progreso, en cuya cima vemos la paz, la libertad, y la igualdad" (what moves me and many of my colleagues is the idea that we're ants carrying our grains of sand to the mountain of progress, at whose summit we see peace, liberty, and equality). For Tierno, then, this mountaintop of "peace, liberty, and equality" was, more than a fanciful bit of political rhetoric, intended to be a real mechanism for deciding policy: that which quite literally impelled his actions as mayor, as he himself noted. In "Otra idea de Madrid," the introductory section to a 1983 edition of *Villa de Madrid*, a magazine published as often as three times yearly by the Ayuntamiento de Madrid between 1958 and 1992, one reads, with respect to what would eventually be formalized as the Plan General de Ordenación Urbana of 1985, that after decades during which Madrid's urbanization process had been effectively thrown to the economic wolves, "[p]or vez primera no sólo se tiene una idea precisa de la ciudad sino que toda la gestión va a conducir a ese objetivo" (8) (not only is there a clear idea of the city but its management will be directed toward the achievement of that idea), and further on in the same introductory article the promise that the municipal government's "actuaciones a corto y medio plazo han cobrado un sentido en función del futuro Plan de la ciudad" (9) (short and medium-term actions take their meaning as a function of the future Plan for the city). For Tierno—again, if only in theory—policy making would be determined *not* by short-term exigencies but rather by a long-term vision of that "future perfect" city described years earlier in *El País*, and to one version or another of which Tierno frequently returned in discussing his own municipal regime.

And while Tierno may not have accomplished as much in this regard as Ugarte would have liked—nor, probably, as much as Tierno himself would have liked—the processes of non- or even counterneoliberal urbanization undertaken during his administration should not be overlooked, in particular given the national PSOE's commitment to setting not just Madrid but all of Spain on the "path to neoliberalism" (Stapell 189). The Tierno administration opposed speculation, resisted the deindustrialization of central Madrid, strove to reduce disparities in living standards and infrastructure between the northern and southern sectors of the city, and jealously guarded "suelo rural" (rural land not available to urban-style development) from profit-hungry real estate developers seeking to deregulate the same. One more specific example of these counterneoliberal processes is the extent to which "urban renewal" under Tierno was at times as much a matter of what was not produced as of what was. "[B]etween 1979 and 1983," Stapell notes, "the municipal administration did not permit the construction of the Torres de Valencia, the Torres de Colón, or a significant part of the large-scale commercial project destined for Azca," all projects that would "benefit only a select few at the expense of society as a whole" (53–54). Even Ugarte identifies the construction of Madrid's Kio Towers (1989–1996) as the "ultimate expression" of the Azca project, serving as a "threshold to the capital of Spain," in the double sense of the word, and an emblem of that capital's "eagerness to join the corporate empire of the 'global economy'" (118). Furthermore, Tierno and those responsible for the rhetorical trappings of his administration explicitly connected the counterneoliberal thrust of their refusal of building permits and suppression of further large-scale development in Azca to what Tierno famously termed the "motor utópico" (utopian engine) firing it (qtd. in Prieto). So, in accounting for what is thus designated "la parte 'invisible' de la gestión [de Madrid]" (10) (the "invisible" part of Madrid's management)— that is, the refusal of building permits and suppression of further large-scale development in Azca—writers for the aforementioned edition of *Villa de Madrid* insist that "ha sido preciso tener una 'idea' de la ciudad" (10) (it's been necessary to have an "idea" of the city) toward which "toda la gestión de la ciudad" (8) (all of the management of the city) is oriented. My contention that this "idea" continued to belong to the category of McManus's "future perfect" utopia, that is to say, to not only a given set of values but also the achievement of the city as their actual and definitive embodiment, finds what I see as its most poetic confirmation in what the Tierno administration eventually identified, in its own broadsheet-style *Villa de Madrid: Informativo quincenal,* as the "objetivo principal" (principal objective) of 1985's definitive Plan General de Ordenación Urbana: "Acabar Madrid" ("La cara oculta" 4) (Finish Madrid).

Before proceeding, I would like to briefly address the contention that the legend of Tierno—whether as utopian visionary or as patron saint of the post-Franco, postmodern "Madrid of living for the moment, a city no longer concerned with keeping order or remaining in strict control of the nation but with displacing that order and centrality" (Ugarte 103)—was, as Ugarte argues, more myth than reality. In short, my response to this accusation is "So be it, and perhaps all the better": as myth, Tierno's legacy retains the potential to do precisely what myths do, which is to provide intellectual and rhetorical resources for political actions and material practices.

My final reason for advocating for reading Millás's inscription of *El mundo*'s narrative within the horizon of a "future perfect" utopia of achievement and completion as modeling one very situated, particularly Madrilenian, possibility for what Peck, Theodore, and Brenner call "more progressive, democratic reappropriations of city space" (65) engages directly with arguably the most common objection to such a "potentially legislating, substantive" (McManus 1) utopianism: namely, the suspicion that the consequences of any political "quest for perfection . . . are almost necessarily totalitarian" (Levitas 7). Harvey fleshes out this suspicion in his 2000 *Spaces of Hope*. Anything other than a kind of "intransitive" (1) utopianism of the sort championed by McManus, Harvey writes, necessarily implies a certain sacrificial violence inasmuch as "to materialize one design, no matter how playfully constructed, is to foreclose, in some cases temporarily and in other instances relatively permanently, on the possibility of materializing others" (196), and consequently any effort to so materialize such a design implies a corresponding effort to foreclose on those potentially innumerable others. While I take the tendencies of any such end-state or "future perfect" utopia to pervert its own promises of collective flourishing into nightmares of brutal exclusion (and exclusion by brutality), I believe that, much as the Tierno administration's legacy provides intellectual and rhetorical resources on the basis of which to construct such a politics today, another legacy provides the rhetorical and intellectual resources for arming that politics against such catastrophe. My reasons for this are twofold, the first more generic to the city as such, and the second specific to the case of Madrid. As for the first, in a penetrating reading of Luis Martín-Santos's *Tiempo de silencio* in his "Madrid's Palimpsest: Reading the Capital against the Grain," Joan Ramon Resina highlights the manner in which the novel's protagonist, Pedro, an immigrant from the provinces like so many other residents of the capital, finds himself—even in spite of himself—"constantly in danger of being integrated" into the fabric of the city or, even more, "[y]a . . . incorporado a una comunidad de la que, a pesar de todo, forma parte y de la que no podrá deshacerse con facilidad" (qtd. 71) (incorporated into a community of which, in spite of everything, he forms a part, and from which he cannot easily detach himself).[9] In so integrating them, cities indeed take possession of their inhabitants, building them into themselves and building themselves out of their inhabitants, but this dynamic can also be read in reverse: at every moment, cities, not as symbols or strategic nodes in the vast politico-economic system but as living entities, are constituted as the product of their inhabitants, and there is as such never any city of which to speak, apart from the incessantly fluctuating convergence of those inhabitants. In this regard, a city can pursue its own self-realization or self-actualization only as a space of shared and collective flourishing along a path continuously adjusted, and then at once readjusted, and then readjusted once more ad infinitum, to its present composition. Admittedly, this rather optimistic interpretation of the "tentacular" nature of the city, as Resina characterizes it by way of Martín-Santos, overlooks the fact that in many cases a city's own history provides the foundation for portraying the matter altogether otherwise, identifying that collective to whom an imagined future of collective flourishing applies with particular and exclusionary identity groups—be they defined ethnically or otherwise—in which case inhabitants not included in those groups may be cast as parasitical, resource-sucking obstacles standing in the way of that idealized end state, and their removal and exclusion converted in an essential part of, if not *the* essential part of, the labor of achieving the same. But as Resina writes in "Palimpsest," "Madrid became the [Habsburg] empire's metaphysical center *because* it was not a city, and this irregular origin left a profound mark on its self-awareness" (61). Consequently, while as the *capital* Madrid is indeed linked at its historical inception to a particular identity—namely, that of the Habsburg empire—in reality, and despite the Franco regime's efforts to appropriate certain "images and symbols" of the city as the basis for "a uniformly imposed Spanish national identity, or official Spanishness" (Stapell 24), it possesses no such pedigree as a *city*, precisely because at that same origin it was not only not a city but decidedly a noncity, chosen by Philip II as the site of a new capital precisely *because* of a "historical and economic irrelevance [that] facilitated the seclusion of power" (Resina 60). That legacy, I would argue, provides the rhetorical and intellectual resources with which to defend the municipal utopianism the legacy of Tierno Galván makes thinkable for Madrid against, as Richard Rorty puts it, the "seductions of totalitarianism" (211).

In View of an Ending

Presently, Madrid's mayor is Manuela Carmena, elected to the post as the leader of Ahora Madrid, an "instrumental" party convened for the May 2015 municipal elections in association with the emergent Podemos, a state-level party included by its own secretary general, Pablo Iglesias, among the contemporary "adversaries [of] neoliberalism" ("Introducing"). In the run-up to those May 2015 elections, many of Carmena's supporters went to great lengths to compare her to Tierno Galván. Among them was Iglesias himself, who in a preelection speech recalled the pride his grandmother took in having Tierno as the mayor of her city and declared, "Necesitamos volver a estar orgullosos de un alcalde en esta ciudad, necesitamos Manuela Carmena como alcaldesa" (qtd. in López, "Iglesias dispara") (We need to once again be proud of our mayor in this city; we need Manuela Carmena to be our mayor). After those elections successfully delivered Carmena to the mayor's office, the comparisons continued, including on the Web site for the magazine *Cambio 16*, which over the course of its long history has featured both Tierno and Carmena on its covers. There, former editor-in-chief and current director of institutional relations and ombudsman Gorka Landaburu notes, apropos of a comparison between a cover from 1985 featuring Tierno and another from 2015 featuring Carmena, that "ambos provienen del mundo de la judicatura, su prestigio y su trayectoria son indiscutibles. Su compromiso con los más débiles y vulnerables, y su afán por una mayor justicia también los une" (both come from the judicial world, and their prestige and career paths are indisputable. Their commitment to the most disadvantaged and vulnerable and their passion for greater justice also unite them). Later in the same article, Landaburu acknowledges critics who, "aún reconociendo su condición de buenas personas, argumentan que no es posible distinguir a Enrique Tierno Galván y a Manuela Carmena por su capacidad de gestión política. Nunca fueron animales políticos y, en consecuencia, sus propuestas se sitúan más cerca de la utopía que del aparato" (even while recognizing them as good people, argue that neither Enrique Tierno Galván nor Manuela Carmena is characterized by a capacity for political administration. They were never political animals, and their proposals are therefore situated closer to utopia than to the existing political apparatus). Landaburu counters that "resulta imposible transformar la sociedad e impulsar el auténtico cambio sin ilusión y sin esperanza" (it is impossible to transform society and impel genuine change without hope and aspiration). Going still further, what I have tried to suggest in this essay is that successfully extricating Madrid from the punishing machinery of neoliberal urbanization may well require, more than ambitions that exceed the range of possibilities offered by extant political realities, a recuperation of a genuine political will to *acabar Madrid*.

NOTES

1. See, for example, Millás's 2014 *La mujer loca*, which reprises the postmodern playfulness that typifies his mature oeuvre.
2. I borrow this terminology from David Harvey, who in *The Enigma of Capital and the Crises of Capitalism* argues that capitalism requires a minimum of 3 percent compound growth to survive.
3. The term, of course, also has historically been used to designate the ideology, a kind of "free-market utopianism" with roots in the Chicago school of economics, that continues to lend the congenitally ongoing neoliberal project a sheen of common sense or, recalling that most famous of Thatcherisms, fatal inevitability.
4. See my "The Alchemists: On the Rise of Podemos" for further discussion of the 15-M movement as a movement in defense of the commons.

5. For a discussion of Beckett's incipient postmodernism, see Richard Begam, *Samuel Beckett and the End of Modernity*.

6. Blanco's remarks were made in the context of his participation in the 2013 Nueva Economía Fórum. They were published in numerous newspapers via the EFE wire service.

7. See Bermúdez for a particularly useful description and delineation of "Constitutional" Spain.

8. See Stapell for a lengthy discussion of this tension.

9. This translation is Resina's.

WORKS CITED

Ayuntamiento de Madrid. "La cara oculta del Plan." *Villa de Madrid: Informativo quincenal* 65 (1 Apr. 1985): 7–10. Web. 15 Feb. 2014.

_____. "Otra idea de Madrid." *Villa de Madrid* 76 (1983): 4. Web. 15 Feb. 2014.

Begam, Richard. *Samuel Beckett and the End of Modernity*. Stanford: Stanford University Press, 1996. Print.

Bermúdez, Silvia. "La España constitucional: Democracia y cultura, 1978–2008." *Revista de Estudios Hispánicos* 44.3 (2010): 533–43. Print.

Evans, Eli. "The Alchemists: On the Rise of Podemos." *Field Day Review* 11 (2015): 32–50. Print.

Gaffney, Christopher Thomas. "The Mega-Event City as Neo-liberal Laboratory: The Case of Rio de Janeiro." *Precurso Acadêmico* 4.8 (2014). Web. 12 Jan. 2016.

Harvey, David. *A Brief History of Neoliberalism*. Oxford: Oxford University Press, 2005. Print.

_____. *The Enigma of Capital and the Crises of Capitalism*. Oxford: Oxford University Press, 2010. Print.

_____. *Spaces of Hope*. Berkeley: University of California Press, 2000. Print.

Iglesias, Pablo. "Understanding Podemos." *New Left Review* 93 (2015). Web. 8 June 2015.

Klein, Naomi. *The Shock Doctrine: The Rise of Disaster Capitalism*. New York: Holt, 2007. Print.

Landaburu, Gorka. "De Tierno a Carmena." *Cambio 16*. Web. 26 Jan. 2016.

Levitas, Ruth. *Utopia as Method: The Imaginary Reconstitution of Society*. Basingstoke: Palgrave Macmillan, 2013. Print.

López de Miguel, Alejandro. "Iglesias dispara contra Aznar y Aguirre." *Público*. 13 May 2015. Web. 13 May 2015.

Martín-Santos, Luis. *Tiempo de silencio*. Barcelona: Seix Barral, 1973. Print.

McManus, Susan. "Fabricating the Future: Becoming Bloch's Utopians." *Utopian Studies* 14.2 (2003): 1–22. Print.

Méndez, Ricardo. "Globalización, neoliberalismo y dinámicas metropolitanas en Madrid." *DAAPGE* 12.19 (2012): 29–49. Web. 8 Jan. 2016.

Millás, Juan José. *El desorden de tu nombre*. Madrid: Alfaguara, 1992. Print.

_____. *Dos mujeres en Praga*. Madrid: Espasa, 2000. Print.

_____. *El mundo*. Barcelona: Planeta, 2007. Print.

Peck, Jamie, Nik Theodore, and Neil Brenner. "Neoliberal Urbanism: Models, Moments, Mutations." *SAIS Review* 29.1 (2009): 49–66. Print.

Peck, Jamie, and Adam Tickell. "Neoliberalizing Space." *Antipode* 34.4 (2002): 380–404. Print.

Prieto, Joaquín. "Enrique Tierno: 'Frente al capitalismo, la única alternativa es el marxismo." *El País*. 22 June 1979. Web. 12 Feb. 2014.

Prouse, Carolyn. "The Jock Doctrine." *Jacobin*. Oct. 2014. Web. 5 Feb. 2016.

Resina, Joan Ramon. "Madrid's Palimpsest: Reading the Capital against the Grain." *Iberian Cities*. Ed. Joan Ramon Resina. Hispanic Issues 24. New York: Routledge, 2001. 56–92. Print.

Rorty, Richard. *Philosophy and Social Hope*. New York: Penguin, 1999. Print.

Stapell, Hamilton M. *Remaking Madrid: Culture, Politics, and Identity after Franco*. New York: Palgrave Macmillan, 2010. Print.

Tierno Galván, Enrique. "Vamos a dejar una ciudad limpia, culta y con una circulación libre." Interview. *El País*. 29 July 1979. Web. 12 Feb. 2014.

Ugarte, Michael. "From 'Años del hambre' to Years of Desire." *Iberian Cities*. Ed. Joan Ramon Resina. Hispanic Issues 24. New York: Routledge, 2001. 93–121. Print.

CHAPTER 5

Trash as Theme and Aesthetic in Elvira Navarro's *La trabajadora*

Susan Larson

> La basura se siente bien contigo.
> Hazla metáfora.
> O deja aquí, entre plástico, los ojos
> para que otro los use.
>
> (Trash feels good with you.
> Make it a metaphor.
> Or leave it here, between plastic, eyes
> for someone else to use.)
>
> "Basura" (Garbage) is a poem by Carlos
> Pardo from *Echado a perder* (Spoiled)[1]

The social movements and participatory urbanism in Madrid in the wake of the economic crisis of 2008 resulted in a storm of social protest centralized in the Puerta del Sol that has since spread out in real space into all manner of neighborhoods and symbolically into a wide variety of artistic forms. This essay focuses on one example of this collective desire to articulate new ways of thinking about and inhabiting urban space: Elvira Navarro's 2014 *La trabajadora (The Worker)*, a novel that directly confronts the human cost of austerity measures in Spain by addressing the indignation experienced by those whose life plans have been altered by economic instability and labor precarity. Specific attention is paid to the notable presence in contemporary works of urban social criticism of references to garbage, trash, waste, and detritus of all kinds.[2] In many of these works, garbage and its recycling appear as recurring themes but also function at the conceptual level to propose an aesthetic all their own. *La trabajadora* is a direct response to the material conditions of the city and serves as a prime example of art that envisions the reuse and repurposing of refuse within urban space. It's a novel about contemporary life in Madrid that suggests there *are*

viable alternatives to the accumulation strategy of debt-driven financial capital
It's also a work that explores how human beings find ways to inhabit the cracks
and abandoned areas left behind by the failure of the neoliberal project.[3]

Words, sounds, and images exist in a reciprocal relationship to urban space,
creating meanings that are constantly being renegotiated and fought over. Urban culture is invariably tied up in the "production of social space," to use Henri
Lefebvre's term. As Álvaro Sevilla-Buitrago points out in "'This Square Is Our
Home!'" the 15-M movement combined some of the already existing political
answers to Spain's problems from the left-wing parties making up Spain's parliamentary government with very different (and oftentimes conflicting) calls for
self-government that came from more radical groups.[4] Even if only for a short
period of time, on the municipal, national, and global scales the Puerta del Sol
spatially embodied a set of radically new political possibilities. Luis Moreno Caballud subsequently identifies a post-crisis shift in Spanish culture toward what
he terms a "culture of anyone":

> The economic disaster has generated such a huge drop in the credibility of politi-
> cal institutions that it has begun to affect this hierarchical cultural system, thus
> compromising the very authority of those "in the know." This has driven many
> people "in the dark" to trust in their own abilities to collaboratively construct the
> knowledge they need in any given situation and to generate effective answers to
> the problems that confront them. In the process, they avoid having to weigh down
> their ways of knowing with the monopolistic, exclusive, hierarchical ambitions
> that accompany the tradition of the "experts." (3)

15-M, as Moreno Caballud explains, sparked a social movement that
spawned a host of grassroots collectives that have ever since been bringing
together people who want to reimagine urban space and artists that look to
the everyday to create meaningful connections that are more accessible and
inclusive.

La trabajadora can be understood as part of this artistic response to 15-M in
that it directly confronts the effects of austerity measures in Spain by addressing
the indignation and frustration experienced by two women, Susana and Elisa,
whose life plans have been destroyed by economic instability and labor precarity. As the title of the novel indicates, the women's identities are irrevocably
tied to their work, their economic status, and their debt. Their identities evolve
over the course of the novel as their work situations worsen and they are subsequently disconnected from traditional notions of urban space and pushed to
the periphery of society. One explanation for changing social perceptions of

work and workers in Spain can be found in anthropologist Irene Sabaté's ethno-graphic study of individual responses to the economic crisis of 2008—responses that hinge on what she calls the "failure of the central concept of the 'moral economy'" (109).[5] Sabaté argues that the moral economy has traditionally de-pended on the perception of mortgage overindebtedness as an illegitimate con-dition. As indebtedness becomes an increasingly common experience, however, the condition of being in debt is now more widely shared and rearticulated. The effects of violating moral economies include the collapse of life projects, the renunciation of promised futures, and the perceived "regression" of debtors to earlier stages of life. The current economic crisis has made people feel as though they have lost the futures promised to them through the years of financial pros-perity. According to Sabaté, those involved in her study increasingly feel that the moral economy has been violated, promises broken, and their long-term life plans devastated. Many are now left with unpayable debts and feel disillusioned with and frustrated by capitalist credit-debt agreements that have sold off their futures and left them tarnished by negative stereotypes.

Elvira Navarro's *La trabajadora* is, then, a work that considers how the 2008 economic crisis in Spain, coupled with the aggressive privatization of pub-lic space and increasingly precarious labor situations for both working- and middle-class workers, has affected Madrid's citizens. It's a model of what Jon Snyder calls a "poetics of opposition": a work that actively reappropriates and resignifies urban space. Snyder explains that the events that first transpired on May 15, 2011, in the Puerta del Sol have had a lasting impact on how people read and resist the rhetoric of austerity.

> Although the protesters' reshaping of the city may be precarious, forever on the shore of its own disappearance . . . what persists when demonstrators no longer occupy the square, and when the urban milieu may succumb again to routine commerce, private enterprise, and property speculation, are the transformative practices of protesters who *read* their common subjugation critically and, in the process, make the sources of domination *legible* as a collective circumstance, with material consequences. . . . Reading, it seems, plays an important role in constitut-ing and reconstituting multitudes that mobilize toward change. (2–3)

Snyder's argument is that the social movements stemming from 15-M in 2011 gave protesters the tools to read and subsequently denounce the rhetoric upholding processes such as gentrification and the privatization of the urban landscape, forced evictions, and a whole host of other policies that were recast in the media as outcomes of the personal failings of the poor.

In the wake of the highly visible 15-M demonstrations across Spain, Navarro's novel is one of many examples of the proliferation of small-scale grassroots endeavors that work toward creating new ways of living in and theorizing the city, and it accomplishes this by questioning some very basic assumptions about what a city is. Both individually and collectively, 15-M has resulted in a consideration of what some have termed a "new ecology of urban space."

Many urban geographers interested in theorizing a more socially just organization of space in the wake of the 2008 economic collapse have begun to explore what they call "degrowth" in both fiction and grassroots initiatives of the kind mentioned above.[6] They have dissected the depoliticizing effects of the growth discourse (Swyngedouw, 2015) and have investigated how cities can adapt to the prolonged and foreseeable absence of growth. Central to this conceptualization of the new city and its economies of degrowth are trash, waste, and reuse in the wake of urban (and, by extension, regional) shrinkage. The degrowth movement is particularly strong among activists and intellectuals in southern Europe who share a vision of an alternative to capitalist socioecological relations. The concept signifies a ruthless critique of the ideology of economic growth and its material effects as well as a search for alternatives to the teleological progression marching toward ecological disaster.[7] The terms mentioned here—"degrowth" (D'Alisa, Demaria, and Kallis; Prádanos-García, "poetics of resistance" (Snyder), "cultures of anyone" (Moreno-Caballud), and an "aesthetics of trash and recycling" (Feinberg and Larson)—have all been used in recent years to identify a set of collective political and closely related cultural tactics that articulate the unraveling of the social fabric in Spain in general and propose radical changes to urban life in particular.

Elvira Navarro's 2014 novel *La trabajadora* comes in at a relatively short but remarkably dense 150 pages. The reader is invited to consider the social and psychological impact of Spain's 2008 economic crisis through a plot that hinges on the everyday realities of part-time labor contracts, rising rents, and severely weakened social services. The existence of young women in abandoned, provisional nonspaces in the novel is made even more precarious by the decentralized experience of the informal and increasingly digital environment in which they work and conduct some of their most important intimate relationships. Mental illness brought on by this alienation and the effects of anti-depressants on an entire generation of young Spaniards are closely related themes thoughtfully developed in *La trabajadora*.[8]

The urban imaginary created in Navarro's novel is one where Madrid's working- and middle-class citizens alike are pushed into abandoned and peripheral spaces. The main protagonist of *La trabajadora* is Elisa Núñez. She is a well-educated copy editor for a major publisher based in Madrid whose short-term contracts become further and further apart after Elisa is named an independent contractor (the official term in Spanish is, significantly, "colaboradora externa") who works increasingly from home. The company she works for is part of the Grupo Editorial Término (allusions to Melville's Dead Letter Office come to mind with this nomenclature, of course, as does Bartleby's famous phrase, "I would prefer not to"). As her work situation becomes increasingly precarious (she is paid by the hour and loses her designated office space), her economic situation worsens and she is forced to move from her rented apartment in the rapidly gentrifying Tirso de Molina neighborhood in Madrid's historic city center to an apartment found for her by the city's Sociedad Pública de Alquiler in Aluche (on Madrid's southwest side), which is the only place she can afford.

Though Elisa is a highly educated author, ghost writer, editor, and translator, these skills are not enough to earn her a place in Madrid's middle class. Spanish geographer Jorge Sequera has described how Madrid's neoliberal economy has stripped a generation of hope for the future. To compete as a global city, Madrid has capitalized on its culture industry, with dire implications for its citizens and its use of public and private space. In the process of becoming a global city, Sequera writes, Madrid is

> tratando de conformar un entorno urbano propicio para la creación de *clusters creativos* en el centro histórico de Madrid. Este tipo de políticas urbanas materializa distritos creativos y culturales y recurre para ello a la potencialidad de la cultura, basada en el arte, la contracultura, el "artivismo" o la multiculturalidad. . . . La cultura, por lo tanto, se pone al servicio de la producción capitalista, en el centro de las dinámicas de la ciudad global que "debe ser Madrid": la marca Madrid. (128)

> (trying to shape an urban environment that fosters the creation of creative clusters in Madrid's historical center. This type of urban politics creates creative and cultural districts and, to that end, makes use of the potential of culture, based on art, the counterculture, "artivism," or multiculturalism. . . . Culture, then, is put at the service of capitalist production, in the center of the dynamics of global culture of "what Madrid should be": Madrid as a brand.)[9]

In Aluche, Elisa is forced to find a roommate to make ends meet. Her cotenant is Susana, a woman some ten years her senior whose portion of the narration on the first page of the novel uses the advent of the Internet and cell phones (15) as essential temporal markers with the phrase "Acababa de regresar a Madrid, no existía Internet y tenía que recurrir a los periódicos" (11) (I had just returned to Madrid; the Internet didn't exist yet, and I had to resort to newspapers). Technological advances are used to temporally mark and signify the timeline of her life in Madrid. Significantly, Susana couples this life change with her parallel mental illness diagnoses and their treatments: "Para entonces ya me habían cambiado el Risperdal por el litio: mi categoría pasó de esquizofrénica a bipolar" (13) (Back then they had already changed my prescription from Risperdal to lithium: my category changed from schizophrenic to bipolar). These changes in geographical location, in mass communication and technology, and in the main characters' psychological conditions are therefore linked and interconnected from the very first pages of the novel, making the work an exercise in following the evolution of both characters as they change jobs and learn to manage their personal relationships, finances, and mental illnesses through a series of major shifts in work, home, technology, and medical treatments.

Susana's version of her life as an urban citizen involves her moving from what she calls a "cuchitril" (dump) in Madrid's Plaza Mayor close to the iconic Chocolatería San Ginés to Usera, a neighborhood on the south side of the city between Arganzuela and Orcasitas. *La trabajadora* goes into great detail about Susana's pre-Internet, pre–cell phone period (from the mid-1980s through to approximately the year 2000) in Madrid from the perspective of a young woman who spends much of her time either working or simply wandering the streets of the capital's city center. Susana narrates a period in her life when she was recovering from a violent trauma, undergoing therapy, and taking strong medication. From the very first pages of the novel, she describes the source of her depression through the use of urban metaphors. She explains to Elisa, "[N]o sabes hasta qué punto deprime que lo real, o tu cabeza, sea un pedazo de vidrio roto, opaco, abandondado al borde de una acera" (13) (you don't know how depressing it is to have what's real, or what's in your head, be a piece of broken glass, opaque, abandoned on the edge of the sidewalk). This fragmentation and lack of clarity best describes Susana: a broken object that exists within but has been thrown aside by the city. Susana explains that the only thing that helped her get through this difficult period in her life was taking out classified ads inviting the exchange of what can be termed idiosyncratic sexual favors: "El objetivo me centraba. Me daba cierto aire de amazona y la ilusión de que llevaba en mi mano una brújula" (13) (This goal centered me. It made me feel powerful and gave me the sense of having a compass in my hand). In its very first pages, then, the novel presents the female characters as fragile, sharp but beautiful objects cast aside as urban waste. They have been dirtied by everything life has thrown at them, leaving them isolated, abandoned, and alone. Each character survives these difficult conditions by voicing her desire: in this case of Susana, a desire to make a human connection with another person, no matter how fleeting, is described as holding a compass in her hand—a way to trace a route for herself on the urban map.

Elisa, the figure of the author within the text, experiences a significant connection to spaces making up the urban periphery just as she loses her ability to make out the details of even the most iconic monuments in the city center. On the ride back to her apartment in Usera after a particularly difficult conversation with her boss about her lack of a long-term contract, for example, Elisa states, "Al llegar a Cibeles y a la Gran Vía tuve la impresión de que había menos estatuas coronando las fachadas. No habría sido capaz de precisar qué estatuas faltaban" (65) (When I got to Cibeles and the Gran Vía, I had the feeling that there were fewer statues on top of the fronts of the buildings. I wouldn't have been able to say exactly which statues were missing).

Susana also reflects on how the cost of rent has changed the city of Madrid since the 1980s, saying of her attic apartment in the Plaza Mayor, "Ahora pienso que las condiciones en las que habitaba mi buhardilla preconizaban lo que iba a pasar veinte años después con las viviendas. . . . Me podría haber alquilado una casa de cinco habitaciones en el barrio de Salamanca por el precio de mi habitación en tu piso" (19) (Now I think that the living conditions I experienced in my attic apartment foreshadowed what was going to happen twenty years later. . . . I could have rented a five-room home in the Salamanca neighborhood for the price of my room in your apartment). In a segment of this first part of the narration that belongs to Susana, we learn why she chooses to live in the more expensive city center during the most difficult period of her mental illness and during the worst heat of summer. Searching for open space and silence in the city, she inevitably finds herself in the Sabatini Gardens: "Algo en mis nervios me impelía a moverme, sobre todo durante la noche, y ese movimiento no solo era una necesidad de los músculos tensos, sino que el día cercado por las paredes de mi buhardilla y las de mi cabeza buscaba la amplitud de los espacios abiertos" (27) (Something inside compelled me to keep moving, especially at night, and that movement wasn't merely a result of my tense muscles, but of the day spent hemmed in by the walls of my attic apartment and of my mind, looking for the openness of open spaces). Susana carefully details the route she takes on these August evening walks by herself, starting in the Puerta del Sol, walking down Arenal toward Ópera to the royal palace, where she stands on the viaduct over Calle de Segovia and looks out over the Casa del Campo.

Si me concentraba lo suficiente durante las noches cerradas perdía el sentido de la lejanía. Las luces de Somosaguas se tornaban en farolas repartidas en cerros, al igual que los ranchos de Caracas. Me daba una tranquilidad mustia, como si me hubiesen envasado en un vacío aburrido y acogedor, imaginarme que estaba en otro lugar, o bien pensar en los trayectos de mi infancia en el coche, con mis padres y hermanos. (21)

(If I concentrated hard enough during the close nights, I lost the sense of distance. The lights of Somosaguas became streetlights distributed over the hills, just like the ranches of Caracas. It gave me a musty tranquility, as if I'd been bottled up in a boring and cozy emptiness, to imagine that I was in another place, or else to think about the trips I used to take with my parents and brothers when I was a kid).

At another point in this narrative segment, Susana shares this view with her lover and reflects on the fact that "daba gusto llegarse a la Almudena y contemplar cómo caía la tarde con esos filos de nubes fugaces sobre la Casa del Campo, el paseo de Extremadura y Somosaguas. El cielo aproximaba; parecía querer contarle algo a los pedazos de urbanizaciones que asomaban sus cuerpecitos histéricos de ladrillo entre la maleza y la lejanía" (30) (it was great to go to the Almudena and contemplate how the afternoon fell with those sharp edges over the Casa del Campo, the road to Extremadura and Somosaguas. The sky got closer; it seemed to want to say something to the fragments of housing developments that thrust out their hysterical little brick bodies amid the brush and the distance). Susana's walks in the 1990s are then described not in visual but in tactile terms: "me aplicaba en recorrer con las manos la turgencia de los bojes, las espinas de los rosales sin rosas, la tierra negra y seca y también, si tenía el día atrevido, los cabellos y los fútiles chándales de manga larga de los pasantes . . . y el silencio, pues eso también era fundamental para llegar a mi casa con sensación de espacio: el campo sonoro" (21–22). (I dedicated myself to running my hands over the firmness of the boxwoods, the thorns of the roseless rosebushes, the black, dry earth, and also, if I was feeling daring, the hair and futile long-sleeved tracksuits of the passersby . . . and the silence, since that too was fundamental in order to arrive at my house with a sense of space: the sonorous open air). *La trabajadora* contains several descriptions of women walking through the city looking for brief moments of respite. Places to recover and reflect on where exactly they are in time and space. In the passage quoted above, Susana hungers for a real connection to the space around her through touch and hearing. These moments contrast with her desire to find a connection to those around her in the digital age, where she is more disconnected from her body and lives much of her life looking at a screen.

La trabajadora is divided into several fragments, told in different styles and from the points of view of different narrators. Immediately after the first segment of the narration laying out Susana's life and mental illness issues, the second segment consists of a short story written by author-in-the-text Elisa—a short story called, curiously enough, "La trabajadora." It consists of four pages, and the segment ends with the words (in caps) "RELATO PUBLICADO EN UN EXTINTO DIARIO ESPAÑOL" (48) (STORY PUBLISHED IN A NOW-DEFUNCT SPANISH NEWSPAPER). It's a miniature version, so to speak, of the novel the reader holds in his or her hands and an autobiographical narration of Elisa's trajectory as a culture worker fallen victim to gentrification and labor precarity in Madrid, some twenty years after Susana's experience in the late 1980s and 1990s in the same location. The mixture of narrators, styles, and lengths of each segment of the novel give the impression that it is a piecing together of found texts that have been salvaged from the trash. This almost accidental piecing together of whatever is at hand by the amateur artists in the text works at both the thematic and stylistic levels.

A particularly well-crafted section of *La trabajadora* in which the precarious, provisional nature of life on the city's periphery is interwoven with a reflection on the construction of objectivity suffered by all authors occurs in chapter 8. Elisa is a runner and puts on her warmest clothing to go on nightly runs throughout the most abandoned and empty spaces she can find. As Michel De Certeau explains in *The Practice of Everyday Life* (in the chapters "Walking in the City" and "Spatial Stories" in particular), pedestrians, in effect, tell urban stories through their movements. They give their own particular shape to spaces and weave together places in ways that potentially transgress, from within, the abstract map imposed from above by the panoptic gaze and administrative strategies of corporate and government interests. For De Certeau, the physical act of walking (or running, in this case) realizes the radical possibilities of refashioning the urban spatial order (the network of streets, for example), in the same way that a speaker or an author uses language to create articulate meaning. This creative process "affirms, suspects, tries out, transgresses, respects, etc., the trajectories it 'speaks'" (De Certeau 99). Walking is framed as an elementary and embodied form of experiencing urban space—a productive, yet relatively unconscious, speaking/writing of the city. *La trabajadora*, then, highlights how the characters move through, write down (in the case of Elisa), and remake the map (literally, in the case of Susana) of Madrid's periphery.

The periphery of Madrid highlighted in most of the novel is not the globally competitive tourist center nor even the more central gentrifying areas where the cultural industry is housed. Susana and Elisa do run into each other in one such neighborhood at one moment at the Café Barbieri in Lavapiés, but the two pretend not to know each other. Their relationship has no place in the city center, and they cannot share the same community. They belong to a part of the city where there are a variety of abandoned or unfinished housing developments. Elisa explores these areas every night, assuming that she is passing through block after block of abandoned or unfinished housing construction projects until she notices that as night falls, lights turn on inside, powered by almost-invisible cables that are taking electricity illegally from the few streetlights that remain on the street. "Siempre pensé que estos proyectos fracasados estaban en mitad de páramos, o a unos reglamentarios kilómetros de la línea de costa. No imaginaba que tal cosa sucediera en la ciudad" (76) (I always thought that these projects were in the middle of moors, or at a regulated number of kilometers from the coastline. I didn't imagine that such things happened in the city). "Vivienda clandestina" (clandestine housing), "viviendas sin permiso de habitabilidad" (housing without an occupancy license), "cooperativa de viviendas habitada por los timados a pesar de su construcción inacabada" (a housing cooperative occupied by those who were scammed despite their being unfinished), "urbanizaciones fantasma" (ghost developments), and "el fenómeno de la auto-construcción" (do-it-yourself construction) (76–77): this is the new vocabulary of postcrisis housing in the southernmost areas of Madrid. The inhabitants of this area "se comportaban como los que viven al pie de un volcán y llevan años atentos a los suaves hilos de humo que atraviesan los días claros" (78) (behave like people who live at the foot of a volcano and spend years carefully watching the soft plumes of smoke that cut across the clear days). Madrid's citizens increasingly live in spaces where they are not supposed to live, in unplanned, half-constructed developments that are neither entirely urban nor rural because they are falling into ruin and degenerating into their natural state.

Allusions to trash, recycling, and abandoned spaces are prevalent in *La trabajadora*. There is a recurring reference to a group of gypsy scavengers—"los del camión" (57) (the guys with the truck)—who are constantly crossing paths with Elisa along her nightly jogging routes. Elisa at one point goes through the clothing that her deceased mother left her years ago when she needs to find something more professional to wear. Elisa's apartment is furnished by her "recogidas de muebles en el barrio de Salamanca" (86) (furniture pickups in the Salamanca neighborhood). We learn that Elisa is herself a published author of prose only when her roommate Susana happens upon a crumpled-up short story of Elisa's being used to pack ceramic mugs during Susana's move from Italy to Spain. In the few hours a day when Elisa is not working or sleeping, the reader follows her wanderings by bus and on foot through the empty boulevards and urban wastelands on the periphery of Madrid. For weeks, the protagonist travels to a park called Eugenia de Montijo to watch the demolition of the Carabanchel Prison, "un deforme hueso urbano" (71) (a deformed urban bone), saying that she stayed in front of its "piedras . . . un buen rato, pues aquella desolación me resultaba consoladora" (47) (stones a good while, since that desolation was comforting to me). Elisa enjoys riding the practically empty buses at night that run from La Colonia San Ignacio de Loyola past General Fanjul, Carpetana, and Plaza Elíptica and down the empty boulevards "que me dejaban una agradable sensación de estar en otra parte" (47) (that always gave me the agreeable sensation of being somewhere else).

These are just some of the numerous references to trash and abandoned, isolated spaces in the novel. They work together to create a series of interwoven impressions and experiences that hinge on the narrator's desire to find something real, something solid to connect to in her daily life. But the real contribution—the startling originality of *La trabajadora*—is the description of the narrator's experience of abandoned, urban ruins in Madrid's noncentral, semi-industrial or more residential neighborhoods. The novel expertly critiques the reasons behind the abandonment of peripheral urban space on a massive scale in Madrid's metropolitan region since the bursting of the real estate bubble, and the ways that people are now occupying these informal and difficult-to-define areas.

The novel's first mention of her new neighborhood of Aluche is secondhand: "me dijeron que se trataba del cerro donde Antonio López pintó uno de sus cuadros, pero lo único que encontré en mi búsqueda internauta fue un paisaje de Vallecas y otro que rezaba MADRID SUR, que no concordaba con lo que veía desde la ventana" (78) (they told me that it was the hill where Antonio López painted one of his paintings, but the only thing I found with my Internet search was a landscape of Vallecas and another that read SOUTH MADRID that didn't match what I saw out of the window). The image of the typical city street—full of people, traffic, small businesses—is elusive throughout much of *La trabajadora*. There is some question as to whether or not the periphery of Madrid (where, after all, the majority of Madrid's citizens actually live) is faithfully represented in the urban imaginary. Antonio López's iconic paintings of the periphery of Madrid come up again in the novel when Elisa looks out the fifth-floor window of the Vallecas Library. She looks out on the M-30 and M-40 and notices that a eso se parecía aquel paisaje, a un puro recuerdo, y también a una impresión general de soledad, como si los edificios estuvieran deshabitados o los ocupara el desierto. Aquellas vistas me llevaban de nuevo a repasar los cuadros de Antonio López en Internet, esos cuadros con su exactitud delirante, de cuajo echado a la existencia. La ciudad parecía congelada, pero no por el frío, sino por la luz y el calor. Desde aquella cuarta planta jamás se veían transeúntes a lo lejos. No es que no los hubiera, sino que resultaba imposible reparar en ellos. La soledad de los edificios erguidos, la precariedad tan eficaz con la que se multiplicaban unas cuantas formas, como las amebas y otros organismos cuando un rayo fecundó los océanos, hacía que la vista borrara la vida, y todo funcionaba como un revés de ese origen, pues la tierra se resecaba. Por eso, me dije, el cuadro que buscaba, ese cuadro que estaba segura de haber contemplado, había simplificado la forma hasta resolverla con unas líneas escuetas. (78–79)

(that's what that landscape looked like, a pure recollection, and also like a general impression of loneliness, as if the buildings were uninhabited or were inhabited by the desert. Those views brought me back to looking over the paintings of Antonio López on the Internet, those paintings with their dizzying exactitude, fully immersed in existence. The city seemed frozen, not with cold but with light and color. From that fifth floor you never saw passersby from afar. It's not that there weren't any, it was just impossible to get a fix on them. The loneliness of the straight buildings, the efficient precarity with which certain forms were multi-plied, like the amoebas and other organisms when a bolt of lightning brought life to the oceans, made the gaze seemingly erase all life, and everything worked as if in reverse from that origin, since the land was drying out again. That's why, I told myself, the painting that I was looking for, that painting that I was sure I had seen, had become more simplified in shape until it was reduced to a few stark lines.)

Elisa, gazing out the window in Vallecas, is looking for a way to describe and understand the space she sees. She describes the landscape as a product of the drying out of an ocean and has a difficult time comprehending what remains. What is its plan? Its rationale? How do humans inhabit this space? Is it urban at all? If not, how can it be categorized? Her point of reference is painting: Anto-nio López's visualization of the region. Indeed, Benjamin Fraser says of López's neorealist paintings of Madrid and its periphery that they do nothing less than "reorient our urbanized consciousness. . . . López's urban scenes remind us that paintings are not only surfaces but entire worlds that overlap with and stand in contrast to our own" (2). The references to the López paintings here are another opportunity for Navarro to remind us that our own perception of space—urban space, in this case—is intricately bound up in and informed by the competing images and discourses of the urban already in our heads. The narrator in this segment of the novel is lost and looking for direction in a rapidly changing urban environment that does not resemble what she has been led to expect the city to look like. Its planning seems to have been undone; its housing and infrastructure are not being used in the ways for which they were built. The city has been decentralized and seemingly overtaken by nature—a kind of devastated ruin or rubbish heap slowly reverting back to nature. Antonio López's paintings, then, seem to contain a nostalgic form or structure that the narrator looks for in real life but cannot find.

The very structure of *La trabajadora* reinforces and provides a model for how to produce art that draws on everyday life. The second part of the novel, five pages long, consists of a story about a young woman whose work situation becomes increasingly precarious over time. Only later do we learn that this is Elisa's first published short story, an accomplishment that Elisa refuses to talk about with anyone. Significantly enough, the newspaper pages where the story was published are discovered by accident (as mentioned above) when Susana finds that it has been used to wrap her coffee mugs during her move. Elisa's one and only published work narrowly escapes making its way into the trash, only to be recycled by her roommate/friend/artistic competitor, Susana. Only when the novel is finished does the reader find the note on the last page that states that this second section was indeed published in the "Cuaderno de Verano" section of a Spanish newspaper called *Público* in August 2010 with the title "Un ejemplo deplorable de estructura circular" (157) (A deplorable example of circular structure). The euphemism "circular structure" paired with the phrase "deplorable example" alludes to the trash can as the ultimate destination of the hard work and incipient literary creations of young authors such as Elisa.

At one point in the novel, Elisa finds Susana hunched over the northernmost section of a map of Madrid issued by the Entidad Estatal del Suelo (State Land Commission), with tiny nail scissors in hand. She has for years assiduously been cutting out and classifying miniscule, millimeters-wide images of Madrid's buildings, monuments, cars, people, and plants from a variety of publications into envelopes entitled "Trees," "Gardens," "Tall Buildings," and "Low Buildings," leaving only the trace of the form of the city left in the pockmarked and incomplete maps. When asked why she obsessively collects these miniature depictions of essential urban landmarks, Susana states that she wants to make her own maps of Madrid by changing the locations of all of the buildings: "Su pretensión era que el mapa permaneciera igual en su estructura, pero con todos sus elementos traspuestos. Iba a componer varios mapas" (79–80) (Her aspiration was for the map to maintain the same structure, but with all of its elements rearranged. She was going to put together several maps). Significantly, when Susana is asked why she doesn't use a computer program to cut out these images and paste them back together, she replies by saying that she knows that it would be much faster and the computer would enable a large number of different combinations, but the problem for her is that "quedaría perfecto, y a mí me gusta que se note el trabajo. La suciedad" (80) (it would be perfect, and I like for the work to be visible. The dirt). Susana makes a series of these maps, saying during the creation process that she will either burn them or show them in an exhibit. Much of the last third of the novel is devoted to how she works her way into the art world in Madrid and how Elisa struggles with feelings of jealousy that ultimately motivate her to change her life in significant ways. The two protagonists are looking for ways to make meaningful lives in a city that keeps changing the rules. Pushed into the periphery and subject to the whims of the ever-changing labor market, they look for ways to restructure, reorder, and remake the city, resorting to image and text. Out of necessity, both women resort to *bricolage* or do-it-yourself techniques that empower them by enabling them to take some control through their ability to combine the objects around them in new ways that speak to their own experiences. It is significant that Susana and Elisa find outlets for their creative impulses only when they are able to reject the virtual world and its digital culture. While the Internet is constant in the novel (the main characters spend most of their working hours sitting in front of a computer screen; they conduct their long-distance relationships over Skype; they look for entertainment and social connection through Facebook, Netflix, and other resources) both very consciously fight against Internet addiction to create their own subjectivity, to forge their own path through the layers upon layers of cultural references they use to communicate their feelings to one another.

La trabajadora is the result of one character telling the life story of another: Elisa's fictional version of Susana's autobiography, with Elisa's own fictionalized account of her own precarious work situation thrown in seemingly haphazardly as a fragment unconnected to the rest of the story. The very structure of the novel is highly asymmetrical—seemingly put together from found fragments of narrative that serve very different purposes and are written in very different styles and for different purposes. The novel begins with an aside in italics, presumably written by Elisa, the author within the text: "*Este relato recoge lo que Susana me contó sobre su locura. También anoto algunas de mis reacciones, en verdad no muchas. Huelga añadir que su narración fue más caótica*" (11, italics in the original) (*This story compiles what Susana told me about her madness. I will also jot down some of my reactions, but really not many. I should perhaps mention that her telling of the story was much more chaotic*). This unevenness and fragmentation is highly significant because it underlies many of the issues discussed throughout the novel: the fact that we make the stories of our lives out of what we encounter around us, and that our lives themselves are a mixture of the otherworldly and the mundane, of the beautiful and the ugly, of high culture and low, of the digital and the material, of the intensely private and the social. The novel amounts to a moment of quiet tranquility and reflection in a loud, fast-moving, and chaotic city. David Shields argues in his *Reality Hunger: A Manifesto* that contemporary writers tend to take larger and larger pieces of the real world and use them in their work because they are "obsessed by real events because [they] experience hardly any" (16). The aesthetic of *La trabajadora* is very much in tune with Shields's proposal in *Reality Hunger*. Some have described Shields's book and its deconstruction of the modern novel as an insightful breath of fresh air, others call it a fraud, but still others have called it a good-faith presentation of what literature might look like if it caught up with the present-day strategies being used in the other arts to revive its outdated forms.[10] Shields argues,

> Painting isn't dead. The novel isn't dead. They just aren't as central to the culture as they once were. Skeptical of the desperation of the modernist embrace of art as the only solution, and hyperaware of all artifacts of genre and form, we nevertheless seek new means of creating the real. Suddenly everyone's tale is tellable, which seems to me a good thing, even if not everyone's story turns out to be fascinating or well told. (22)

La trabajadora is a novel whose purpose is to tell the stories of the everyday women being left behind by Spain's austerity economy. In terms of urban space, both the young artists and white-collar participants in the culture industry are pushed out of the city center by gentrification. The style of the novel can be considered to be as hyperrealist as an Antonio López painting, and its structure is a piecing together of seemingly disparate episodes, texts, and registers. The main characters struggle to find ways to express themselves in a world where every feeling and experience is mediated through popular culture (music, film, television, visual art, literature) and their most meaningful relationships are conducted via Facebook, Skype, and e-mail.

It is significant that the women of the novel invariably explain their past lives and their aspirations by comparing them to films and television series. Susana's lover, Fabio, is compared to Señor Galindo from the television program *Crónicas marcianas*, Elisa compares her Christmas-associated angst to a well-known commercial for El Almendro turrón, Susana's cartographic montages are compared to the work of Hieronymous Bosch and Ivan Zulueta, and there are a number of references to musicians whose songs provide the soundtrack to the protagonists' lives. *La trabajadora* describes the lives of women awash in a sea of information in the form of texts, images, and sounds circulating with increasing speed and frequency. It explores how women creatively piece together their own survival tactics in this dehumanized urban environment where one's emotions are closely related to a sense of place, which in the twenty-first century city is simultaneously material, symbolic, and virtual. Against this backdrop, the novel ultimately stresses that one's life in the city is made up of a collection of found objects and relationships pieced together with care to form one's particular subjectivity.

Elisa and Susana are redundant, peripheral, and living on the outskirts of a city that has expelled them from its center as they have grown older and increasingly unable to find a foothold in the middle class to which they fully expected they would belong. They are walking, breathing financial problems. In his 2004 book *Wasted Lives: Modernity and Its Outcasts*, the sociologist Zygmunt Bauman draws a distinction between the use of the term "unemployed" in previous decades (with its implication that those without work belong to a "reserve army of labor" that would soon be called back into active service) to the more recent term "redundant." He explains that "to be declared redundant means to have been disposed of because of being disposable. . . . 'Redundancy' shares its semantic space with 'rejects,' 'wastrels,' 'garbage,' 'refuse'—with *waste*" (12). Expanding on Bauman's concept of human redundancy, Spanish philosopher José Luis Pardo's 2010 *Nunca fue tan hermosa la basura* extends the idea into a theory of everyday life: "'Nunca fue tan hermosa la basura' . . . y si lo que llamamos basura no lo fuera en realidad? Entonces no tendríamos que preocuparnos porque nos devorase, no nos sentiríamos asfixiados por los desperdicios si dejásemos de experimentarlos como desperdicios y los viviéramos como un nuevo *paisaje urbano*" (170) ("Trash was never so beautiful" . . . and what if what we called trash wasn't trash at all? Then we wouldn't have to worry about it devouring us; we wouldn't feel strangled by waste if we stopped experiencing it as waste and lived in it as if it were a new urban landscape). Pardo, like Bauman, points out that for the first time in human history we are living in a period in which there is not enough space for the waste that the world's population produces. Historically, Pardo argues, the more refuse that modern societies created (in terms of both quality and quantity) the wealthier, bolder, and more energetic they were considered to be. Wealth meant squandering, wastefulness, and surplus. In the past, he claims, modern societies needed ever-growing spaces to deposit trash so they could carry on with life and keep on wasting in the midst of their own waste. These *non-places* (to use Marc Augé's term) became necessary and by extension even gave rise to social *non-places*, locations where segments of the population are transferred that the systems of production and consumption cannot absorb (in the form of suburbs, shacks, *favelas*, ghettos, and camps, for example). "Trash" for Pardo is that which does not have a place, that which is misplaced, and, therefore, that which has to be moved to another place in the hope that it might disappear as trash there, that it might be reactivated, recycled, extinguished: trash is that which searches for another place. The movement of people from one place to another is no longer a feasible solution, as both Bauman and Pardo argue, because almost all the places in the world are now occupied, and there is nowhere to put those who are not wanted. Pardo's philosophy of trash, then, and its concomitant "new urban landscape" require anyone interested in cities and urban culture to focus not on the monumental public spaces of the historic city center (such as Madrid's Puerta del Sol) but on the more peripheral non-places that are difficult to define because they don't fit into traditional ways of imagining the city.

Afterword

Equally as rich as her novels is Elvira Navarro's blog *Periferia. Vallecas – Usera – Hortaleza – Carabanchel – Las Tablas*. It's an open-access portal, updated frequently, that pairs descriptions of peripheral urban spaces (all of which are detailed in *La trabajadora*) with photographs. More photojournalism than fictional narrative, Navarro's digital space is an exploration and celebration of what grows between the cracks of Madrid's crumbling infrastructure.

> Quizás no sea gran cosa, pero tranquiliza saber que todavía está permitido generar lugares en estos no lugares. Y que la vegetación crezca alguna vez en los cilindros del ecobulevar, que buena falta hacen aquí el fresco y el arropo.

> (Maybe it's no big deal, but it's a relief to know that making places in these non-places is still allowed. And that vegetation grows every once in a while in the cylinders of the ecoboulevard, that fresh things and groundcover are direly needed here.)

Navarro's novel and other satellite projects such as her blogs often feature such manifestos directed specifically to all of those struggling to understand their place during this era of austerity and neoliberalization. By focusing on the trials and survival tactics of women who have been stripped of their dignity and self-esteem as workers, Navarro's fiction is part of an attempt to create a new social space: a space where people who have been suddenly disqualified, refused, and expelled by the political and economic system are coming up with new rules for the game at the heart of the experience of living in the city.

The author would like to thank the members of the Fall 2016 Texas Tech University Women Faculty Writing Group for their camaraderie, support, and incredibly contagious energy during the writing of this essay. Formidable *trabajadoras* indeed.

NOTES

1.   The English translation of this selection is that of Curtis Bauer. All other translations are the author's.
2.   See Amago for a study of the political and cultural implications of the popular response to the week-long sanitary workers' strike that took place for several weeks in November 2013.
3.   See Feinberg and Larson for an essay that takes as its point of departure Swyngedouw's concept of cultural ecology to look at architectural manifestos, philosophical essays, and occupied green spaces in Madrid since 2008 that call into question basic assumptions of what a city is and can be by offering proactive understandings of natural/artificial oppositions that privilege the interconnected role of culture and community in previously discarded, abandoned, or otherwise unused city spaces.
4.   See "Geografías de 15-M: Crisis, austeridad y movilización en España" for a discussion among eleven young academics from different disciplines and activists on how the highly localized and largely symbolic occupation of the Puerta del Sol for a short time in 2011 worked its way into larger-scale and longer-term struggles over the privatization of public space and the future of Spain's housing, health, and education (Díaz Cortes and Sequera 1–9).
5.   The concept of the "moral economy" stems from the eighteenth century but was more recently elaborated by E. P. Thompson (1971). He may be best known for exploring how it is possible for groups of people to construct a "non-capitalist cultural mentality using the market for its own ends" (97).
6.   The term *décroissance* (degrowth) was first coined by André Gorz in a debate organized by *Le Nouvel Observateur* in Paris in 1972. Participants included the philosophers Herbert Marcuse and Edgard Morin, the ecologist Edward Goldsmith, and then President of the European Commission Sicco Mansholt. Gorz used the term to question the compatibility of the capitalist system with the "degrowth of mate-

rial production," and he underscored the importance of reducing consumption and promoting values such as frugality, autonomy, and conviviality. The intellectual genealogy of degrowth also includes the thinking of Ivan Illich, Cornelius Castoriadis, and Hannah Arendt, and there are many parallels with Murray Bookchin's libertarian municipalism (Demaria, Schneider, Sekulova, and Martínez-Alier, 195).

7.   Prádanos-García extends this degrowth proposal to the level of a pedagogy that guides students toward "unlearning ingrained commonplaces about economic growth, technology or progress. Only after such unlearning occurs can the floor be opened to deep critical discussions about posthuman environmental ethics and alternatives to growth that are socially desirable and environmentally sustainable" (154).

8.   See Benéitez Andrés for a thorough analysis of the theme of mental illness in *La trabajadora*, Murray for a broad theorization of the representation of neoliberal urban space in Spanish fiction after 2008, and García for a discussion of hybrid digital and real worlds in Navarro's fiction.

9.   Sequera points out that Madrid is the city in Spain with the highest concentration of what can be called highly educated "culture workers" belonging to what he calls a "creative class" whose noted presence in revitalized (gentrified) parts of the historic city center are a key component of the city's strategy to compete on a global scale (125–28). See "Geografías de 15-M" (Díaz Cortes and Sequera, eds.) for a more detailed description of the long-term impact that the social movement has had on Spanish political discourse and efforts to rethink the use of urban space.

10.   Elvira Navarro's 2016 novel *Los últimos días de Adelaida García Morales* is a fictional biography that presumes to recount some of the reasons behind the death of one of Spain's most respected, reclusive, and mysterious novelists. The work was immediately embroiled in a heated debate over the ethics of writing about well-known, real-life people whose surviving family members demand that the "truth" of their loved one's stories be told. See Víctor Erice's denouncement of Navarro's fictional appropriation of García Morales's life story in *Babelia* (26 Oct. 2016).

WORKS CITED

Amago, Samuel. "Basura, cultura, democracia en el Madrid del siglo veintiuno." *ALCES XXI* 2 (2014–2015): 33–69. Web. 14 July 2016.

Bauman, Zygmunt. *Wasted Lives: Modernity and Its Outcasts*. Cambridge: Polity Press, 2004. Print.

Benéitez Andrés, Rosa. "Crisis y violencia psicosocial: *La trabajadora* de Elvira Navarro." In *Narrativas de la violencia en el ámbito hispánico: Guerra, sociedad y familia*. Eds. Miguel Carrera Garrido and Mariola Petrak. Sevilla: Padilla Libros, 2015. 193–204. Print.

Cotella, Giancarlo, Frank Othengrafen, Athanasios Papaioannou, and Simone Tulumello. "Socio-Political and Socio-Spatial Implications of the Economic Crisis and Austerity

Politics in Southern European Cities." *Cities in Crisis: Socio-Spatial Impacts of the Economic Crisis in Southern European Cities*. London: Routledge, 2016. 27–47. Print.

D'Alisa, Giacomo, Federico Demaria, and Giorgos Kallis. *Degrowth: A Vocabulary for a New Era*. New York: Routledge, 2014. Print.

De Certeau, Michel. *The Practice of Everyday Life*. Trans. S. F. Rendell. Berkeley, CA: University of California Press, 1984. Print.

Demaria, Federico, Françoise Schneider, Filka Sekulova, and Joan Martínez-Alier. "What Is Degrowth? From an Activist Slogan to a Social Movement." *Environmental Values* 22 (2013): 191–215. Print.

Díaz Cortes, Fabia, and Jorge Sequera. Introduction. "Geografías de 15-M: Crisis, austeridad y movilización en España." *ACME: An International Journal for Critical Geographies* 14.1 (2015): 1–9. Print.

Erice, Víctor. "Una vida robada." *Babelia* (supplement of *El País*). 26 Oct. 2016. Web. 28 Oct. 2016.

Feinberg, Matthew, and Susan Larson. "Cultivating the Square: Trash, Recycling and the Cultural Ecology of Post-Crisis Madrid." In *Ethics of Life: Contemporary Iberian Debates*. Hispanic Issues Series Vol. 42. Eds. Katarzyna Beilin and Willian Viestenz. Nashville: Vanderbilt University Press, 2016. 113–42. Print.

Fraser, Benjamin. *Antonio López's Everyday Urban Worlds: A Philosophy of Painting*. Lanham, MD: Bucknell University Press, 2014. Print.

Furió-Sancho, María-José. "Evocación y reivindicación de las vanguardias artísticas en la arquitectura moderna con ambición social en las novelas *Catálogo de formas*, de Nicolás Cabral, y *La trabajadora*, de Elvira Navarro." *Dissidences* 6.11 (2015): n.p. Web. 8 June 2016.

García, Noelia S. "La desaparición del exterior en *La trabajadora* de Elvira Navarro." *LL Journal* 11.2 (2016): 1–15. Web. 15 Aug. 2016.

Lefebvre, Henri. *The Production of Space*. 1974. Trans. Donald Nicholson-Smith. Oxford: Blackwell, 1991. Print.

Moreno-Caballud, Luis. *Cultures of Anyone: Studies on Cultural Democratization in the Spanish Neoliberal Crisis*. Liverpool: University of Liverpool Press, 2015. Print.

Murray, Michelle N. "Capital Ruptures: Economies of Crisis and Urban Space in Javier Moreno's *2020*." *425ºF* 15 (2016): 71–92. Print.

Navarro, Elvira. *Periferia. Diario ligero de una que se pasea por la periferia madrileña*. Blog. *madridesperiferia.blogspot.com*. Web. 8 July 2016.

_____. *La trabajadora*. Barcelona: Random House, 2014. Print.

_____. *Los últimos días de Adelaida García Morales*. Barcelona: Random House, 2016. Print.

Pardo, Carlos. "Basura." In *Echado a perder*. Madrid: Visor, 2007. 17. Print.

_____. "Garbage." Trans. Curtis Bauer. *The Dirty Goat* 25 (2011): 68–69. Print.

Pardo, José Luis. *Nunca fue tan hermosa la basura*. Barcelona: Galaxia Gutenberg, 2010. Print.

Prádanos-García, Luis. The Pedagogy of Degrowth: Teaching Hispanic Studies in the Age of Social Inequality and Ecological Collapse." *Arizona Journal of Hispanic Cultural Studies* 19 (2015): 81–96. Print.

Sabaté, Irene. "The Spanish Mortgage Crisis and the Reemergence of Moral Economies in Uncertain Times." *History and Anthropology* 27.1 (2016): 107–20. Print.

Sequera, Jorge. "#Redecoramos tu barrio: Gentrificación cultural en la ciudad." *El paseo de Jane: Tejiendo redes a pie de calle*. Eds. Susana Jiménez Carmona and Ana Useros. Madrid: Modernito Books. 127–31. Print.

Shields, David. *Reality Hunger: A Manifesto*. New York: Vintage, 2011. Print.

Snyder, Jonathan. *Poetics of Opposition in Contemporary Spain: Politics and the Work of Urban Culture*. New York: Palgrave Macmillan, 2015. Print.

Swyngedouw, Erik. "¡La naturaleza no existe! La sostenibilidad como síntoma de una planificación despolitizada." *Urban. Nueva Serie* 1 (2011): 41–66. Print.

_____. "Urbanization and Environmental Futures: Politicizing Urban Political Ecologies." *Handbook of Political Ecology*. Eds. Tom Perreault, Gavin Bridge, and James McCarthy. London: Routledge, 2015. 609–19. Print.

Thompson, E. P. "The Moral Economy of the English Crowd in the Eighteenth Century." *Past & Present* 50 (1971): 76–136. Print.

PART II

Sites of Memory

CHAPTER 6

Institutional Sites of Remembrance: Monuments and Archives of the 11-M Train Bombings

Jill Robbins

This essay examines the monuments and archives that took the place of the spontaneous grassroots memorials that arose at the sites of the March 11, 2004, train bombings in Madrid, known as 11-M, along the doomed commuter line that originated in Alcalá de Henares and passed through a series of stations in working-class neighborhoods before arriving at the Atocha station. The line had been constructed thanks to the Urban Development Plans of 1985 and 1997, whose goal was to transform Madrid from a third-level European city, or what Neil Brenner has called a "national urban center," into a "global city" (262). The plans brought about the neoliberal redesign of the city, eliminating the *chabolas*, or shantytowns, in the traditionally leftist districts of Villa de Vallecas and Puente de Vallecas and encouraging the incorporation of these exurban districts into the capital proper and the construction of new housing, hospitals, schools, parks, and shopping centers in them.[1] The development of an elaborate network of commuter trains and the transformation of the Atocha station into a gleaming international hub were vital elements of this project:

> La alta velocidad contribuye a la especialización funcional de Madrid como "ciudad de negocios," "ciudad de las compras y de la moda" y "ciudad del ocio-cultura y turismo." Dentro de sus objetivos está llevar el tren al centro de la ciudad, lo que en Madrid se ha concretado en la ubicación de sus terminales en Atocha y Chamartín. (*Evaluación del Plan Urbanístico de 1997* 31)

(The high-speed train contributes to the functional specialization of Madrid as a "city of business," a "city of shopping and fashion," and a "city of leisure culture and tourism." Among its objectives is to bring the train to the center of the city, which in Madrid has taken the form of locating its terminals in Atocha and Chamartin.)

Ironically, the logistical and symbolic success of this project facilitated the attacks on March 11, 2004, when terrorists placed bombs on commuter trains heading to the central station from working-class neighborhoods during the morning rush hour. Of the ten bombs, only three exploded at Atocha, Madrid's central station and the headquarters of RENFE, the national railroad company. The remaining seven bombs did not affect Atocha: four bombs exploded in a train near Téllez Street, some 800 meters away; one went off at the Santa Eugenia station; and two, on a train that was just leaving the El Pozo del Tío Raimundo station, where immigrant workers lived alongside Spanish nationals.

This essay focuses on some of the monuments and archives dedicated to these events, arguing that they do not simply represent the kind of petrification of living memory that Pierre Nora's concept of *lieux de mémoire* brings to mind. In the case of 11-M, for example, an Archive of Mourning was created by Spanish anthropologists in part as a way for them to process their own feelings, and in a sense their work embodies that affective relationship to the people and places they studied and preserved. Some of the texts from the grassroots memorials, moreover, have not remained in the isolated space of the archive, but have come to be literally inscribed on and in monuments in public places, where they may continue to be read. Others, such as the poems that were posted in the window of the Rafael Alberti bookstore soon after the attacks or those written by schoolchildren in the poor working-class district of El Pozo, have made their way into anthologies, with the proceeds going to victims' associations. Here, I suggest that these archives and monuments represent complex processes of embodiment, mourning, and performance that reveal dynamic processes of cultural memory in which class issues are brought to the fore.

The Archive of Mourning in the RENFE Library of the Train Museum (Delicias Neighborhood)

Following the removal of the materials spontaneously placed at the original site of a grassroots memorial, the collection, cleaning, and cataloging of the artifacts by academics and museum experts contributed to a process of "heritagization" and institutionalization of the structures (Margry and Sánchez-Carretero

17). Indeed, every archive, Jacques Derrida reminds us, "is at once institutive and conservative. Revolutionary and traditional. . . . [I]t keeps, it saves, but in an unnatural fashion, that is to say in making the law (nomos) or in making people respect the law" (7). It has also been argued that the archiving process desacralizes the memorial, in much the same fashion as the display of religious artifacts in museums and libraries reappropriates them for history by separating them from the context in which they are or were sacred: "As the paradigmatic institution of passive cultural memory, the archive is the opposite of the memorial space of the church: It is the unhallowed bureaucratic space of a clean and neatly organized repository" (Assmann 102). The archive also does a poor job of preserving affect because it is precisely the trauma—as registered in the emotions and shattered bodies—that escapes the classificatory drive of the endeavor. What is more, the archive is selective—though less so than the canon, as Aleida Assmann explains (103)—and its omissions reflect the ways in which institutions marginalize certain individuals as they create a unified body of citizens.[2] In this sense, Ann Cvetkovich reminds us that "trauma can be used to reinforce nationalism when constructed as a wound that must be healed in the name of unity," and it is important to remember that archives of trauma do not house "the forms of violence that are forgotten or covered over by the amnesiac powers of national culture, which is adept at using one trauma story to suppress another" (16).

The archive removes objects from circulation, storing them in a place hidden from public view. The Archive of Mourning, for example, is housed in the small library maintained by RENFE in the very back of the Train Museum, located in the working-class Delicias neighborhood, not far from Atocha. Las Delicias is one of the seven wards (or neighborhoods) into which the District of Arganzuela, located in central-southern Madrid, is divided. As with most libraries in Spain, the stacks are closed, and investigators must obtain prior permission to access the materials of the archive, which the staff of the library brings out to the tables. The library itself is open to the public, however, and it is visited often by parents and grandparents with small children in tow, who come to look at the materials and juvenile literature available on the shelves. These individuals sometimes encounter a scholar like myself leafing through archival materials and may thus chance upon the documents and objects that have been stored away, of whose existence they had been previously unaware.

All of this does not necessarily imply, however, that the archive's founders and employees are entirely indifferent to the original traumatic event or that they view their endeavor from a cold, distant remove. Rather, we might see in their work the kind of contradiction that Avery Gordon discusses in relation to sociology in her book *Ghostly Matters: Haunting and the Sociological Imagination*, where she describes how she came "to understand the real as an effect (as something produced) and as an *affective relation* between analyst and analyzed, between I and it or them or you" (38). Indeed, when I consulted the archive, one of the librarians shared with me his own experience of the 11-M attacks, including the ways it personally affected all of the library and museum employees. In a similar fashion, Cristina Sánchez-Carretero's introductory essay to her edited volume of anthropological studies related to 11-M combines an objective, scientific approach with a description of the investigations' affective roots and intended social effects:

> De alguna manera, el ir a las estaciones para documentar lo que estaba ocurriendo era también la forma de responder, desde nuestra profesión, a una necesidad de acción ante una situación traumática. . . . El dolor ante la muerte es un mecanismo que puede dar lugar a acciones muy diversas, incluyendo el inicio del proyecto de investigación El Archivo del Duelo. (19)

> In some sense, going to the stations to document what was happening there was also a way of responding, by means of our profession, to a call to action when faced with a traumatic situation. . . . The pain of confronting death can give rise to very different activities, including the initiation of the Archive of Mourning research project.

What we see here, and what I felt in my own research in the archive, was, in the words of Avery Gordon, the turn toward

> the places where our discourse is unauthorized by virtue of its unruliness. The detour takes us away from abstract questions of method, from bloodless professionalized questions, toward the materiality of institutional storytelling, with all its uncanny repetitions. The detour takes us away from abstract questions of method into what lies outside the metadiscursive talk about method, which is, well, us, our involvement. (40)

Thus, despite the fact that the archive is highly ordered, with each item preserved in a plastic sleeve inside a folder and/or box, the desperately scrawled messages and the objects the archive contains can retain their emotional impact and continue to circulate in unexpected ways.

Ramón Mayrata's poignant poetic/narrative text, "Entre escombros, fragmentos de aquellos días" (Amid the rubble, fragments of those days) also illustrates how the archive may be an affective site.[3] The work appears in the volume *Homenaje a las víctimas 11-M* (Homage to the 11-M victims), put together by the workers' union, Comisiones Obreras Unión Sindical de Madrid-Región (Workers' Union Commission of the Madrid District), which places artworks alongside narrative and poetic texts.[4] Mayrata's contribution is set in the context of the Alcalá de Henares branch of the Spanish National Library, where he conducts research, and the Atocha train station in Madrid, which is 500 meters from his home. As he puts it, "Durante años he vivido, aún vivo, entre una y otra ciudad, llevando conmigo un equipaje de sensaciones coincidentes o encontradas" (Comisiones Obreras Unión Sindical de Madrid-Región 63) (For years I lived, I still live, between one city and the other, carrying with me the baggage of coincidental or accidental sensations). His piece is divided into several parts: "Atentado" (The attack), "Horas antes" (Hours earlier), "Por la tarde" (In the afternoon), "A otras personas" (To other people), "Manifestación (al día siguiente)" (Protest march [the next day]), "Días después" (Days later), Carta al poeta J. L. Moreno" (Letter to the poet J. L. Moreno), and "Qué vuela?" (What flies?). Most sections contain an autobiographical narrative component that explains how the author experienced "those days," and a poem or two. The penultimate section is a letter, addressed to a poet, that ends with the final text, a poem dedicated to two artists. Each of the genres contributes distinctly to the text, with the poems taking over like a flash to communicate the affective component when the narrative seemingly can no longer go on. The verse sections thus seem to allow the speaker to give some order to the emotions that come upon him and thereby step out of the immediacy of the trauma, the shock of his realization that people he sees every day might suddenly have disappeared forever. The effect of the entire text is to convert the library from a mere repository of archival documents into an affective site, characterized by the interactions among the people working there in various capacities, bound together by the threads of metaphor.

Monuments

Although the bombs exploded along the route of the commuter trains and in the stations of Santa Eugenia (Villa de Vallecas) and El Pozo del Tío Raimundo (Vallecas), along the same doomed line, the world's attention fell on Atocha, and to a large extent remains there, with the other locations almost completely forgotten. This section on monuments, then, will begin with Atocha and the other sites in the city and region of Madrid that are associated with cultural heritage and thus with the distinguished, global image that the architects of the 1997 urbanization plan hoped to project to the world.

The grassroots memorial inside the Atocha terminal building originally contained the mix of objects and texts that typify what Jack Santino has termed "spontaneous shrines": candles, stuffed animals, flowers, religious symbols, and other objects (Margry and Sánchez-Carretero 25). The Madrid train stations were papered with original or copied poems and song lyrics in much the same fashion as what came to be known as "Ground Zero" after the 9/11 attacks (Rowland 108), but the Atocha station was also adorned with the Spanish flag, black ribbons, white hands, prayer cards, and hymns. These objects were removed on the request of the workers in the station and replaced with a computerized "Espacio de Palabras" (Word Space) (Sánchez-Carretero, "The Madrid Train Bombings" 252), which remained in place until 2007.[5] One could argue that the technology of the site dramatically alters the act of writing there. Rather than reading other peoples' discourse and then adding to the chorus of voices, visitors interact with a computer screen and keyboard individually or with small groups of family members or friends. This technology also requires a certain degree of computer literacy—minimally, the ability to type—whereas even an illiterate person could leave an object at the original sites. Even those with the capability of writing on the computer, moreover, lose the kind of physicality that handwriting involves, and the particular textures and connotations of writing materials. Thus, in some senses, the technology changes the relationship between visitors to the physical site and the original objects placed there by mourners, even if some of these may be visible at the location.

The technology, however, allows for a continued physical interaction with the site, as the visitors must first touch the screen with their hands, adding their own imprint to the iconic symbol of solidarity with the victims, before contributing their own words. At the same time, that symbol, which was developed in response to ETA violence, and the other images on and surrounding the screen (taken from some of the original texts at the memorial) may condition visitors' interpretations of the events and even their writing. The act of touching evokes a kind of physical contact with the dead, even if what the writers touch is a cold screen rather than the textures of paper, clothing, and cardboard. The writing materials in the original shrine consisted of such objects, many of which had been in intimate contact with the everyday existence of mourners and, in some cases, the dead, and therefore metonymically represent them.

The texts written on this electronic site are likewise conditioned by its technological characteristics. Of the tens of thousands of messages archived by the Consejo Superior de Investigaciones Científicas (Spanish National Research

Council, or CSIC), most take the form of brief messages, almost like e-mails directed to the bereaved and the dead, but there are nonetheless several poetic entries, including brief lyrical texts, quotes from poems and songs, and even full-length poems. The content of these texts contrasts strongly with the rather cold image of the site's mechanical output, which, like the other objects and texts from the memorials, is housed in the Archive of Mourning. The writers would not see this output, however: rather, they would send the messages off into cyberspace, which could be felt as a way of sending them to the dead in another world, or directly, like an e-mail, to the living who were still suffering. Also recorded on the site are the geographical origins of the authors, so that the messages come to represent a coming together of far-flung bodies in a commemorative act.

The materiality of the body is a key feature of the most well-known 11-M monument: the crystal cylindrical structure that pierces the roof of the Atocha station, channeling light to the interior space below. The monument can be seen from the street, a shimmering transparent tower of clear glass blocks jutting out of the station at an angle, visually recalling the explosions. Inside the layer of glass blocks is a clear membrane on which messages to the victims in numerous languages are inscribed in a continuous, spiraling text. The architects, FAM Arquitectura y Urbanismo S.L., describe the rhetoric of this linguistic presentation in relation to concepts of transparency, light, absence, and structure, but also in part as a metaphorical representation of the body's connective tissues, membranes, and skins, tattooed with poetic messages and encased in a glass structure that explodes like a frozen blast out of the building and into the Madrid sky. The thin membrane and absolute transparency of the building (the architects write, "Tan solo brillos, reflejos y luz formarán materialmente el monumento" [Only gleams, reflections, and light will give material form to the monument]) allows for continued communication between the living and the dead on the thin membrane that separates the individual from the collective. The inner cavity of the memorial, meanwhile, forms a meditation room embedded in the body of the Atocha station and separated from the rest of the station by a soundproof glass wall, creating "un espacio vacío, en silencio, con la luz como protagonista" ("Monumento homenaje a las víctimas de los atentados de 11-M") (an empty space, in silence, with light as the protagonist). The silence and the vacuum represent the ghosts of the disappeared bodies,[6] and the names of the dead, etched into the glass walls, are symbolically linked with the messages on the membrane above.

The list of the victims' names preserves a trace of identity in a gesture that is typical of monuments to the dead. Carole Blair notes in particular that, in contemporary memorials, the inscriptions "name individuals whose lives and/or deaths have been rendered outside the cultural mainstream" (Blair 282). She is thinking of the AIDS Memorial Quilt, the Civil Rights Memorial, and the Vietnam Veterans Memorial. The names on the 11-M memorial are largely of the economically and legally marginalized: working-class citizens and un-documented foreign workers living on the outskirts of the capital. If we look at another monument, an interactive page on the Web site of the newspaper *El Mundo*, we see another approach to the memorialization of individuals. Here we have a virtual wall of images, which, when clicked, bring up the portrayed individual's biography, another way of evoking bodies and lives. This gesture appears in 11-M poetry as well. The poem "Elegy" by Guillermo López Gallego, for example, lists the names of the dead, with "Guillermo," "López" and "Ga-llego" in bold as they crop up in others' names. Likewise, two books of poetry— Juan Castrillo's *Dolor de luz* (Light's pain; 2005) and Pedro Provencio's *Onda expansiva* (Shock wave; 2012)—dedicate a poem to each of the victims.

Along with the Atocha station, other sites symbolic of Madrid's history as the national, imperial, and Catholic capital received considerable government funding and media attention. We find the Bosque del Recuerdo (Memorial Forest), with one tree for each of the dead, in Retiro Park, a space that was created by Queen Elizabeth I as part of a monastery but became a palatial garden during the reign of King Philip II. It is at this silent memorial that the victims' association most closely tied to the conservative Popular Party and anti-ETA sentiment, the Asociación Víctimas del Terrorismo (Association of the Victims of Terrorism, or AVT), holds its annual 11-M memorial ceremonies.

Alcalá de Henares, the birthplace of Miguel de Cervantes and a bishopric before becoming part of the diocese of Madrid, is also an historic site associated with Spain's imperial past, designated as a UNESCO World Heritage Site in 1998. The original location of the Complutense University, it is the home of the University of Alcalá, the Archivo General de la Administración (General Administration Archive) and the Cervantes Institute, which promotes Hispanic culture. None of the bombs exploded in Alcalá, but the commuter line along which the trains exploded has its origin there, and the city was thus affected by the attacks. The monument outside the Alcalá de Henares train station includes a group statue of what appear to be typical Spaniards, slightly smaller than life size, though the victims included immigrants and the station itself is located in an immigrant neighborhood. In the small square outside the station, which has been renamed the Plaza 11 de Marzo (March 11 Square), we find an enormous abstract sculpture and a column listing the residents of the city who perished on the doomed commuter train.

Distant and distinct from the sites associated with cultural heritage, the train stations and neighborhoods of El Pozo and Santa Eugenia have remained largely invisible in the government actions taken to recognize those affected by the bombings. This neglect extends to the benefits accorded to the victims, including the construction of monuments, which have been erected and funded by the government only thanks to the determination and concerted effort of people living in the neighborhoods.

The abstract concrete monument to the 11-M victims in El Pozo, designed by the architect José María Pérez González (Peridis) and inaugurated in 2011, towers above visitors to the site. Looking through the structure from one end of it, you feel the power of an enormous train, but from the side you see that it is broken into pieces, like the trains themselves on that fateful day. This static monolithic structure is bathed at night in soft light and surrounded by the flowing waters of a fountain, suggesting the continuity of life, with death looming in its midst. In the background is a mosaic of artworks by the painter Juan Genovés (1930) and the graphic artists El Roto (Andrés Rábago García, 1947) and Forges (Antonio Fraguas de Pablo, 1942), embedded behind panes of glass in a great wall. Some of these pieces also appear in the collaborative book edited by the Comisiones Obreras, *Homenaje a las víctimas 11-M*, along with the texts by Ramón Mayrata (described above) and other well-known writers (Luis Antonio de Villena, Moncho Alpuente, Luis del Val).

Perhaps more than any other neighborhood in Madrid, El Pozo del Tío Raimundo embodies resistance, resiliency, and class consciousness. Indeed, we find a narrative of this collective spirit in the introduction to the anthology *11-M: Palabras para el recuerdo* (11-M: words for remembering), a collection of texts written primarily by local schoolchildren and compiled by the Asociación de Vecinos y Amigos de El Pozo del Tío Raimundo (Association of Residents and Friends of El Pozo del Tío Raimundo). After a brief presentation by famed journalist and TV anchor Iñaki Gabilondo (1942), the book begins with a narrative text authored by the neighborhood association as a group, which offers a genealogy beginning with the founding of El Pozo when Tío Raimundo ("Uncle" Raimundo) arrived from Asturias in the late 1920s. In the postwar period, "[a]ños de vencedores y humillación de vencidos; de cárceles repletas de los derrotados; de mujeres de media España con la cabeza rapada a modo de escarnio y escarmiento, ante el recocijo de los caciques y las bendiciones del clero" (Asociación de Vecinos y Amigos del Pozo del Tío Raimundo 10) (years of the victors and the humiliation of the vanquished; of jails filled with the defeated; of women from half of Spain with heads shaved to shame and punish them, to the delight of the strongmen and with the blessing of the clergy), El Pozo continued

to grow as a marginalized community of poor, hardworking migrants who together built and maintained a space where they could "levantar la cabeza y pro-
clamar la dignidad de pueblo trabajador" (13) (raise their heads and proclaim
the dignity of the working class). In this reading, the *chabolas* (slum dwellings)
were "puntas de lanza" (14) (spearheads) in a class war, refuges for a persecuted
class of people in the Spanish postwar. It was in that community, the narrative
continues, that a true democratic spirit was formed (17). Far from the image of
filth and delinquency that justified the dismantling of the *chabolas*,[7] the last of
which collapsed in 1986, this text highlights the intellectual and political nature
of its residents through the 1960s.

As the introduction explains, poetry (particularly social poetry) played an
important role in this process. Not surprisingly, then, many of the texts (not
all are poems) in the collection reflect concepts of democracy, solidarity, and
class consciousness. Rubén Sánchez, a fourth-grader, writes of how the Spanish people protested the decision of then-President José María Aznar to inter-
vene in the Iraq War (Asociación de Vecinos y Amigos 98–99). Another poem,
collectively written by 11-year-old sixth-graders, decries the death of innocent
people due to the President's ill-fated "error" (41). Cristina Maseda, another
11-year-old, writes of solidarity leading to a peaceful world (53). Another poem
likens the dead to a defenseless flower destroyed for the sole reason that they
belonged to the working class, echoing Neruda's "Explico algunas cosas" (Let
Me Explain a Few Things) from his 1938 anti-fascist book, *Spain in My Heart*.
The author, Cruz Moreno Aranda, wrote it on March 26, 2004, when he was
a student at Padre Mariana Public School, in the neighborhood of Entrevías,
another stop on that ill-fated commuter train line. It is written in the ballad
form (eight-syllable lines with assonant rhyme in the even verses), symbolically
placing its young author in the traditional role of the minstrel, declaiming his
verse in the public square to a popular audience. In using this form to recount
the violence that the working class suffers, he recalls the tradition of Federico
García Lorca's *Romancero gitano* (*Gypsy Ballads*; 1928). The allusion to Lorca,
who was assassinated by right-wing nationalists in 1936, at the beginning of
the Spanish Civil War, also appears in this poem's final lines—"Si somos hojas
caducas / cuando el viento nos cimbrea" (Asociación de Vecinos y Amigos 64)
(For we are expired leaves / when the wind sways us)—which bring to mind the
ending of the Andalusian poet's *Lament for Ignacio Sánchez Mejías* (1935).[8] It is
worth remembering in this context that the repression of the postwar years also
had a cultural expression in the censorship of authors and aesthetic tendencies,
including those of poets such as Lorca and Neruda.

Elsewhere, frustrated by the lack of material support from the Popular Party government of the Community of Madrid and angered that the victims of the poorer communities had not been consulted in the design of the other sites, the neighborhood association of Santa Eugenia raised money to create its own memorial ("Monumento a las víctimas del 11-M"). The statue, completed in 2007, seems not to be a wholly effective remembrance: the small statue is not prominently displayed on the grounds of the station, but across the street, in an isolated, weedy patch. Nonetheless, the residents host commemorative events at the site, including an annual memorial ceremony with local schoolchildren. In 2012, for example, they left flowers and sang a well-known pop song, "No dudaría" (I wouldn't hesitate) by Antonio Flores (Guernica), whose theme is antiviolence. Flores, born in Madrid in 1961, was the son of singer Lola Flores, who played the Franco-era prototype of the Andalusian gypsy in numerous films, and Roma guitarist Antonio González.[9] Although Flores might have easily lived isolated by his parents' wealth, he instead immersed himself in the local street life, and he was a popular figure with residents. Furthermore, as stated earlier, immigrants fleeing extreme poverty in Andalucía had flocked to the neighborhoods surrounding the El Pozo and Santa Eugenia stations during the dictatorship, so the choice of an artist with strong roots in Andalucía is not surprising.

Conclusions

In addition to the exclusions that archives and monuments produce, an essential dilemma underlying many of the institutional responses to violence is that their definition of the dead as victims and the attackers as terrorists may be used to justify future violence. This kind of thinking has underpinned the global "war on terror," which has eroded civil rights and undermined national and international law as well as national sovereignty even as it has sought to defend nations and their citizens from external perils. Indeed, it was arguably Spain's participation in the preemptive war against Iraq that precipitated the March 11 bombings, which in this context would be construed not as terrorism but as an act of war. And we have learned that the U.S. drone attacks alone, justified by 9/11 and the failed Iraq War, have killed many more civilians, including hundreds of children, than the 11-M bombings. Within Spain itself, meanwhile, the official gatherings at the monuments and memorials have been opportunities for political speech making that turns the victims' groups against one another, negating and thereby exacerbating the pain of many people affected by this act of violence, whose wounds (literal and figurative) have not healed and, in some cases, never will. Despite these disputes, linked to the origins of archives and monuments in institutional and political practices, the practices of reading and writing in archives and monuments resist reductionism, preserving to some degree the affective link to the traumatic events and their aftermath.

NOTES

1. Unfortunately, these changes also contributed to the dramatic rise in rents and overall economic precariousness for working-class people in those very neighborhoods (Méndez 35; Vives and Rullan 405), which arguably represents a form of violence, and the mortgaging practices underlying them would be a major factor in the debilitating economic crisis that began in 2008.

2. For this reason, theorists from Jacques Derrida to Diana Taylor to Ann Cvetkovich have suggested alternatives to the traditional concept of the archive, including anti-archives, digital archives, repertoire, and counter-archives, that might resist the incorporation of the artifacts of radical and grassroots political movements into the institutionalizing, historicizing, conservative, and/or neoliberal thrust of the traditional archive.

3. Mayrata is now known principally as a novelist, most famous for his book about the Western Sahara, *El imperio desierto* (The desert empire; 1992), which combines elements of autobiography, anthropology, history, and fiction. He began his career, however, as a poet, and his fiction remains quite lyrical. He explained to me that he does not generally write poetry immediately in response to traumatic experiences, preferring to return to them from a reflective distance, but that the poems in this text came upon him almost unheeded, out of necessity, much as the structure implies (personal interview, November 13, 2015).

4. In the Exposición Trazos y Puntadas para el Recuerdo (Exhibition Strokes and Stitches for Remembrance), inaugurated on March 11, 2014, the emotions and moods of the victims are explored through works organized according to four colors: red for terror and violence, yellow for solidarity and citizens' embraces, green for the hope of emerging from the black tunnel of despair, and blue for peace and respect for human rights. In addition to other donated works, the exhibition contained thirty-eight paintings, five sketches, two sculptures, and three books from the Asociación de Pintores Realistas de Madrid (Madrid Association of Realist Painters), created for their own exhibition in 2005.

5. These interactions were filmed over the course of several months and then studied by the anthropologist, Gerôme Truc. In his article, he focuses primarily on the ages and genders of the participants and the dynamics of the various groups that visit the site and inscribe texts there, which include traditional families, children and teachers on school excursions, tourists, and groups of young people (Truc).

6. It is hard to know what to say, however, about the failure of this project, as the membrane has collapsed and the memorial is often closed for maintenance.

7. See, for example, the article in *El País* dated May 29, 1986 (Fresneda).
8. "Alma ausente" ("Absent soul") the last text in Lorca's four-part elegy, ends thus: "Yo canto su elegancia con palabras que gimen / y recuerdo una brisa triste por los olivos" (I sing his elegance with words that moan / and recall a sad breeze through the olive trees). The Web site of this school explains that Entrevías, a neighborhood in the district of Puente de Vallecas, was populated by the waves of immigrants who came to Madrid fleeing the poverty of Extremadura and Andalucía, and it is now also the home to a growing population of Asian, Moroccan, Eastern European, and Latin American immigrants ("Quiénes Somos | C.E.I.P. 'Padre Mariana' | EducaMadrid").
9. Although this particular song does not form part of the flamenco tradition, we should also keep in mind the important work done by Lorca, along with composer Manuel de Falla, in promoting so-called "gypsy music" to an art form in their conference on *cante jondo* (the Andalusian "deep song") in 1922. In his poetry and plays, Lorca also combated social prejudice against against the poor and marginalized Roma people, at the receiving end of much state violence represented by the famous Civil Guards that appear in the *Romancero gitano*.

WORKS CITED

Asociación de Vecinos and Amigos del Pozo del Tío Raimundo, ed. 11-M: *Palabras para el recuerdo*. Madrid: Punto de Lectura, 2004. Print.

Assmann, Aleida. "Canon and Archive." *A Companion to Cultural Memory Studies*. Eds. Astrid Erll and Ansgar Nünning. New York: De Gruyter, 2010. 97–107. Print.

Blair, Carole. "Reflections on Criticism and Bodies: Parables from Public Places." *Western Journal of Communication* 65.3 (2001): 271–94. Print.

Brenner, Neil. "Global Cities, 'Glocal' States: Global City Formation and State Territorial Restructuring in Contemporary Europe." *The Global Cities Reader*. Eds. Neil Brenner and Roger Kell. London: Routledge, 2006. 259–66. Print.

Comisiones Obreras Unión Sindical de Madrid-Región. *Homenaje a las víctimas 11-M*. Madrid: Ediciones GPS, 2005. Print.

Cvetkovich, Ann. *An Archive of Feelings: Trauma, Sexuality, and Lesbian Public Cultures*. Durham, NC: Duke University Press, 2003. Print.

Derrida, Jacques. "Archive Fever: A Freudian Impression." Trans. Eric Prenowitz. *Diacritics* 25.2 (1995): 9–63. Print.

Evaluación del Plan Urbanístico de 1997. N.p.: n.p., n.d. Print.

Fresneda, Carlos. "El Pozo del Tío Raimundo dice adiós a las chabolas." *El País*. 29 May 1986. Web. 1 Nov. 2014.

Gordon, Avery F. *Ghostly Matters: Haunting and the Sociological Imagination*. Minneapolis: University of Minnesota Press, 2008. Print.

Guernica. "El blog del Guernica: Homenaje al 11- M." *El blog del Guernica*. 9 Mar. 2012. Web. 20 Oct. 2015.

Margry, Peter Jan, and Cristina Sánchez-Carretero. "Introduction." *Rethinking Memori-alization: The Concept of Grassroots Memorials*. New York: Berghahn Books, 2011. 1–47. Print.

Méndez, Ricardo. "Globalización, neoliberalismo y dinámicas metropolitanas en Madrid." *Documentos y aportes en administración pública y gestión estatal* 19 (2012): 29–49. Print.

"Monumento a las víctimas del 11 M." *Minube*. N.d. Web. 6 Nov. 2014.

"Monumento homenaje a las víctimas de los atentados de 11-M." FAM. *Estudio de arqui-tectura*. 2007. Web. 20 Oct. 2015.

"Quiénes somos C.E.I.P. 'Padre Mariana' EducaMadrid." N.d. Web. 28 Oct. 2015.

Sánchez Carretero, Cristina. *El archivo del duelo: Análisis de la respuesta ciudadana ante los atentados del 11 de marzo en Madrid*. Madrid: Consejo Superior de Investigación Científicas, 2011. Print.

_____. "The Madrid Train Bombings: Enacting the Emotional Body at the March 11 Grassroots Memorials." *Grassroots Memorials: The Politics of Memorializing*. Eds. Cristina Sánchez-Carretero and Peter Jan Margry. New York: Berghahn Books, 2011. 244–61. Print.

Truc, Gérôme. "Espacio de palabras y rituales de solidaridad en Atocha." *El archivo del duelo: Análisis de la respuesta ciudadana ante los atentados del 11-M en Madrid*. Ed. Cristina Sánchez-Carretero. Madrid: Consejo Superior de Investigaciones Científicas, 2011. 209–26. Print.

Vives, Sònia, and Onofre Rullan. "La apropiación de las rentas del suelo en la ciudad neo-liberal española." *Boletín de la Asociación de Geógrafos Españoles* 65 (2014): 387–408. Print.

◆　　CHAPTER 7

The Politics of Public Memory in Madrid Now: From an "Olympic Capital of Impunity" to "Omnia sunt communia?"

Scott Boehm

On January 9, 2014, an editor for Google Maps approved an unknown user's suggestion that Berlin's Theodor-Heuss-Platz should properly be labeled Adolf-Hitler-Platz. A day later Google corrected the mistake and issued a public apology, but for nearly twenty-four hours the square named in honor of Germany's first post–World War II president was identified by its Nazi name ("Google Maps Apologizes"). As *Der Spiegel* reported, "Anyone using Google Maps on Thursday evening could have been treated to an unfortunate trip down memory lane. The popular online mapping service mislabeled Theodor-Heuss-Platz, in the western Charlottenburg district of Berlin, with the name it held from 1933 to 1945: Adolf-Hitler-Platz" ("Berlin Blunder"). This unexpected flash of memory illuminates how historical memory and cultural politics intersect in public space (of both the physical and virtual varieties), producing radically different structures of feeling via the symbolic power of naming—and renaming—urban squares and city streets. It is no accident that in 1963 this particular *platz* was chosen to commemorate Germany's first federal president, after its name had been changed back to its pre-Nazi name of Reichskanzlerplatz during denazification. Carried out through directives issued by the Allied Control Council in the wake of WWII, the goal of denazification was to rid Germany (and Austria) of all remnants of National Socialist ideology. While the Nuremburg Trials are its most remembered component, denazification was a sweeping program that included purging the press, judiciary, economy, and politics of Nazi influences. Due to the critical role symbols play in the formation and maintenance of ideological fantasies, the program also included the physical removal of Nazi symbols across the war-torn German-speaking landscape.[1]

Thus, when strolling through the German capital today, it is impossible to stumble upon a swastika on a city plaque or Hitler's name on a street sign; not only were the markers of German fascism removed by the Allies, but their public display remains prohibited by German law. For this reason, Google Maps' return of the most repressed signifier of Nazism ("Hitler") to the city's map nearly seventy years after its defeat was shocking since it went against not only German, but even global common sense. It is simply inexplicable that the Name-of-the-Father of German fascism and the Holocaust could appear on the Berlin cityscape—*even in virtual form*—so many decades after the streets were cleansed of Nazi symbols.

But what is inexplicable in one country can be perfectly normal in another, and compared to Germany, Spain has a long history of being "different" when it comes to dealing with its own legacy of fascism and genocide. In Spain, forty years after the death of "El Generalísimo" Francisco Franco, otherwise referred to as "El Caudillo de España," "defrancofication" is a term yet to be coined and the streets of its capital city are replete with symbols of Spanish fascism. In fact, in Madrid people stroll through the Plaza del Caudillo, the Spanish equivalent of "Der-Führer-Platz," every day without demonstrations of shock or outrage. A tree-lined square fitted with a fountain and several benches, the Plaza del Caudillo's persistence adjacent to the Palacio Real de El Pardo—Franco's residence throughout the dictatorship—is symptomatic of the politics of public memory in postdictatorship Madrid. It is also far from an isolated case in Spain, which counts eight villages still named in Franco's honor.[2]

The example of Reíllo, a small village in Cuenca, puts the politics of public memory in Madrid in a broader national context. In January 2008, the village government decided to change the name of its main street from "Calle El Generalísmo" to "Calle José Mondéjar" in commemoration of a beloved schoolteacher who also served as the village's mayor from 1963 to 1972. In April 2014, however, a new government led by the conservative Partido Popular decided to change the street name back to "el nombre que tenía antes" (the name it had before), according to Pablo Campillo, the PP mayor. Defending the decision to reporters, Campillo stated that "en el pueblo los vecinos no se han pronunciado ni a favor ni en contra" (in the village, the neighbors haven't spoken in favor or against) and asserted, "[Y]o soy nacido en los ochenta y para mí eso es historia de España, al igual que hay otra calle que se llama Isabel I de Castilla" (qtd. in"Franco vuelve") (I was born in the eighties, and for me this is the history of Spain, just like there's another street that's called Isabella I of Castile). Thus, only months after the virtual Adolf-Hitler-Platz incident elicited an immediate apology from Google, a conservative mayor of a Spanish village put Franco's name back on the map and on the street itself, quite unapologetically and without media uproar.

The stark contrast in the politics of public memory related to fascism in Germany and Spain highlighted by this case is largely the result of the fact that the Allies chose not to topple Franco after defeating Hitler and Mussolini with the help of exiled Spanish republicans, who were among the first troops that liberated Paris. For it should be remembered that denazification was a project imposed upon a defeated state occupied by the Allies. In contrast, Franco enjoyed the support of the United States from the early 1950s until his death in 1975. Putting aside the Allies' decision to leave Franco in power, however, it becomes clear that the Transition following Franco's death has dictated the politics of public memory in Spain during forty years of postdictatorship. The pacts of silence and forgetting forged by "the regime of 1978" during the Transition are ultimately responsible for the fact that Madrid could be accurately denounced as an "Olympic capital of impunity" by human rights organizations during the city's 2013 bid to host the 2020 Olympic Games (Moraga).[3]

And yet, two years later, historic elections ended twenty-four years of the Partido Popular's control of Madrid's city hall, signifying a seismic shift of political power in Madrid, and opening the door to the possibility of confronting the culture of impunity that has characterized the city for decades. In those May 2015 municipal elections, Manuela Carmena—a former judge, cofounder of Judges for Democracy, and a survivor of the 1977 Atocha massacre who had reluctantly agreed to run as the mayoral candidate for Ahora Madrid (Now Madrid), an electoral platform created through an agreement between Podemos and Ganemos Madrid, a collective of progressive social movements and organizations—shocked her main rival, Esperanza Aguirre, the longtime president of the Partido Popular in Madrid, by replacing Ana Botella—the wife of former Spanish president and staunch conservative José María Aznar—as Madrid's new mayor.[4] Not surprisingly, one of the first major controversies sparked by the new city government involves precisely the politics of public memory related to Spanish fascism in Madrid.

In this chapter, I will examine the memory politics that have flashed up in Madrid during the first real moment of danger for the regime of 1978. My position is that unless the emergent leftist political formations that exploded onto the Spanish political scene in 2014 and 2015 achieve national—or plurinational—hegemony, the politics of public memory related to Spanish fascism will remain highly contentious, particularly in Madrid thanks to the city's symbolic significance as the Spanish capital, even if fascist symbols are removed from the cityscape en masse. Following Raymond Williams, this is because the Transition—understood here not as a discrete historical period (typically dated from somewhere between 1973 and 1975 to 1981 or 1982), but as an ideological cultural process—is still dominant, in the sense that it continues to serve as "the ruling definition of the social" in postdictatorship Spain (Williams 125). Even if the regime of 1978 is facing, for the first time in its history, the threat of being reduced to a residual force in Spanish politics, the "Culture of the Transition," or "CT," as outlined by Guillem Martínez and other cultural critics, is sustained by institutionalized power that has proven remarkably resistant to critiques from the left and new challenges from a mobilized electorate.[5] Indeed, the battle over public memory in Madrid may prove decisive in the consolidation of a cultural process that is currently emerging in Spain against all odds. Yet it remains to be seen whether this new cultural process—with roots in both the 15-M and the historical memory movement—can establish itself as a historical bloc capable of definitively transforming the structure of feeling in Madrid in addition to removing the fascist names and symbols that adorn its streets.[6] While the latter is a prerequisite to achieving the former, the asymmetry of institutionalized power in postdictatorship Spain—a symptom of the Transition—means that such an outcome is far from guaranteed, even if there are signs that optimism, however cautious, is warranted.

Anatomy of a Controversy

On July 6, 2015, less than a month after Manuela Carmena was sworn in as Madrid's mayor, Rita Maestre, the spokesperson for the new city government, announced its intention to apply the Law of Historical Memory to the Madrid cityscape. The announcement was consistent with Ahora Madrid's electoral program, which stipulated the following action line: "Garantizar la aplicación de la Ley 52/2007 de Memoria Histórica, en especial en lo referente a la simbología y al callejero" (Programa Ahora Madrid) (Guarantee the application of the Law of Historical Memory 52/2007, especially in regard to symbols and street names). Ahora Madrid's goal was to enact the first clause of Article Fifteen of the 2007 Law of Historical Memory, which reads as follows:

> Artículo Quince. Símbolos y monumentos públicos.
> Las Administraciones públicas, en el ejercicio de sus competencias, tomarán las medidas oportunas para la retirada de escudos, insignias, placas y otros objetos o menciones conmemorativas de exaltación, personal o colectiva, de la sublevación

militar, de la Guerra Civil y de la represión de la Dictadura. Entre estas medidas podrá incluirse la retirada de subvenciones o ayudas públicas. (Boletín Oficial de Estado, Ley 52/2007)

(Article Fifteen. Public Symbols and Monuments.
The offices of Public Administration, in the exercise of their authority, shall take appropriate measures to remove all shields, insignia, plaques, and other commemorative objects or references that extol, individually or collectively, the military uprising, the Civil War, and the Dictatorship's repression. These measures may include the withdrawal of public subsidies and support.)

While the language of the law explicitly calls for the removal of public symbols and monuments related to Spanish fascism, the Partido Popular administrations in Madrid headed by Alberto Ruiz-Gallardón (2003–2011) and Ana Botella (2011–2015) failed to comply with the law even though Madrid is replete with such public symbols and monuments, particularly when it comes to street names, as Ahora Madrid emphasized in its electoral program. Such noncompliance with the law is consistent with the Partido Popular's hostility toward the Law of Historical Memory, which it vigorously opposed from the beginning.

In February 2015, Eduardo Ranz Alonso, a Madrid human rights lawyer, filed a lawsuit against thirty-eight Spanish mayors for disobeying Article Fifteen of the law. Primarily directed at Ana Botella and the situation in Madrid, the lawsuit included a number of socialist mayors as well. The inclusion of PSOE mayors confirmed longstanding claims by leftist critics of the law that it is little more than a symbolic document meant to pacify the historical memory movement, rather than a law to be taken seriously or broadly interpreted, even by the party that was in power when it passed. In 2008, Spanish judge Baltasar Garzón learned this lesson the hard way when he was forced to close his investigation of crimes against humanity committed during the Francoist dictatorship, suspended from the Spanish judiciary, and charged with perversion of justice, which led to his high-profile Supreme Court case.[7] Within such a juridical context, it is unsurprising that Judge María Belen Sánchez dismissed the lawsuit; however, the speed with which she did so—just fifteen days later—was certainly uncharacteristic of a justice system roundly criticized for sluggishness ("Archivan la denuncia"). Ranz Alonso, who has claimed that the historical memory law "está derogada de facto" (is de facto repealed), also points to the singularity of the Madrid cityscape when it comes to the public memory of Spanish fascism:

Madrid es la única ciudad del mundo que tiene un monumento, como es el caso del Arco de la Victoria, que recuerda o refuerza la victoria de un bando frente a otro. No ocurre en ninguna otra ciudad del mundo. Otro ejemplo es el Valle de los Caídos, donde están enterrados los dictadores. Mussolini está enterrado en una tumba muy humilde, Hitler no se sabe dónde está y el general Francisco Franco está en una construcción megalómana que se ve a kilómetros por la carretera de A Coruña. (qtd. in Escribano)

(Madrid is the only city in the world that has a monument, as is the case of the Victory Arch, which remembers or reinforces the victory of one group over another. This doesn't occur in any other city in the world. Another example is the Valley of the Fallen, where the dictators are buried. Mussolini is buried in a very humble tomb, it's not clear where Hitler is, and General Francisco Franco is in a megalomaniacal structure you can see for kilometers from the A Coruña highway.)

Ranz Alonso cites two of the most important sites of Spanish fascist memory, the Victory Arch erected in honor of Franco's victory over the II Spanish Republic in 1939—a victory that was not secured until Franco's troops were able to take Madrid after two and a half years of popular resistance, an important fact to remember when considering Madrid's symbolic importance to contemporary battles over public memory—and the Valley of the Fallen, the monumental resting place of both Franco and José Antonio Primo de Rivera, the founder of La Falange, Spain's fascist party—located in La Comunidad de Madrid near El Escorial, the burial site of Spanish kings. Operated by the Patrimonio Nacional, the Valley of the Fallen remains nearly the same as it did when it opened in 1959 to celebrate "twenty years of peace" after the Spanish Civil War. Tellingly, the Patrimonio Nacional has never advertised the fact that the Valley of the Fallen was built with the slave labor of the defeated and contains the remains of thousands of *los desaparecidos* (the disappeared) regardless of which political party has been in power during the postdictatorship. In 2013, the Spanish government decided to restore the façade of the fascist monument, at a cost of 214,847 euros, after having eliminated the budget for mass grave exhumations of *los desaparecidos* disappeared by rebel troops and La Falange during the 1936 coup ("El Gobierno adjudica").

Another highly symbolic site of Spanish fascism in Madrid operated by the Patrimonio Nacional, the Palacio Real de El Pardo—Franco's residence throughout the dictatorship—remains relatively untouched since Franco's death, full of artifacts from El Caudillo's daily life that have been eerily preserved more or less as they were at the time of his death (Rodríguez). Unlike the Eagle's Nest—Hitler's famous residence in the Bavarian Alps, which contains a museum explaining the site's important relationship to German fascism—Patrimonio Nacional fails to connect the Palacio Real de El Pardo to Spanish fascism. Thus, its history is not contextualized for visitors and, as CNN reported in 2013, during tours of the site, "anecdotes about Franco's home life are conspicuous by their absence" (Whitley). This impression is due, in part, to the 2010 order by the Comisión de Seguimiento de la Memoria Histórica to close Franco's personal rooms to tourists "porque no aportan nada" (because they don't contribute anything) (Calero). Thus, far from signifying a more rigorous approach to the site's fascist history, the commission's order mirrors the information offered on Franco's relation to it by the official website of El Pardo: "El Palacio Real de El Pardo fue la residencia del anterior Jefe de Estado, el general Francisco Franco, hasta 1975. En la actualidad se destina a la visita turística, así como a residencia de los Jefes de Estado extranjeros de visita oficial en España" (Palacio Real de El Pardo) (The Royal Palace of El Pardo was the residence of the previous head of state, General Francisco Franco, until 1975. Currently, it is maintained as a tourist site, and used as the residence for foreign heads of state on official visits to Spain).

Such a seemingly matter-of-fact description belies the ideology within which it is embedded. For while it is true that Franco was the previous head of state—before he personally appointed Juan Carlos I as his successor—he was also a fascist dictator who came to power through a military coup that unleashed genocide, ignited a civil war, and led to massive state repression for nearly forty years. Quite infamously, Franco reviewed the death sentences of political prisoners over coffee from the comfort of the palace and hunted on the surrounding grounds. In addition, the Web site copy omits the fact that before Franco took up residence in El Pardo, it served as the headquarters of a division of the Republican army during the civil war. Another building on the grounds housed members of the International Brigades, who defended the city against the fascist offensive at the Ciudad Universitaria, and Colonel Segismundo Casado, who led the March 1939 coup against the besieged Republican government, also has ties to the site. Casado's coup allowed Franco to enter Madrid without firing a shot, bringing the civil war to an end a few weeks later. Ironically, it was also Casado, in his role as the director of presidential security, who escorted President Manuel Azaña from El Pardo—which Azaña used as a summer residence—to the safety of the Palacio de Oriente in the center of Madrid during the July 1936 coup.[8] Yet none of this history is mentioned on the El Pardo Web site.

Like the 317 streets across Spain still named after Franco, the fact that El

Pardo, the Victory Arch, and the Valley of the Fallen remain much as they were when Franco's corpse was ceremoniously lowered into the crypt dedicated to his "crusade" is a symptom of the Transition and a reminder of the extent of its ideological dominance forty years later.[9] Encapsulated in the frequent injunction to "no remover el pasado para no re-abrir heridas" (don't stir up the past so as not to reopen wounds), the Transition as cultural ideology is alive and well even after the 2014 death of former Spanish president Adolfo Suárez, one of the central figures of the (historical) Transition whose name now posthumously graces Madrid's Adolfo Suárez-Barajas airport. The fact that Suárez suffered from Alzheimer's during the last decade of his life seems tragically appropriate since the disease coincided with the emergence of the historical memory movement in Spain.

Inspired by the exhumation of mass graves related to the political genocide that took place during the Spanish Civil War, the historical memory movement can be interpreted as a cure to the enforced forgetting fostered by the Transition. Such forgetting was in the interest of the cultural and political elites who oversaw the transfer of power after Franco's death. The pacts of silence and forgetting they forged behind closed doors served to protect their privileged status in postdictatorship Spain while ensuring Spain's smooth integration into Europe by minimizing the potential for social conflict that a reckoning with the traumatic past might have produced at that time. Suárez, who held various high-level posts under Franco—including director-general of the Spanish Radio and Television Corporation—before becoming the first democratically elected Spanish president since the days of the Second Spanish Republic, embodied the contradictions implicit in a democracy founded on a state policy of forgetting the crimes committed in Franco's name. Ironically, the cultural forgetting that Suárez helped propagate in the public realm seems to have privately manifested itself in the disease that plagued his personal memory to death. Appropriately, the inscription on Suárez's tomb, "La concordia fue posible" (Social harmony was possible), encapsulates the cultural fantasy at the heart of the Transition, declaring a state of affairs that never existed in reality, since social harmony depends on a context of social justice, which was absent from the historical Transition and is antithetical to Transition ideology.

Indeed, along with the injunction "not to reopen wounds," invocations of "social harmony" and "reconciliation" discursively embody the much-revered "spirit of the Transition." Far from an attempt to inadvertently evoke the ghosts hiding in the closet of the regime of 1978, calling on the "spirit of the Transition" is a more diplomatic way of saying "¡¿Por qué no te callas?!" (Why don't you shut up?!) when attempts to challenge or go beyond Transition ideology are made.[10]

Typical of the disciplinary function of the strategic deployment of ideological discourse, these particular "keywords" and phrases of the Transition appear frequently in the public memory battles that have taken place in Spain recently as a result of the emergence of the historical memory movement. Opponents of that movement rely on such invocations to delegitimize an argument (or an adversary) that dares to suggest a more inclusive politics of memory based on ethics rather than impunity. Their deployment further masks the pacts of silence and forgetting upon which cultural fantasies of national consensus and unity have been propagated throughout the postdictatorship by discursively delimiting the terms of such debates.[11] Following this logic, the passage of the Law of Historical Memory, far from representing a break with such cultural fantasies, marked an attempt to legislate from within their imaginative boundaries, and is essentially a product of Transition ideology. This is evident in the language found in the law's preamble, which begins by citing "el espíritu de reconciliación y concordia" (the spirit of reconciliation and concord) as its inspiration.[12]

It is within this context that the Ahora Madrid government's desire to apply the Law of Historical Memory in Madrid—and the polemic it has provoked—should be understood. The desire to be in compliance with the law reveals itself as an ethical act in opposition to a dominant ideology maintained by institutionalized power, particularly within the Spanish judicial system and mainstream media. Furthermore, the desire to begin to reshape Madrid's structure of feeling by removing the city's fascist symbols goes far beyond legal questions and echoes the sentiment of David Harvey when he writes:

> The question of what kind of city we want cannot be divorced from the question of what kind of people we want to be, what kind of social relations we seek, what relations to nature we cherish, what style of life we desire, what aesthetic values we hold. The right to the city is, therefore, far more than a right of individual or group access to the resources that the city embodies: it is a right to change and reinvent the city more after our heart's desire (4).

Thus, Ahora Madrid's initiative to rid the capital of its fascist symbols can be seen as a first step in an attempt to reinvent the city according to a set of values radically different from those represented by the names on the street signs targeted for removal in accordance with the law (El Caudillo, José Antonio Primo de Rivera, General Mola, etc.). But such values are also significantly different from those responsible, one way or another, for their continued existence on Madrid streets (Ana Botella, Alberto Ruiz-Gallardón, Adolfo Suárez, etc.)

Whereas Manuel Fraga Iribarne, minister of information and tourism during the dictatorship, was able to claim with impunity "¡La calle es mía!" (The streets are mine!) as minister of the interior in 1976 to justify the violent repression of popular demonstrations *after* Franco's death, forty years later Ahora Madrid is asserting its right to shape Madrid's streets in a more inclusive fashion. The desire to reimagine the city based on communal values within the *municipalista* sector of Ahora Madrid was signaled during the swearing-in ceremony for members of the new city government when two councilmembers, Pablo Carmona and Guillermo Zapata, swore to uphold the city constitution with the phrase "Omnia sunt communia." This Latin phrase, associated with Thomas Aquinas and the sixteenth-century protestant reformer Thomas Müntzer, which means "All things are held in common," reflects Ahora Madrid's ties to urban occupations and the squatter's movement, which have adopted it as a motto. This is especially true for Carmona and Zapata, both of whom have strong ties to Patio Maravillas, the Malasaña occupation conceived of as a space for the production of democracy during the Week of Social Struggle in 2007. Several years before the 15-M and Podemos transformed Spanish political discourse, that self-managed, multipurpose social laboratory sought to substitute the traditional left–right conception of politics with a top–bottom political paradigm during a period marked by the increasingly extreme consolidation of economic wealth and political power in the hands of a few ("Historias"). Not coincidentally, in one of her last acts as mayor, Ana Botella ordered the eviction of Patio Maravillas.

In 2012 Botella also proposed that Madrid should name a street after Fraga—in contradiction to the Law of Historical Memory—after his death. As Emilio Silva, president of the Association for the Recovery of Historical Memory, stated, the law "habla de proteger los espacios públicos para que no representen a quienes formaron parte de un regimen que secuestró la democracia durante cuarenta años. Y en este caso hablamos de un hombre que fue entre otras cosas ministro de la dictadura. . . . Fraga nunca se arrepintió de su participación en la dictadura" (qtd. in "Dar el nombre") (speaks of protecting public spaces so that they don't represent those who formed part of a regime that kidnapped democracy during forty years. And in this case, we're taking about a man who was, among other things, a minister of the dictatorship. . . . Fraga never repented his participation in the dictatorship). Despite opposition from Izquierda Unida, the proposal passed with PSOE's support, and Avenida Manuel Fraga Iribarne now runs parallel to Terminal 4 of Adolfo Suárez-Barajas Airport in Hortaleza.[28] Likewise, as president of the Comunidad de Madrid, Esperanza Aguirre honored Fraga with the Gran Cruz de la Orden del Dos de Mayo—without irony—and named a high school after him in the neighborhood of Sanchinarro.[29] The posthumous veneration of one of the most high-profile Francoist ministers is indicative of the politics of public memory in Madrid inherited by Ahora Madrid and Manuela Carmena at the time of her inauguration. Mediated by Transition ideology, which facilitates the disavowal of Fraga's Francoist past by insisting solely—*and uncritically*—on his role during the Transition, such politics are incongruent with a city government that values the common good. Thus, Ahora Madrid's announcement that it intended to change Madrid's fascist street names came as a shock to a system run for decades on impunity and ideological forgetting.

For example, the government delegate in La Comunidad de Madrid, Concepción Dancausa, responded to the news by calling it a "mistake." She elaborated by saying that "if we don't learn from the past, we will repeat the same mistakes," that "history is what it is" and "it can't be changed." Therefore, "to ignore what happened, to ignore the symbols or to try to erase them, [is] a mistake" ("Aguirre"). The fact that Dancausa is the daughter of Fernando Dancausa, a Falangist politician who served as the mayor of Burgos during the dictatorship, from 1965 to 1973, and was also a founding member of the Fundación Francisco Franco, helps explain the delegate's particular philosophy of history. Yet, far from being an exceptional response, her comments typified the reaction among key figures of the Partido Popular. For her part, Esperanza Aguirre, the spokesperson for PP in the Madrid city hall, denounced the measure as "absurd" ("Aguirre"). Five months later, in December 2015, when the Madrid city council voted to change thirty street names—with the support of Ahora Madrid, PSOE, and Ciudadanos but not PP—Aguirre deployed the disciplinary discourse of Transition ideology by criticizing what she perceived as a lack of "the spirit of reconciliation" referenced in the first article of the Law of Historical Memory, even though the list of street names included the Plaza del Caudillo, Avenida del Arco de la Victoria, Plaza Arriba España, Pasaje del General Mola, Calle de General Yagüe, and Avenida del General Fanjul ("El PP").

In contrast to the reactions of Dancausa and Aguirre, Celia Mayer, the city council member in charge of culture and responsible for the implementation of the measure, stated the following:

> Ni las presencias ni las ausencias en el callejero son neutras. Forman parte de una Historia de parte, y lo que queremos es recuperar para la narración de la historia de Madrid a las personas olvidadas que merecen un reconocimiento por su trayectoria y biografía, los acontecimientos de relevancia que produjeron los avances sociales, y los lugares que fueron significativos históricamente. Son evidentes los déficits [en el callejero, como] las mujeres, que son absolutamente in-

visibles en el callejero; profesiones, oficios y labores que han construido la riqueza de la ciudad y no encuentran ni tan siquiera reconocidos; personas, madrileños y madrileñas de a pie de calle, que han contribuido a construir esta ciudad; y, sobre todo, luchas colectivas y vecinales que han luchado por los servicios públicos y no se encuentran reconocidos en estos elementos. (qtd. in García Gallo)

(Neither the presences nor the absences on the street map are neutral. They form part of a history that is partial, and what we want is to recover for the narration of the history of Madrid the forgotten people who deserve recognition for their trajectory and biography, the important events that produced social advances, and the places that were historically significant. The deficits are evident [on the street map, like] women, who are absolutely invisible on the street map; professions, trades, and tasks that have built the richness of the city and are not found or are even recognized; people, everyday men and women of Madrid, who have contributed to the construction of this city; and, above all, collective and neighborhood struggles that fought for public services and are not found in these elements.)

Here we have a vision of history that echoes Walter Benjamin's "Theses on the Philosophy of History." Opposed to Dancausa's claim that "history is what it is," Mayer follows the Benjaminian injunction that "nothing that has ever happened should be regarded as lost for history," while turning her gaze toward those figures forgotten by the victors of the Spanish Civil War and suppressed by the long tradition of celebrating militaristic patriarchy in Spain at the cost of recognizing the contributions of women and the working class (Benjamin 254). It is precisely Ahora Madrid's elevation of the common people of Madrid, particularly those engaged in popular struggles for the public good in lieu of figures associated with fascism and crimes against humanity, that is so threatening to those who have enjoyed the privileges of political power and impunity for so many decades thanks to a Francoist inheritance that remains prosperous to this day as a result of the Transition and its continued ideological import. To return to Emilio Silva's critique of Manuel Fraga, the figure recently honored with his own street in Madrid was "uno de los grandes responsables de la esperanza de vida de lo que se llamó franquismo sociológico. Y que trajo hasta nuestros días. . . . Lo que hizo fue formar parte de una élite en la dictadura y seguir formando parte de una élite en la democracia" (qtd. in "Dar el nombre") (one of the major figures responsible for the life expectancy of what was called sociological francoism. And he brought it into our time. . . . What he did was form part of an elite during the dictatorship and continued forming part of an elite in democracy). The elite that Silva refers to is precisely the historical bloc that feels threatened by the transformation of Madrid's politics and cityscape by Ahora Madrid.

If it is true, as Celia Mayer claims, that the presences and absences in Madrid's cityscape are not neutral, the question of historical interpretation is not neutral, either, and the polemic over one particular name on the list of thirty streets to be changed further illustrates the confrontation between Transition ideology and the emergent cultural process taking place. Calle del Comandante Zorita, named in honor of Demetrio Zorita Alonso, became a source of controversy as a result of two different interpretations of history. For Esperanza Aguirre, Zorita was "el primer aviador español que rompió la velocidad [del sonido]" ("Zorita") (the first Spanish pilot who broke the sound barrier), which is historically accurate. Yet, as Mayer made clear, he was also "un aviador español sublevado contra la República en 1936, que vulneró pues un regimen legítimamente democrático mediante las armas, y que combatió con los nazis en la Segunda Guerra Mundial" ("Zorita") (a Spanish pilot who rebelled against the Republic in 1936, who damaged a democratically elected regime through armed conflict, and who fought alongside the Nazis during World War II), which is also historically accurate. The ability to celebrate the former while disavowing the latter is a symptom of Transition ideology that allows for a highly selective interpretation of history in which inconvenient facts related to the Spanish Civil War and the dictatorship are actively forgotten, just as in the case of Manuel Fraga.

To cognitively map the Madrid cityscape, one must comprehend the degree to which ideology shapes public space and memory. In keeping with Louis Althusser's assertion that "ideology has a material existence," a comprehensive cartography of Madrid must trace the role ideology has played in the production of its contested spaces.[13] Along those lines, it is bears mentioning that one of Madrid's most emblematic sites, the Puerta del Sol, is devoid of any historical marker that would indicate the historical significance of the Casa de Correos, the square's most famous building, as a site of state repression during the dictatorship. While anything but an anomaly, the Casa de Correos is perhaps the most egregious example in a city full of spaces used by the dictatorship to systematically repress opposition. The other major site of state repression in the city, Carabanchel prison—which, like El Valle de los Caídos, was built by political prisoners after the Spanish Civil War—was demolished at night in October 2008, despite protests demanding that part of the prison be converted into Spain's first museum of Francoist repression, which the country still lacks. Host to the nationally televised New Year's festivities every year, the Casa de Correos served as the National Security Headquarters during the dictatorship, where the detention and torture of political dissidents were a matter of routine. For decades, demonstrations were prohibited in the Puerta del Sol, and it was not uncommon for passersby to hear screams echoing up from the basement detention cells when walking past the building. Yet while historical markers on the exterior of the building memorialize the popular uprising against Napoleon's troops (May 2, 1808) and the terrorist attack (March 11, 2004), and the "Kilometer Zero" marker on the sidewalk in front of the building is a favorite spot for tourist selfies, there is no mention of the site's significance as a central part of the dictatorship's repressive state apparatus. Again, to cite Celia Mayer, this state of affairs is not "neutral," but yet another manifestation of Transition ideology in the Madrid cityscape. For to officially remember the torture and systematic repression that occurred in one of Madrid's most photographed buildings would violate the "pact of forgetting" at its heart. Contesting such officially sanctioned forgetting, the Plataforma Contra la Impunidad del Franquismo has convened a demonstration every Thursday from 7 p.m. to 8 p.m. in the Puerta del Sol since the summer of 2010, one year before the 15-M took over the space. A cultural practice that subverts the normalization of Transition ideology, the demonstration temporarily transforms the largely commercialized space into a public confrontation with the specters of genocide haunting postdictatorship Spain. Inspired by the Mothers of the Plaza de Mayo in Buenos Aires, protesters— many of whom are former political prisoners and family members of the more than 114,000 *desaparecidos*—denounce the crimes against humanity committed by the dictatorship and the existence of mass graves across Spain, while specifically recalling the sordid history of the Casa de Correos.

Yet, unlike in the Argentine capital, where survivors and the family members of the disappeared can visit the Parque de la Memoria—which commemorates the victims of state terrorism during the military juntas—there is no such memorial in Spain's capital that honors the victims of state terrorism carried out during the Francoist dictatorship. Such a glaring absence in the Madrid cityscape is another material manifestation of Transition ideology that contrasts with that of not only Buenos Aires but also Santiago de Chile (Memorial del Detenido Desaparecido y del Ejecutado Político), Montevideo (Memorial de los Detenidos Desaparecidos), and São Paulo (Monumento em Homenagem aos Mortos e Desaparecidos Políticos). Despite the fact that state repression was exponentially greater and lasted significantly longer in Francoist Spain than in the Southern Cone, there is no equivalent public marker of this historical trauma in Madrid, which serves as a testament to the durability of the asymmetrical balance of power established between the victors and the vanquished of the Spanish Civil War.

Not surprisingly, then, on February 1, 2016, the controversy surrounding Ahora Madrid's plans to change Madrid's fascist street names exploded when the government removed the Monolito al Alférez Provisional from the Plaza Felipe IV.[14] The monument, dedicated to volunteers who enlisted in the Nationalist army during the Spanish Civil War, features the Francoist motto "Por Díos y por España" ("For God and Spain") and has stood near Retiro park since 1960. Spontaneous protesters interrupted the removal of the monument after workers had cut the monolith into sections and knocked it to the ground. Those same workers fled the scene before completing the removal process, and protesters covered the downed monument with a Spanish flag. The sections of the monolith were removed early the next morning (Olaya).

Three days later, the Fundación Francisco Franco filed a lawsuit against Manuela Carmena and Celia Mayer as well as the administrators of the company hired to remove the monument, claiming that they constituted the "presuntos autores de un delito sobre patrimonio histórico y colaboradores del delito de prevaricación" (Olaya) (presumed perpetrators of a crime against historical heritage and the perversion of justice). After two weeks of intense scrutiny by mainstream media, pressure from the Partido Popular, and internal conflict within Ahora Madrid, the mayor responded to the lawsuit on February 15 with a letter sent to the foundation on her behalf by City Legal Consultant Ángel Luis Ortiz, stating that the monument would be returned to its place in the same condition before its removal, but that over the next few months City Hall would develop rules for how to properly implement the Law of Historical Memory, hinting that the monument could be removed once again in the near future, following an approved protocol ("Carmena"). Ironically, the letter was sent to the foundation's office located on Avenida Concha Espina, named after one of the canonical writers of Spanish fascist literature, who also joined the Sección Femenina in 1936, another street name that should be changed under the Law of Historical Memory. After the monument was restored, the Fundación Francisco Franco along with other far-right extremist organizations such as the Falange Española, Manos Limpias, and Fuerza Nueva organized a fascist rally at the site to celebrate their victory. The rally ended with "Cara al sol" (the Spanish fascist anthem), fascist salutes, and chants of "Arriba España" and "Viva Franco" on February 20, 2016, forty years after Franco's death (Maestre).

To return to the comparison with which I began this chapter, it is simply unimaginable that such a turn of events could take place in Germany now. "The Adolf Hitler Foundation Sues Berlin Government over Removal of Nazi Monument" is simply not a conceivable headline, for reasons previously discussed. Yet such stories regularly appear in Spanish newspapers, running next to a steady stream of political corruption scandals and soccer scores. Despite decades of democracy, public reminders of Spanish fascism coexist in Madrid alongside pockets of fascists and "sociological Francoism" that still permeate sectors of Spanish society well into the twenty-first century. As I've attempted to make clear, this is due to the fact that the architects of the Transition purposely avoided a reckoning with Spanish fascism and state repression during the dictatorship, converting the concept of *concordia* into a code word for impunity. The cultural common sense produced by the dominance of Transition ideology in postdictatorship Spain, reinforced on a regular basis by the mainstream media, makes actions that are not only legal but also ethically grounded seem like partisan revenge and worthy of the controversy they elicit, when in fact what should be polemical—such as the various ways institutional power supports the persistence of fascism in Spain—isn't sufficiently interrogated by the mainstream media or counteracted by government policies. All too frequently, the opposite is the case. For example, Spanish president Mariano Rajoy eliminated government funds for the exhumation of mass graves containing the remains of the disappeared when he took office in 2011, and the Fundación Francisco Franco, an organization dedicated to exalting the ideals and memory of the dictator, received 150,840 euros from the government between 2000 and 2002 under former president José María Aznar (Hernàndez). Such asymmetry of institutional support has material effects that help explain why the Madrid cityscape contains so many egregious markers of Spanish fascism, from the Plaza del Caudillo to the Monolito al Alférez Provisional to the Avenida Concha Espina, and why there is such fervent resistance to their renaming or removal.

Conclusion

I will end with the story of another Madrid monument that has become a source of controversy. On October 22, 2011, a modest modernist monolith dedicated to the International Brigades—the 35,000 volunteers from more than fifty countries who fought against fascism during the Spanish Civil War—was erected on the grounds of the Universidad Complutense, marking the seventy-fifth anniversary of their formation. The university still bears scars of the fighting that took place there in 1936, when it served as a key site in the defense of Madrid, and international volunteers—particularly Germans who had fled from the Nazis—played a crucial role in pushing back the advance of the Nationalist army. The simple monument, which is easily overlooked and located not far from Franco's grand Victory Arch, immediately came under fire by many of the same far-right groups that protested the removal of the Monolito al Alférez Provisional. Following an administrative complaint filed by Miguel García Jiménez, a lawyer and Francoist, the Tribunal Superior de Justicia de Madrid ordered the monument's removal seven months later, claiming that it was not properly licensed. When reaching its decision, the court ignored the fact that university officials had requested the appropriate planning permission from the city government—while Ana Botella was mayor—on three separate occasions but received no response. The court decision sparked outrage around the world, most notably in the United Kingdom, where fifty-six members of Parliament signed an early day motion denouncing it, citing that the case involved British citizens (Cros). Bolstered by international support free from the cultural common sense produced by Transition ideology, the university has successfully resisted the court's decision, and the monolith remains standing five years after its inauguration.

Despite surviving legal battles, however, this singular Madrid monument that recalls the city's historical significance as the emblematic site of international antifascist solidarity efforts quickly became a target of twenty-first-century fascist resentment. Just a few days after its inauguration, the monument was covered in red paint and tagged with the word "asesinos" (murderers). Not surprisingly, then, the monolith became the site of symbolic retribution in the wake of Ahora Madrid's removal of the Monolito al Alférez Provisional. On February 17, 2016, the monument was defaced with graffiti that read "Carmena, hija de puta" (Carmena, daughter of a bitch) and "rojos, asesinos" (reds, murderers) ("Nueva pintada"). After volunteers of the university's Colectivo de Jóvenes Comunistas cleaned the monument, another round of graffiti attacking the mayor appeared on February 21, including "Carmena, más fea que un orco" (Carmena, uglier than an orc) and the Francoist slogan "Arriba España" ("El monumento").

It is no coincidence that a monument to the International Brigades has been converted into a canvas for fascist resentment, nor that animosity toward Manuela Carmena and the new Ahora Madrid government has manifested itself in this way. In a city marked by a deficiency of public sites honoring the memory of Madrid's historic resistance to fascism, there is a generalized lack of appreciation for a legacy considered heroic in other parts of the world. Perhaps this situation will change when Ahora Madrid begins the process of renaming the city's fascist streets and removing more monuments that celebrate the victors of a war waged against democracy. Hopefully, such actions will follow an approved protocol and be announced in advance so that the process of "defrancofication" in Madrid is conducted openly and deliberately. Ideally, these democratic alterations to the cityscape will be accompanied by public acts designed to involve residents in the resignification of public space. Only then will Spain have a capital whose cityscape reflects a commitment to the common good, rather than the culture of impunity Madrid has perpetuated until now.

NOTES

1. It should be noted that denazification was not devoid of *realpolitik* or hypocrisy on the part of the Allies, nor did it occur without its own share of enforced forgetting for Germans. Indeed, the 1960s generation of Germans who broke the cultural silence surrounding the Third Reich by inquiring about what their parents did during the Nazi period were responsible for the transformation in German approaches to its fascist past that is so markedly different from the Spanish case. For further information on this topic, see Taylor, *Exorcising Hitler: The Occupation and Denazification of Germany.*
2. Llanos del Caudillo, Bembézar del Caudillo, Águeda del Caudillo, Alberche del Caudillo, Bárdena del Caudillo, Guadiana del Caudillo, Villafranco del Guadalhorce, and Villafranco del Guadiana.
3. For further analysis of this campaign, see Boehm, "Specters of Genocide: Mass Graves, Horror Film, and Impunity in Post-dictatorship Spain."
4. The 1977 Atocha Massacre took place on January 24, 1977, when a group of far-right terrorists attacked the offices of lawyers affiliated with the Spanish Communist Party and Comisiones Obreras, the communist trade union, which were located at Calle Atocha, 55. Four lawyers and a union member were killed and four other lawyers were wounded during the attack. Manuela Carmena was spared because Luis Javier Benavides had requested to use her office for a meeting that day. Benavides was shot and killed in the massacre.
5. See Martínez, *CT o la Cultura de la Transición: Crítica a 35 años de cultura española.*
6. To quote Stephen Gill commenting on the Gramscian concept: "An historical bloc refers to an historical congruence between material forces, institutions and ideologies, or broadly, an alliance of different class forces politically organized around a set of hegemonic ideas that gave strategic direction and coherence to its constituent elements. Moreover, for a new historical bloc to emerge, its leaders must engage in conscious planned struggle. Any new historical bloc must have not only power within the civil society and economy, it also needs persuasive ideas, arguments and initiatives that build on, catalyze and develop its political networks and organization —not political parties such" (58).
7. For more on the Garzón case and the Spanish judiciary, see Saez, "Los jueces y el aprendizaje de la impunidad, a propósito de los crímenes del franquismo."
8. See Rojas, *Diez figuras ante la guerra civil*; de la Cierva, *1939: Agonía y Victoria*; and Cabanillas, *Historia de mi vida: Memorias.*
9. According to the Callejero del Censo Electoral from July 2015, some 1,171 streets

in 637 towns are named after figures with Francoist ties. Three hundred seventeen are named after Franco, and 373 are named after José Antonio Primo de Rivera. For more information, see Escudero, "Franco aún 'vive' en 317 calles."

10. "¡¿Por qué no te callas?!" ("Why don't you shut up?!") was King Juan Carlos I's infamous retort to Venezuelan president Hugo Chávez during the 2007 Ibero-American Summit when Chávez denounced former Spanish president José María Aznar as a fascist who had supported the 2002 coup attempt against his democratically elected government and put his life in jeopardy.

11. For more on the role of national consensus in postdicatorship Spain, see Delgado, *La nación singular*.

12. The first three paragraphs of the law are indicative of its manifestation of Transition ideology:

El espíritu de reconciliación y concordia, y de respeto al pluralismo y a la defensa pacífica de todas las ideas, que guió la Transición, nos permitió dotarnos de una Constitución, la de 1978, que tradujo jurídicamente esa voluntad de reencuentro de los españoles, articulando un Estado social y democrático de derecho con clara vocación integradora.

El espíritu de la Transición da sentido al modelo constitucional de convivencia más fecundo que hayamos disfrutado nunca y explica las diversas medidas y derechos que se han ido reconociendo, desde el origen mismo de todo el período democrático, en favor de las personas que, durante los decenios anteriores a la Constitución, sufrieron las consecuencias de la guerra civil y del régimen dictatorial que la sucedió.

Pese a ese esfuerzo legislativo, quedan aún iniciativas por adoptar para dar cumplida y definitiva respuesta a las demandas de esos ciudadanos, planteadas tanto en el ámbito parlamentario como por distintas asociaciones cívicas. Se trata de peticiones legítimas y justas, que nuestra democracia, apelando de nuevo a su espíritu fundacional de concordia, y en el marco de la Constitución, no puede dejar de atender. (Boletín Oficial de Estado. *Ley 52/2007*)

(The spirit of reconciliation and harmony and of respect for pluralism and peaceful defence of all ideas, which guided the Transition, enabled the establishment of a Constitution for us, that of 1978, which legally expressed the desire of Spaniards for reunification, forming a social and democratic state of law with the clear wish for integration.

Thus the spirit of the Transition gives meaning to this constitutional model offering the most fruitful coexistence that we Spaniards have ever enjoyed and it also explains the various measures and rights which have been recognized over time from the very beginning of the entire democratic era, for the benefit of those persons who, for the decades prior to the Constitution, suffered the consequences of our devastating civil war and the dictatorship that succeeded it.

Notwithstanding that legislative effort, there still remain initiatives which should be adopted to give effect and a definitive response to the demands of those citizens, presented both through parliament and through various civic associations. These constitute legitimate and just demands to which our democracy, calling again upon that founding spirit of harmony and in the context of the Constitution, cannot fail to respond.) (Translation by Equipo Nizkor; see works cited.)

13. See Althusser, "Ideology and Ideological State Apparatuses."
14. The removal of the monolith coincided with the removal of two other historical markers related to the Spanish Civil War: a headstone in memory of José García Vara, a right-wing unionist, and a plaque commemorating the execution of eight Carmelite friars in 1936. While the removal of those historical markers also provoked controversy for different reasons, the monolith elicited the most dramatic response from the Far Right. It should be noted that aside from not having an approved protocol in place for the removal of fascist monuments, the other major complaint levied against Ahora Madrid, with some degree of legitimacy, was that the removal of the monolith and other markers had not been publicly announced in advance. Although Celia Mayer claimed the action had been announced at the December plenary session during which Ahora Madrid had announced its decision to remove 30 fascist street names, it is clear that the news came as a surprise on the day the monolith was removed. Mayer has come under scrutiny for her management of the process, including from Manuela Carmena. Problems with both the contract and work of Mirta Núñez Díaz-Balart, the Chair of Historical Memory at the Universidad Complutense and the person hired as a consultant to lead the identification of fascist street names, only complicated Mayer's position and added to the controversy surrounding Ahora Madrid's plans to apply the Law of Historical Memory in Madrid. Núñez Díaz-Balart resigned from her position because of her role in the controversy. While there was significant pressure for Mayer to resign as well for issues that went beyond historical memory, at the time of writing she remained the city council member responsible for culture and sports. However, as if to highlight the volatility of the on-going "culture wars" in Madrid and within Ahora Madrid itself, Manuela Carmena removed Mayer from that position in March 2017, putting her in charge of gender and diversity while placing the area of culture under her personal control as mayor. Likewise, there have been several important developments related to the politics of public memory in Madrid between the time of writing and publication of this chapter, including the approval of the removal of fifty-two fascist street names in April 2017. Further changes, and controversy, are likely, especially if Ahora Madrid remains in power after the 2019 elections.

WORKS CITED

"Aguirre ve un 'disparate' eliminar los nombres franquistas del callejero de Madrid." *20minutos.es*. 20 minutos. 10 July 2016. Web. 26 Apr. 2016.

Althusser, Louis. "Ideology and Ideological State Apparatuses." *Lenin and Philosophy and other Essays*. Ed. Louis Althussar. New York: Monthly Review Press, 1971. Print.

"Archivan la denuncia contra Ana Botella al no ver delito en el mantenimiento de símbolos franquistas en Madrid." *elmundo.es*. El Mundo. 26 Feb. 2015. Web. 26 Apr. 2016.

Benjamin, Walter. *Illuminations*. New York: Schocken Books, 1969. Print.

"Berlin Blunder: Google Maps Brings Back 'Adolf Hitler Square.'" *Der Spiegel*. Der Spiegel. 10 Jan. 2014. Web. 26 Apr. 2016.

Boletín Oficial de Estado. *Ley 52/2007*. Ministerio de la Presidencia. 2007. Web. 26 Apr. 2016.

Boehm, Scott. "Specters of Genocide: Mass Graves, Horror Film, and Impunity in Post-dictatorship Spain." *The Ethics of Remembering and the Consequences of Forgetting: Essays on Trauma, History, and Memory*. Ed. Michael O'Loughlin. New York: Rowman & Littlefield, 2015. 249–72. Print.

Cabanillas, Alfredo. *Historia de mi vida: Memorias*. Sevilla: Espuela de Plata, 2011. Print.

Calero, J. G. "Patrimonio cierra al público las habitaciones de Franco en El Pardo." *ABC.es*. ABC. 10 Dec. 2010. Web. 26 Apr. 2016.

"Carmena obliga a Mayer a reponer el monolito del Alférez Provisional." *elconfidencial.com*. El Confidencial. 16 Feb. 2016. Web. 26 Apr. 2016.

de la Cierva, Ricardo. *1939: Agonía y victoria (El protocolo 277)*. Barcelona: Planeta, 1989. Print.

Cros, Almudena. "Hands off the Madrid Monument!" *The Volunteer*. Abraham Lincoln Brigade Archive. 14 Sept. 2013. Web. 26 Apr. 2016.

"Dar el nombre de Manuel Fraga a una calle va 'contra la ley.'" Público. 19 Jan. 2012. Web. 26 Apr. 2016.

Delgado, Luisa Elena. *La nación singular: Fantasías de la normalidad democrática española (1996–2011)*. Madrid: Siglo XXI, 2014. Print.

"El Gobierno adjudica por 214.847 euros la restauración de la fachada del Valle de los Caídos." 19 Aug. 2013. Web. 26 Apr. 2016.

"El monumento a las Brigadas Internacionales vuelve a aparecer con insultos a Carmena." El Confidencial Autonómico. 22 Mar. 2016. Web. 26 Apr. 2016.

"El PP de Aguirre vota contra el cambio de nombre de las calles que ensalzan el franquismo." infoLibre. 22 Dec. 2015. Web. 26 Apr. 2016.

Equipo Nizkor. "Full text of the aberrant impunity law known as the 'Memory Law.'" *derechos.org*. Derechos.org. 26 Dec. 2007. Web. 26 Apr. 2016.

Escribano, Mario. "Eduardo Ranz: 'La Ley de Memoria Histórica está derogada de facto.'" *infolibre.es*. Infolibre.es. 13 Apr. 2015. Web. 26 Apr. 2016.

Escudero, Jesús. "Franco aún 'vive' en 317 calles de toda España; José Antonio Primo de Rivera, en 373." *elconfidential.com*. El Confidencial. 26 Dec. 2015. Web. 26 Apr. 2016.

"Franco 'vuelve': Un pueblo de Cuenca recupera la calle del Generalísimo." *elplural.com*. El Plural. 9 Apr. 2014. Web. 26 Apr. 2016.

García Gallo, Bruno. "Madrid cambiará antes del verano el nombre de 30 calles franquistas." *elpais.com*. El País. 22 Dec. 2015. Web. 26 Apr. 2016.

———. "Zorita, ¿pionero o aviador nazi? *elpais.com*. El País. 22 Dec. 2015. Web. 26 April 2016.

Gill, Stephen. *Power and Resistance in the New World Order*. New York: Palgrave Macmillan, 2003. Print.

"Google Maps Apologizes for Hitler Square Gaffe." *Voice of America News*. Voice of America News. 10 Jan. 2014. Web. 26 April 2016.

Hernàndez, Enric. "El PP rehúsa retirar la ayuda a la Fundación Francisco Franco." *elperiodiodearagon.com*. El Periódico de Aragón. 24 Sept. 2003. Web. 26 Apr. 2016.

Historias en la historia. El Patio Maravillas, 2016. Web. 26 Apr. 2016.

Maestre, Antonio. "Acto fascista contra Manuela Carmena." *lamarea.com*. La Marea. 20 Feb. 2016. Web. 26 Apr. 2016.

Martínez, Guillem, ed. *CT o la Cultura de la Transición: Crítica a 35 años de cultura española*. Madrid: Debolsillo, 2012. Print.

Moraga, Carmen. "Colectivos argentinos antifranquistas bautizan a Madrid como 'Capital Olímpica de la Impunidad.'" *eldiario.es*. eldiario.es. 6 Sept. 2013. Web. 26 Apr. 2016.

"Nueva pintada en el monumento a las Brigadas Internacionales de la Complutense: 'Carmena, hija de puta.'" *eldiario.es*. eldiario.es. 18 Feb. 2016. Web. 26 Apr. 2016.

Olaya, Vicente. "Carmena inicia sin avisar el derribo de los monumentos franquistas." *elpais.com*. El País. 2 Feb. 2016. Web. 26 Apr. 2016.

Palacio Real de El Pardo. Patrimonio Nacional. 2016. Web. 26 Apr. 2016.

Programa Ahora Madrid. Ahora Madrid. 2015. Web. 26 Apr. 2016.

Ramírez, Daniel. "Franco contra Carmena: La fundación se querella por el derribo de un monumento." *elespanol.com*. El Español. 5 Feb. 2016 Web. 26 Apr. 2016.

Rodríguez, Jesús. "El Pardo. Detenido en el tiempo." *elpais.com*. El País. 9 July 2013. Web. 26 Apr. 2016.

Rojas, Carlos. *Diez figuras ante la guerra civil*. Barcelona: Nauta, 1973. Print.

Sáez, Ramón. "Los jueces y el aprendizaje de la impunidad, a propósito de los crímenes del franquismo." *Mientras Tanto* 114 (2010): 41–72. Print.

Taylor, Frederick. *Exorcising Hitler: The Occupation and Denazification of Germany*. New York: Bloomsbury Press, 2013. Print.

Whitley, David. "Hitler's Eagle's Nest and other tyrants' lairs open to all." *cnn.com*. CNN. 24 July 2013. Web. 26 Apr. 2016.

Williams, Raymond. *Marxism and Literature*. Oxford: Oxford University Press, 1977. Print.

PART III

Madrid as Lived Experience

♦   CHAPTER 8

The Train That Gave Women a Voice

Alicia Luna

> *The wind was at our backs,*
> *but they decided to turn it against us*
> *so that the very act of walking would wear us out.*
>
> (Poem written by Alicia Luna inspired by
> the events, translated by Anthony Geist)

It could have been a day like any other but it wasn't—or was it? I realize now that that day could well have been a Saturday like any other were it not for a group of women who decided to immortalize and multiply it. The miracle of multiplication, unlike the miracle of the bread and fishes, was not to be the work of one man named Jesus backed from Heaven by another man, his father. Rather it would be carried out by a group of flesh-and-blood women from every corner of Spain, and some from abroad, aided by cinematographic technology. That is the miracle of the audiovisual. Immortalize and multiply through the ease with which it can be disseminated.

What made that day a day unlike any other was the fact that it all began in a florist shop and from there spread to all the social media. Let me explain. The idea began with a group of women known as *las Comadres* (the Sistahs), whose average age is neither more nor less than sixty and whose height is neither more nor less than four feet nine inches. Not one of those women was going to allow the Minister of Justice to change or annul the law legalizing abortion that had been passed by the previous administration. Do you get what I'm saying? From a flower shop to the national government. It all began with a group of women in their sixties, the wise women of the tribe, who decided in their feminist circle that they would not tolerate a return to a time that had caused so much suffering to so many women who had had to have clandestine abortions with coat hangers, soup spoons, and knitting needles. They were not going to allow any other women to flee to other countries to have an abortion alone in clinics far from their loved ones, their support. They were not going to allow more teenagers to die from primitive abortions to keep their abusive or intransigent parents or parents who looked the other way from being aware of their desperate situation. They were not going to consent to the state or the church taking the decision away from women. They were not going to allow the reproductive rights of women to be controlled by anyone other than the women themselves. They were not going to allow it. A woman's dignity begins in the tiniest pore of the skin that covers her body from the instant she is born. And knowing how and why solidarity among women in this country called Spain finally awoke from the lethargy in which it had lain since they'd joined together in 1930 to fight for the right to vote, which was finally won in 1931.

From social media to an e-mail that called for all Spanish women filmmakers from every clique and corner to join together to film the daring feat of these Comadres. They were going to catch a train. Arrive in Madrid. March on Congress, where men and women representatives meet. Deliver to Spanish politicians a manifesto that would awaken their consciences. They were going to speak up, with the voice of women who exercise their right to be first-class citizens, citizens who do not need to be told how to lead their lives or their reproductive rights.

This daring move came to be known as "el Tren de la Libertad" (the Freedom Train). A train that would leave Gijón (Asturias) and arrive in Madrid. The cry would be unanimous and consist of just two words echoed on thousands of homemade signs: *Yo decido* (I decide).

And the Freedom Train multiplied, departing not only from Gijón but also from Barcelona, Valencia, Sevilla, San Sebastián, La Coruña, Cuenca . . . Thousands of people, mostly women but also men—fathers, husbands, friends, boyfriends, partners—got on planes and buses. And there were caravans of cars as well. And for all of them, the destination was Madrid, on Saturday, February 1, 2014, to share the same hour, share the same cry. A huge demonstration had just been born, and as women filmmakers we felt the need to cry out as we know how to do, using the tools of our craft so that this daring action would transcend, reach every corner of the planet. We were and are *grabajadoras*.[1]

The Trains Revved Their Engines

Two weeks earlier, on a Monday that was not like any other, they'd met in La Corsetería. A physical place, an old corset factory (that garment that held voluptuous female flesh in place but also oppressed and shaped women's bodies to the taste of men), which is now home to the Asociación Nuevo Teatro Fronterizo (Association of the New Borderland Theater) and the Scriptwriting School of Madrid. It was dawn in Tirso de Molina Square, home of La Corsetería. The streets had just been washed down by municipal cleaners, leaving the sidewalks damp. In the square, flower shops were opening their doors and the cobblestones were covered with bright colors and the smell of ozone.

La Corsetería smelled of strong coffee, black tea, pitchers of water, and mixed nuts that the group of women filmmakers sipped and nibbled on during their meeting. The task was to create a documentary that would follow *las Comadres* to Congress. There were scarcely ten or fifteen of us, but everyone was represented there. The tribe of women sat in a circle. One of them—I no longer remember who—read the e-mails expressing support. In just a few seconds, the fifteen of us were sixty. Not one negative response. All the e-mails expressed support and asked for guidelines on how to proceed.

We organized teams. In one group, screenwriters; in another, editors; directors in a third group; and producers in a fourth constituting the largest group, which included directors of production, assistants, executive producers, heads of production, distribution, and publicity. The four group leaders discussed how to give shape to the idea of a documentary on the Freedom Train.

The producers demanded a script: "Without a script, we can't organize the production." The scriptwriters turned on their computers and began to write, brainstorming everything the group suggested. The editors joined in. Someone said, "From indignation to a final, unanimous shout." We now had the original idea we could begin to develop. We would capture the departure from every point in Spain, women boarding trains and buses at dawn. We would film them arriving at train and bus stations, airports, wherever groups of women were to arrive. We would capture the formation of the demonstration. But we would also need to know and show what was happening before they left for Madrid, go and film what was happening in other cities. And lots was happening. In Barcelona, for instance, dozens of women lined up before dawn at the Commercial Property Registration to register their bodies as private property. In this way, neither the state nor the church could make decisions about them. The officials at the registry offices were overwhelmed and, not knowing how to proceed, let the women register their bodies.

Another group of very young women rehearsed a performance. Dressed as flight attendants, their plan was to occupy the cars of commuter trains, giving instructions on flight safety and predicting the fundamental rights that would begin to be lost with the repeal of the existing Law of Abortion Rights: "Ladies and gentlemen, fasten your safety belts. Bring your seats to an upright position and close your minds. We remind you that it is forbidden to think, complain, or have an abortion. . . . We will now demonstrate the abortion counterreformation. There are two emergencies exits. The first is back-alley abortion, hanging between life and death. The second consists of leaving Spain to have a safe abortion. The second emergency exit is reserved for first class passengers . . ."

In another city they organized fake travel agencies whose objective was to reactivate abortion flights to London as though they were a weekend romantic package. To cover all of these different activities in the documentary, the group of directors defined their objectives, including where and when to begin filming, not just on the day of the demonstration.

Finally, the scriptwriters came up with something like a plotline that the producers could begin to use to organize the filming before and during the demonstration. To coordinate the complex logistics, the group of directors inquired about the availability of the rest of the producers: Who could begin filming the actions that were already under way? Who would be available at dawn on the day of the demonstration to catch the departures from the stations and arrivals at the Madrid airport? We received word that another gigantic demonstration in support of the Freedom Train was being organized in Paris. And in Edinburgh and Buenos Aires, in Brussels and Rome and a number of other capital cities. The producers sent on their list of instructions. All the women working on the Freedom Train would wear a vest that said "Women Filmmakers with the Freedom Train." Every woman with a camera would be accompanied by a production assistant with release forms for any demonstrators willing to speak on camera. All camerawomen would have sound equipment. For this we had to rely on our sound colleagues. At a key spot in the demonstration, we would set up a table with laptops where all the directors and producers could download their hard drives. Everyone had to film and send their files in Quicktime format, 25 fps in 1920 x 1080 HD 16:9, to facilitate the conversion of data for editing.

The machinery of the documentary began to function. Day after day, solidarity grew on social media and in the working group that wound up consisting of eighty women filmmakers, the majority Spanish but also women of other nationalities who were willing to film demonstrations in cities in their own countries.

As February 1 approached, there was not a single point on the route not covered by a woman with a camera. Award-winning directors, directors with films in production—all of them, without exception, joined the project. At six in the morning before working on their own films, at the places they were able and needed to be. Everything was captured on film. The arrival of French women from Paris in solidarity with all the women of the world, with their ideals clearly in mind in defense of fundamental rights that cannot be taken away; the arrival of women from Andalucía on trains and buses; the arrival of women from Albacete; the arrival of Catalan women on the high-speed AVE train, of women from Valencia, Extremadura, Galicia, the Basque Country, Rioja . . . the arrival of all the women. Do you now understand the term *grabajadoras*?

They called us from Sans Station in Barcelona: "The station security guards are blocking the door; we don't know if they'll let us in." The next call informed us that the security guards were there in solidarity to escort the women to the platform. The first standing ovation, and the sun had not yet risen. The train from Gijón departed with *las Comadres* on board rehearsing a song they intended to sing, and which they did sing—did they ever!—in the demonstration. Today we know that the directors didn't miss a single detail with their cameras on that train. They had been following the women around for several days beforehand, recording the organization of their departure in the florists' shop; they were waiting to join them on the train at the station in Valladolid and to greet them at their arrival in Madrid.

The producers alerted us that the buses were arriving as the sun was rising over Retiro Park. It was early, and it was February in Madrid. You could see the cold in the steam of the words of joy and encouragement. A bright sun began to shine, and Castellana Boulevard was virtually empty of cars, just a few racing across before it was closed to traffic. At Atocha Station, women of all ages, some men, young couples with baby carriages began to arrive. Groups of students from every corner of the country gathered and held up their signs. Many grandmothers stood arm in arm, with their hats and placards. The access ramp to the station was filling with people and clocks had not yet struck eleven, the scheduled arrival time of the train carrying *las Comadres* and many other women from the north of Spain—Basques, Asturians, Leonese . . . "This is so exciting. Someone should film it," a woman was heard saying. "Look up there, and over there. Do you see them? There are seventy women recording it all on their cameras and twenty more filming outside Spain." You could see the vests of the Women Filmmakers with the Freedom Train scattered throughout the throng of protestors.

> *The wind was at our backs,*
> *but they decided to turn it against us*
> *so that the very act of walking would wear us out.*

But exhaustion crouched down on its heels
when the embraces joined
and our feet moved forward.

Atocha Is a Woman's Name

Inside the lobby of the station you could hear the Solfónica (an activist orchestra and chorus) singing the song of welcome.[2] Outside, another group fastened drums to their belts, drums that would welcome *las Comadres* and escort them during the demonstration. Security guards scurried around, organizing us all. *Here they come!!!* someone shouted and hundreds of women crowded the staircase to the platforms. Inside the train there were also producers filming. Outside, on the platform, was another team that would record the arrival and progress of the group up the stairs. But there was not enough room. The train would stop but there was no room to get off the train or go up the stairs. Once more, the producers and their assistants asked all the women filling the platform and lobby to step back and make room for the women coming from northern Spain to get off the train. But we all wanted to see the brave *Comadres* arrive. The train pulled in, and the unanimous cry of "Sí se puede" (yes we can) rose from among the signs reading "Yo decido."

The Solfónica sang its song. The wise women of the tribe climbed the staircase, looks of surprise and emotion on their faces. Flags from the Basque Country and Asturias, from all the autonomous communities, rose in solidarity with a cause: the fundamental rights of women, the right to interrupt pregnancy in safe and sanitary conditions. Never before had so many women shown such solidarity to such a great effect. *Las Comadres*, standing 4'7", crossed the station lobby to the street. Outside, drums began to beat a rhythm of welcome and gratitude. The demonstration had just begun. The crowd had to part so the *Comadres* could move toward the Congress. All streets leading into the Castellana were crowded with people who had come to see this protest against the regressive law. Helicopters began to fly over the area. People sang, danced, passed out food to the demonstrators. Groups of women of all stripes—teachers, doctors, nurses, judges, politicians, clerks, bakers, cashiers, and students—danced with joy and cried out in indignation: "¡Sacad vuestros rosarios de nuestros ovarios!" (Get your rosaries out of our ovaries) and "We give birth, we decide." They chanted, "Let them arrest us, we are feminists, badass and abortionists, we will not stop." Women with cameras perched atop the fence of the botanical garden, climbed onto fountains, leaned out of windows. Any place was fair game for catching the progress of the demonstration as it moved up the boulevard. There was not a single altercation, no obstacle. The organization went like clockwork. *Las Comadres* arrived at the Congress, which was surrounded by the state security forces. They read their manifesto to the multitude. They entered the politicians' chamber. The women filmmakers, cameras in hand, went with them and recorded every instant.

And Success Came the Day After

As the crowd, exhausted and content, feeling that they had lived a historic moment—which it was—gathered their things to leave with the taste of joy and satisfaction in their mouths, the women filmmakers agreed to meet again to start organizing all the material. Now the hard work would begin. Over 200 hours in the required format had to be downloaded onto the computers on which we would begin to edit. Again we had to outline a script and a concept that would sustain a documentary that would be more than a narration of the facts.

We had to review the enormous number of interviews recorded, organize the filmed material by themes, view and catalogue it all. Later we discarded repetitions and edited the material in chronological order. Editing had begun. This part of creating the documentary took five months of work. We had to put down money and borrow space and computers for editing. It was time to shape emotion with reason. Again we met to discuss the topic, what we wanted to tell, what we wanted to make: a newsreel that simply recounted the demonstration, or a documentary that described the origins and ended with the final cry of victory. There were arguments, controversies, ideas that seemed to be the idea and then went the way of the steam from a cup of coffee, but always with laughter and respect. The editing went on, and little by little the snake began to shed its skin and show an ideal face. The footage from outside Spain began to arrive as well. The interviews were disturbing and moving. There was a great deal of material, too much, and most of it very good. Choosing would be an uncomfortable task.

Toward the end of June, the documentary seemed to be complete. A number of film festivals began to request it. We decided to pick a date to open it in theaters. But solidarity will often trip you up, and the night before the premiere we learned that the widow of the man who'd composed the music of the song *las Comadres* had sung on the train had decided not to grant us the rights. We found a talented and generous composer who wrote music overnight that went with the lyrics. And again we had to return to the editing table to mix the sound with the new melody.

I Decide on the Screen

July 10 was another critical day. Word of the theatrical release spread as though it was a call for another demonstration. *Las Comadres* returned to Madrid from Gijón to recount their memories of the demonstration. The premiere was organized to take place at the same time simultaneously in a number of cities throughout Spain. This time the women in charge of distribution and communication rolled up their sleeves and the machinery of solidarity went into action. Once again the cries of "Yo decido" and "Sí se puede" rang out in dozens of theaters and lobbies. The theaters were packed. And finally the screen lit up with the documentary, *Yo Decido: El Tren de la Libertad* (I Decide: The Freedom Train), which was given to the world in that instant. The press called it "militant cinema."

The same laughter, tears, and chanted slogans heard during the demonstration resounded in the movie theaters. The documentary included archival footage from 1970 that showed a group of Catalan women demonstrating in front of a prison, demanding amnesty for women who had been jailed for having abortions. Indignation swelled again. That handful of courageous women in their twenties and thirties would now be in their sixties. Our *Comadres*, the flower sellers, became indignant at the memory of those days, even though the injustice had been directed not at them but at a handful of Catalan women. The images of those years helped us understand why these women who are now grandmothers had been willing to leave the comfort of their homes on Saturday, February 1, 2014, to go out and reclaim what had been won years before under the blows of Franco's police force.

From that day, the 42-minute documentary *I Decide: The Freedom Train* has been shown at Spanish and international film festivals. It has been screened at forums, assemblies, high schools, universities . . . always introduced by one of the original fifteen women filmmakers, whichever one is willing to ride a train, bus, or airplane to show it. It continues to be in demand today. Since the first time it was shown on July 10, 2014, *I Decide: The Freedom Train* has been accessible for free on the Internet. It can be found on YouTube and Vimeo.[3] Now that nearly three years have passed, I can say that I have never before felt the power of solidarity so intensely. That social movement showed many women filmmakers the tremendous power we have as women and as filmmakers.[4]

NOTES

1. A neologism composed of *grabar*, to record or film, and *trabajadoras* (workers).
2. The Solfónica, a group of musician-activists born out of the 15-M, made its first appearance at Neptune Fountain Square on June 19, 2011, interpreting Beethoven's Ninth Symphony. Since then, they have continued to perform music at protests and mobilizations.
3. Links: *www.eltrendelalibertad.com*; *vimeo.com/99974636*; Facebook: El Tren de la Libertad Film.
4. The Freedom Train's march led Premier Mariano Rajoy to table the reforms in September 2014, forcing the immediate resignation of the Minister of Justice, Alberto Ruiz-Gallardón, who had proposed the radical revisions. At the time of the preparation of this volume, the law is still in the hands of the Constitutional Tribunal. The only modification is in the clause that refers to minors. Now if those women want to claim their right to end pregnancy, it must be with the consent of a parent or guardian.

◆ CHAPTER 9

Madrid Municipal Elections 2015:
A Time of Change

Rosa M. Tristán

The night of May 24, 2015, was a night of change for the city of Madrid. After 24 years under the rule of the Partido Popular (Popular Party, or PP), a leftist candidate emerged in a new social movement. Veteran judge Manuela Carmena (born 1944) was elected to lead the destiny of the capital city for the next four years. A previously unknown coalition called Ahora Madrid (Now Madrid) brought together neighborhood and social platforms, independent personalities, and political parties old and new, among which was Podemos. Leading the charge was Carmena, followed by a groundswell of social activists, young intellectuals, and activists from various leftist parties.

It was cool in Madrid that night, but the Cuesta de Moyano, a street lined with used bookstalls and normally frequented only by day, was a hotbed of people gathered to follow the counting of votes, brought together by the hope that a quarter of a century of the PP in office would end.[1] In fact, many of the thousands who filled the area had known nothing but a conservative mayor in their entire lives, and you could feel in the air the desire to witness the moment firsthand. There were also older people, an indication that messages from Now Madrid had reached a sector that finds it harder to change their vote. Every little while, one of the partners or members of Now Madrid, almost all of them young and wearing jeans and sneakers, came onto the stage that crowned the Cuesta de Moyano to report the latest vote count.

In the end, after a tense wait, the result came at the stroke of 11 p.m.: Now Madrid definitely had won twenty seats in the city council; the PP had gained one, leaving it with a total of twenty-one; the PSOE was in third place with nine (the worst result in its history); and seven went to the newly founded Ciudadanos (Citizens) party, which is defined as centrist but whose economic and social policies are closer to those of the PP than to those of the PSOE. In short, the left added twenty-nine city council members, compared to twenty-eight on the right. The Madrid City Council could change if Now Madrid and the PSOE formed a coalition, and no one doubted that the pact would become a reality. Joy resounded on the street, a few meters from the Atocha train station, while in the PP headquarters windows were closed in order not to hear the rejoicing in the streets as the party leaders began to assess the results that many of them had not been able to foresee.

The Aftermath

Almost a year later, there have been changes in the city—not many, according to some, although the economic situation Now Madrid inherited came burdened with a debt that so far has left little room for maneuvering. Still, Now Madrid has launched major social policies, and neighborhoods in the city have begun to emerge from a long slumber. On the other hand, the lack of experience in some areas of management for those who had never before had the responsibility of running a public institution, which is also the country's largest city government, has been noticeable, disillusioning some and generating tensions within Now Madrid whose consequences remain to be seen. Meanwhile, the mayor, as a lawyer, tries to stay out of the skirmishes and attempts to distance herself from certain positions of Podemos, which has already experienced several major crises, especially since achieving its astonishing sixty-nine deputies in the National Congress in December 2015. As we shall see, Carmena's neutral position and her inclination to recognize and rectify errors is not always understood in her own ranks, where you begin to hear voices calling for greater political commitment from those who were elected.

From Excess to Crisis

What made the conservative parties lose power in a city where they previously ruled for a quarter century? Was it a slow process of attrition, or were there triggers for a turnaround that just a few months before had been unthinkable? Of course, nothing happens overnight. And also, of course, in municipal elections in a capital such as Madrid, many factors, circumstances, and conditions play a role that have little to do with local—but a great deal to do with national—politics. After all, Madrid has been, is, and will continue to be the center stage of the political, economic, and social actions of the country. One indication of the capital importance of Madrid is that previous mayors charged fees to offset the cost of security for street protests organized by citizens from other parts of the country. In 2012 alone, in the depths of Spain's economic crisis, there were more than 2,700 demonstrations in Madrid, with millions of euros spent in cleaning up after them.

Because they are held in the Spanish capital, Madrid elections often reflect national opinion, and voters do not always follow the specific platform of particular candidates or parties. More often they are concerned with larger national issues such as corruption, recession, financial bailouts, and evictions for defaulting on mortgages. There were several factors, however, that made many voters who for years, election after election, had stayed at home, disenchanted with politics, come out to cast their ballots on May 24, 2015. It is significant that Madrid is an aging city where the younger population has been moving to nearby suburbs. The average age in Madrid is 43 years old, and almost 18 percent are over 65. And age influences political positioning: according to the Spanish Center for Sociological Studies, older voters are always inclined to more conservative options such as the PP. That older citizens are more interested in politics and turn out to vote more often than younger ones is nothing new. But it is also true that with the 15-M movement, much of the disaffected youth started coming back to politics, which in the case of Madrid had a direct impact on the results.

With the emergence of the youth vote, a sense arose in Madrid that the PP's days in power were drawing to a close. What happened in Madrid would be a bellwether for the rest of the country. For the PP, losing meant a loss of momentum for the presidential race later in the year; for the PSOE it signified recovering a bastion they'd failed to hold after the death of the mayor Enrique Tierno Galván, a key figure in the transition to democracy after the death of Franco; and for Now Madrid it was the best place to show the rest of Spain that there was another way of doing things.

The last years of the PP's management had not been successful. The visible head of the local government up to the elections had been Ana Botella, who had little in her favor other than being the wife of the powerful former prime minister José María Aznar. Her tenure was marked by a devastating fire, a failed bid for the Olympics, social services that were unable to deal with ever higher levels of poverty, and some errors that sullied the image abroad of a city where tourism is a significant source of income. Another factor that affected the results was the PP's choice of Esperanza Aguirre, former minister and secretary general of the Madrid PP, representing the most conservative and populist element on the Right in her generation, as the replacement for Ana Botella. For the most progressive sector of the electorate, who had historically been less motivated, the possibility that Aguirre might wind up in the mayor's office was an important incentive to turn out and vote. And, of course, an equally important factor was that, for the first time in many years, there was an exciting alternative on the left that was neither of the two traditional options, PSOE and Izquierda Unida (United Left, a coalition that includes the Communist Party), neither of which was able to generate enthusiasm after years of grappling with major problems, not so much for their effectiveness in Madrid, where they had spent many years in the opposition, as for their actions on the national level.

Delving a little deeper into the first of the three factors that made change possible in the Madrid city government on May 24, one could say that Ana Botella's political future was doomed following an incident in a Madrid nightclub on November 12, 2012, in which five teenagers were killed when a Halloween party went awry.[2] Tellingly, Botella had never been elected to office. In fact, she came and left office without any of the locals' approval. She had been appointed to the position in December 2011, three years before the election, to replace her predecessor, also from the PP, Minister of Justice Alberto Ruiz-Gallardón, appointed by Prime Minister Mariano Rajoy when Rajoy came to power. Ruiz-Gallardón left Madrid with a public debt that to this day burdens the city. At the time of the 2015 municipal elections, that debt totaled six billion euros, making Madrid the most indebted of Spain's autonomous regions. That money represents a debt of nearly 2,000 euros per capita for each of the city's just over three million inhabitants.

Madrid's debt stems mainly from the investment of over six billion euros that went to the tunneling of the M-30 beltway that rings the city, on top of which Ruiz-Gallardón built a park. It was a gigantic project that took eight years; one of its outcomes was supposed to be the reduction of environmental pollution, which has not happened. Over the next 30 years, the payment of that debt to the financing entities will generate an expense of one and a half billion euros annually, representing a third of the city's income. The park, named Madrid-River, is spectacular, but many still wonder if it was really necessary to undertake a project of this size. It is true that it began during the economic boom, when expensive public works in Spain were common. In any case, the park was not the only major project of this period: the city government offices also moved to one of Madrid's most emblematic buildings, the Palacio de Cibeles, at a cost of 500 million euros.

But back to Ana Botella. Her second major failure was Madrid's bid for the

Olympic Games of 2020, in which everything indicated that the chances of success were slim. The candidacy cost 11.5 million euros, to which must be added another 500 million in the construction of sports facilities that are currently underutilized. And no, Madrid did not get to host the great sporting event, but Botella's appearance before the Olympic Committee was so embarrassing that nothing could dig her out of that political hole.

This was followed shortly thereafter by a garbage collectors' and street sweepers' strike that left the city buried under heaps of rubbish. The deterioration of public services led to the death of *madrileños* by trees falling on them as a result of careless pruning. Environmental organizations filed complaints about pollution, alleging that the city was manipulating data to avoid having to take action. And the privatization of municipal services aggravated the deterioration of those services and was accompanied by the formation of public companies. One of these was Madrid Destino, which was created to oversee all the museums and public cultural spaces in the city as well as promoting tourism, and whose management was marked by a lack of transparency.

Adding to this failing administration of the city, strongly contested by a growing part of the citizenry, was the unwise choice of Esperanza Aguirre as a mayoral candidate. Aguirre had previously been a minister, president of the Senate, and president of the Autonomous Community of Madrid for nearly a decade (2003–2012). During this last period she had privatized the management of a large number of health, education, and social services. During the real estate boom, construction companies and investment funds built nine hospitals, which the Ministry of Health of Madrid then rented for exorbitant prices. Among Aguirre's difficulties were accusations of espionage within her own party; allegations of censorship and manipulation of the news on Madrid's public television station, Telemadrid, by people who worked there; and especially cases of graft involving public officials whom she had put in power, cases that in early 2016 forced her to resign as president of the PP in Madrid. In fact, in 2012 she had already resigned from her post as regional president, citing personal problems for stepping back from politics, although it was known that behind this decision were other reasons she would not reveal—namely, that the economic crisis was causing such outrage among the country's middle class that the popularity of the president of the PP, Mariano Rajoy, was plummeting. And especially because of a number of cases of corruption in which senior party officials were implicated. It was wise to distance herself from them, with whom she had already clashed, with the idea of returning later as an alternative.

Yet she remained a member of the Popular Party, and in December 2014, with the full support of the PP in Madrid, ran as a candidate for mayor of the capital, a proposal that was accepted with the idea that she would be able to hold the fort; in fact, given her prestige among the most conservative sector of the population, it seemed the only safe bet. The PP did not see that Esperanza Aguirre, after thirty-three years devoted to politics, was too closely tied to the party's past, no matter how much she tried to distance herself from the murkier issues. They failed to see that a new right-wing party had emerged, Citizens, which was clean and was going to take away votes.

On the other side stood Now Madrid, a party created to run exclusively in Madrid's municipal elections and introduced to the public just two months prior to the election. It brought together under a single name parties that had some shared history in common as well as new ones. Among the former were United Left, which underwent an internal crisis because of the party leaders' decision to participate in the coalition, and Equo, an environmentalist party created in 2011 that had failed to take off in the previous election. Among the newcomers were Podemos, which had been the surprise in the European parliamentary elections of 2014, and Ganemos, a citizen assembly platform that had been formally presented the previous November and was largely unknown to the Madrid electorate. Once the pact was reached, it was Podemos that proposed to Manuela Carmena that she run as a candidate in the primaries, and it took considerable convincing, although in the end the pressure bore fruit. She won the primaries handily against the other two candidates.

Until then, Carmena (Madrid, 1944) had been known only in progressive social circles; she was one of the few judges in Spain who had always worked to promote human rights and the defense of freedom, but never was lavish in her public appearances. She had left the judiciary in 2010 after working 30 years as a judge. Even during the Franco dictatorship, she was a defender of workers and political prisoners. In fact, she narrowly escaped an armed attack by the extreme right wing in 1977 that resulted in a massacre of labor lawyers in a firm of which she was a founding partner. She escaped purely by chance. In recognition of her work, in 1986 Carmena received the National Award for Human Rights. Moreover, she was a cofounder of Judges for Democracy, an association that brings together the most progressive members of the judiciary.

Though she was 72, an age at which many have already been retired for years, many understood that in choosing Carmena, Podemos wanted to lend solidity to the project by selecting someone who not only had experience in public institutions but was also new to political activity. In addition, it sought to break the generational gap in the party's leadership, all of whom were very young. The idea was to present a candidate with both proven management skills and deep knowledge of state structures; in addition, the former magistrate could win votes in the electoral niche where, according to all the polls, they had very few supporters: those over the age of 65. Yet the challenge was complicated: having never held political office before and spent years outside the judiciary, Carmena was practically unknown. As was her party, Now Madrid. In addition, compared to the traditional parties, PP and PSOE, it lacked the economic resources to invest in the election campaign. Even the other new party, Citizens, had more funding, with support from the private sector.

Now Madrid, however, had no money and did not want to resort to the banks that it denounced for their role in the economic crisis. The solution was to use microcredits from supporters, an initiative that managed to bring in about 160,000 euros. But aside from that small amount of money, the solution arrived spontaneously with the imagination and good will of supporters of change. And so, under the name Madrid Graphic Liberation Movement, a group of artists filled the social media with illustrations, drawings, and even songs in support of the candidate's campaign, a spontaneous social movement that surprised even the Now Madrid team and the candidate herself. Even as the PP paid for advertising on hundreds of taxis, other taxi drivers offered their vehicles free of charge to Carmena. And, as one would expect, social networks echoed every action and statement of the candidate: the *podemitas*, as followers of Podemos are called in some circles, have proven to be experts at working these new communication channels.

In any case, the determining factor in the unknown Manuela Carmena's securing half a million votes in just three months was her projection of the personality of someone who stood out precisely for not being a politician: not screaming slogans at rallies, not using the common language of confrontation, and simply talking sensibly. Her calm and collected style, which did not attack but instead dissected arguments and recognized her opponents' successes, was winning over supporters at a dizzying pace. Esperanza Aguirre was a case in point. Carmena made it clear from the beginning that although she was running for mayor on the Podemos ticket, she was not a member of that party, and she didn't hesitate to publicly express her differences with its leaders on some issues—and still doesn't. In short, she made it clear that she is independent. While it is true that the support of Podemos voters was essential in getting where she is today, the narrow margin of votes also means that either of the other two Now Madrid candidates running in the primary would have found it more difficult to win the municipal elections, despite the growing dissatisfaction with the previous administration. The result was 519,721 votes for Now Madrid, making it the second most voted list, fewer than 50,000 votes behind the PP and ahead of the PSOE. Enough to end a historic period of two-party rule. And enough, with the support of the Socialists, to begin to transform the city that had lived too long without a clear identity.

It is worth recalling some of the key points from Now Madrid's 68-page platform to understand what it was that shifted half a million votes. There was no talk of great works such as the Madrid-Río or the Olympics, or of spectacular urban renovations such as the previous administration's failed City of Justice. The platform focused on social emergence, the end of organizational centralization, and bolstering districts that had lost prominence. Some objectives did not seem easily achievable in a short time.

The first commitment the electoral platform offered was that all possible municipal means and resources would be mobilized to end evictions and ensure alternative accommodations for those forced to leave their homes for defaulting on their mortgages, a dramatic situation that since the beginning of the crisis has affected 25,000 families in Madrid, according to the Platform of People affected by Mortgages (PAH), a group formed to prevent these evictions that has managed to stop hundreds of them by public support in recent years. Now Madrid announced that it would immediately create an anti-eviction office for this purpose. It also promised to guarantee basic supplies of electricity and water in households that could not afford them; provide health care to all people, even if they were immigrants without proper documents; and immediately halt the privatization of public services and outsourcing of municipal services to private companies as well as the sale of public assets.

Other points on the agenda made it clear that Now Madrid's stance was very different from the previous administration's on issues having to do with the control of public money: a citizen audit of public debt would be conducted to detect "black holes" and renegotiate with financial institutions to try to reduce the amount owed; some sales of municipal assets and urbanistic changes would also be reviewed; utilities would be taken back from the multinationals; a municipal-regional public bank would be created to finance social projects, companies, and cooperatives; some advisory positions would be eliminated (Ana Botella had 162 advisers, and her predecessor, Ruiz-Gallardón, had 310); a citizen-based corruption observatory would be created; and free community school breakfasts would be offered to children in need. These measures were only some among many others proposed, which contrasted with the ten terse points on a single page that constituted the other candidate's electoral platform.

In mid-June, after her inauguration as mayor, Carmena began to take the first steps to implement what she had repeatedly insisted was most urgent: stopping the evictions. Actually, the aim was not to eliminate them, as an eviction is authorized by court order after creditors submit complaints of nonpayment, and the city cannot interfere in the process. Instead, Carmena wanted to facilitate mediation between the parties, seek alternative accommodation for those who wound up on the street, and try to negotiate with banks to provide subsidized rentals of apartments that were sitting vacant as a result of these evictions. To this end, she created the Office of Mortgage Brokerage, which within six months, by December 2015, had been involved in 229 eviction processes, getting 84 of them stopped through the negotiation of an agreement between the parties. Also, as she had announced she would, the mayor met with various financial institutions to try to reach agreement on the aforementioned subsidized rentals, with some success on that front. Another social measure instituted in the first few weeks of Carmena's administration was the opening of school cafeterias during the summer so that children of families with fewer resources would be guaranteed one meal a day, given that some NGOs such as Caritas, run by the Catholic church, had warned that the level of malnutrition among children in the city was increasing.

In the first months, it became clear that it was possible to invest in social improvements and at the same time reduce the debt. In fact, by the end of the year this inherited debt (the 6 billion euros mentioned earlier), was reduced by 871 million euros while the debt of the regional government, which after the elections of May 2016 remains in the hands of the PP, has only increased. This evidence counters the argument that left-wing governments generate public debt. Obviously, to raise funds it has been necessary to raise taxes, as reflected in the budgets for 2016: a tax increase for superstores, companies, and even football stadiums, along with a reduction in property taxes on private homes, which had risen so dramatically in recent years.

The problem is that these first steps immediately raised controversy that had little to do with Carmena's administration and have strained the relations between the mayor and the independent groups that support Now Madrid. The conflicts have to do with the actions of some members of the party leadership and the municipal team that took place prior to the Carmena administration's political activity. The public repercussion of these conflicts has much to do, obviously, with the PP opposition, who will not pass up the chance to disparage members of Now Madrid even if they have to rummage in the past to find anything to taint the ruling coalition's reputation. But it is also true that, as a new political initiative, Now Madrid does not have the necessary experience to address such situations effectively, which on several occasions has done a disservice to the image of the new municipal officials.

Let me provide some examples. The first of the controversies, with ample media hype, took place a few days after the installation of the new municipal government: it was learned that four years before the election, one of the new city councilmembers had tweeted a some very unfortunate messages on Twitter. In these tweets, the newly appointed councilmember for culture and sports, Guillermo Zapata (37 years old) made some derisive comments—"dark humor," as he called them—about Jews and the Holocaust as well as about the terrorist attacks.[3] Although initially he apologized and refused to resign, finally he had no choice but to leave this important department, since Manuela Carmena did not support him publicly, although the party did. Zapata, a member of Ganemos, dropped nineteen of the twenty-one city districts he represented in the Municipal Council: Fuencarral-El Pardo and Villaverde. In fact, he later resigned before having the chance to do anything while in public office. Those tweets caused such an uproar that the news reached the pages of the *New York Times* and ended in a lawsuit, which was later dismissed. The messages were certainly objectionable, but in a country where hundreds of public officials were under suspicion of mismanagement of public funds, was what someone had said on a social network several years ago really so important?

Another case with great impact occurred just a few months later, and this time the protagonist was the spokeswoman for the mayor's office, Rita Maestre (27 years old), a member of Podemos. Maestre had participated in a 2011 student protest against a religious shrine in the university. For this, she was denounced and accused of violating religious feelings. The case went to trial when she was already in the city government, so the opposition asked that she be dismissed. A charge was filed, although for an alleged crime that had nothing to do with her management. In this case, she had the support of the mayor. In the end she was ordered to pay a fine of 4,300 euros, to which she has filed a countersuit. In these two cases, which are not unique, it could be concluded that the first lesson that the new Madrid politicians have had to learn is to justify their behavior when they were not public representatives, something that has not happened with new politicians from other parties.

These new politicians have to understand that even as social networks and new technologies are useful tools for achieving power and publicizing politicians' work, they also expose users to constant public scrutiny, as each message and every gesture immediately becomes a trending topic. The same people who up until a few months ago were real activists on Twitter or Facebook have had to lower the verbal intensity of their profiles, avoiding messages that can be used against them or distorted. In addition, they have spent a great deal of energy countering campaigns on traditional media, the press as well as radio and TV, that have had an impact beyond what the acts themselves merit.

It is also true that other municipal interventions have revealed that improvisation or lack of information in politics can play bad tricks. If anything can generate mistrust among citizens, it is the feeling that actions are being taken without a thorough prior analysis and then having to be rolled back. The first few times correcting a decision might even be positive, because in Spain it is a novelty for political representatives to recognize errors in their management. But when these mistakes occur in quick succession, the perception is different. Could it be that there is too much chaos and lack of coordination? Is it due to the inexperience of the team in public administration? Or is it a failure of communication? Perhaps a little of everything. Several of these events have been associated with the field of culture, one of the major areas of municipal management. The new city government wants to give more prominence to the districts that had lost virtually all power during the governments of Alberto Ruiz-Gallardón and Ana Botella, who had attempted to exercise the greatest possible control over the city. Restoring those districts' roles by increasing their budgets has been the formula chosen to support cultural initiatives in the neighborhoods, especially the less favored areas. There are many underused public spaces in neighborhoods, which are to be made available to social and creative groups of the citizens themselves.

Now there are also cultural events that are more general in nature, and some decisions and subsequent corrections regarding them have generated confusion that the opposition has predictably used to launch further negative media campaigns. In this regard, we must mention the inclusion of a puppet show for adults with certain political messages and scenes of violence in the children's programming organized for Carnival in 2016. The complaint was lodged by only one or two parents who took their children to see the puppet show, but it generated a significant crisis at City Hall.

In the face of criticism regarding the content of the puppet theater, the mayor chose not to support the imprisoned puppeteers; in this, she went against everyone else in Now Madrid, who argued that the puppet show was a satirical work, that as such its content was not real, and that the outcry was therefore an attack on freedom of expression. The party simply noted that there had been an "excess of zeal." In the end, the puppeteers ended up in prison for "glorifying terrorism" even though they had been putting on the same work in cities throughout Spain without any problems for months. This kind of difference of opinion between Carmena and members of her party, including Councilor for Culture Celia Mayer, who comes from a squatter cultural movement, is beginning to generate some tensions in a team that does not always understand the mayor's desire to rectify and apologize publicly for issues that others feel should be defended unanimously.

In fact, something similar has happened as a result of the proposal to change some street names related to the Franco regime, which are still in force, as well as some monuments and commemorative plaques. After Councilmember Mayer announced a list of everything that was going to disappear under the Law of Historical Memory, it was found that some of the names were wrong and some wall plaques could not be eliminated. This was another mistake that could have been less serious but again was used to demand Mayer's resignation and led to an uproar in the media. In the end, Carmena apologized and decided to remove the powers over issues of historical memory from Mayer. For many members of Now Madrid, this was another sign of weakness, of falling prey to schemes promoted by the opposition.

All of the above highlights numerous challenges that lie ahead for the new political project in the capital city. Clearly, Now Madrid has won the city government with a mandate to change and renew the spirit of a city that in the 1980s was the cradle of an innovative cultural movement, known as the Movida, a burst of creativity that eventually died out in the '90s and gave way to a nondescript period, one that was marked by major urban projects but nevertheless left the city with no personality. And so it remained until 2011, when the streets filled with indignation and a desire to take another path. But Madrid has a population of almost 3.2 million people; it is too large and unwieldy to turn fully around in a few months. A year later, citizens who do not depend on social services have not noticed major changes under the new city leaders. Of course, now when pollution is excessive and the actual levels are made public, new speed limits are set, which never happened previously unless the smog was so thick you couldn't see. Most of all, you no longer see evicted families with their furniture on the sidewalk, watching in desperation as the police change the locks on their doors.

NOTES

1. The Cuesta de Moyano is the popular name given to the street named Claudio Moyano, known for its secondhand book stalls located next to the gate of the Botanical Garden. It is situated on a hill, hence the Spanish term "cuesta."
2. Following this incident, many irregularities came to light that exposed the collusion between the promoter of the party and Botella's city government. While the tragedy was due to a huge crowd and the subsequent stampede, an investigation revealed that the security services contracted by the municipality had not properly worked, that health services were insufficient, and, moreover, that there had been another unruly street party in the area that the security forces had done nothing about. Despite the distress caused by this event, the mayor continued her vacation at a spa that weekend, a decision that caused her public image to plummet within a matter of hours.
3. The controversial comments were made by Guillermo Zapata via his Twitter account in 2011, crudely making light of the Holocaust, Jews, and Irene Villa, a victim of an ETA attack in which she lost both legs.

CHAPTER 10

Historical Perspectives: From Madrid as *Villa y Corte* to *After Carmena, What?*

Edward Baker

Quite properly, this volume of Hispanic Issues is anchored in the present. My purpose here is to broaden the historical perspective of the collection. I have tried to do this, with all due brevity, in three parts: a consideration of the asymmetries governing Madrid's status as *villa y corte*, city and capital; a discussion of the symbolic resonance of the Puerta del Sol; and, finally, a reply to an unanswerable question: *after Carmena, what?*

Madrid, Villa y Corte

Sometime in the summer of 1561—we don't know exactly when—King Philip II moved the royal court from Toledo to Madrid. Toledo was the imperial center—it had been the site of the Visigoth monarchy and had therefore, over the course of more than a millennium, accumulated abundant symbolic capital—but Philip abandoned it. From his standpoint, it offered him little in the way of advantages. His father, Charles V, had abdicated in Brussels and retired in ill health to Yuste in 1555, placing Spain and its colonies in Philip's hands. The emperor died three years later, in 1558, but he still cast a deep and wide shadow over both Toledo and the young monarch's spirit. In addition, Toledo was Spain's most clerical city, the seat of the Spanish Church. The Cardinal Archbishop, Primate of Spain, wielded enormous political power in what had become one of the wealthiest dioceses in all of Christendom.

Madrid, on the other hand, offered numerous advantages. On the face of it, it wouldn't seem that way. The city had strongly supported the *comuneros*, but forty years had passed since that day, and the fervor had not survived. Madrid was no less centrally located than Toledo, the climate was relatively temperate, the area was heavily wooded and so the hunting was excellent, a matter of great import. It even had what Quevedo later called an "aprendiz de río," an apprentice river, the unnavegable Manzanares, which, along with underground streams, assured that there would be no shortage of water. The Alcázar, which belonged to the royal patrimony, needed work, then more work, and then still more, in a constant refashioning over a period of some 170 years that rendered the 1561 version unrecognizable when, on Christmas Eve of 1734, it fell victim to a fire that consumed it very nearly in its entirety. But, *faute de mieux*, it served in 1561 as the royal residence, the court, and the seat of government until it shared time with Philip IV's Retiro palace beginning in the 1630s. Finally, Madrid as the *caput regni* boasted two determinate absences that were immensely attractive to Philip and that Toledo could not possibly hope to match: no father, no bishop.

But it didn't boast much of a city, and this, too, was to Philip's advantage. His objective was a new monarchy, yet a *ciudad de nueva planta*, a wholly new city to house it, was economically out of the question. Although for Ferdinand and Isabella as well as for the Emperor, it had been recreationally attractive, Madrid had no significant commerce and little in the way of manufacturing or an agricultural hinterland capable of producing much of a surplus. In the kingdom of Castile, it was neither large nor terribly important, and these two characteristics suited Philip, as did the significant imbalance between *villa* and *corte*, city and State. A powerful State, a strictly political capital lacking both a military and an economic presence dominated a weak and relatively unproductive city. Madrid was, however, to become a city of churches and convents: beginning in the last third of the sixteenth century, numerous religious orders began to situate themselves in proximity to State power. By 1656, when the Portuguese cartographer Pedro Texeira made his map *Topographia de la Villa de Madrid* (Topography of the City of Madrid), he listed no fewer than fourteen parish churches and seventy-five monasteries and convents, along with many other religious establishments, and these figures would remain virtually unchanged until the 1830s. We can easily chart the presence of those establishments all the way into the early nineteenth century by consulting maps and guide books. In their pocket-sized *Plano de la villa y corte de Madrid en sesenta y cuatro láminas* (Map of the City and Court of Madrid in Sixty-four Plates) published in the year 1800, Fausto Martínez de la Torre and Josep Asensio list thirty-eight monasteries and thirty-two convents, for a total of seventy. In the second and third editions of

Ramón de Mesonero Romanos's *Manual de Madrid* (Madrid Manual), 1833 and 1835 respectively, that number remained steady. But Martínez de la Torre and Asensio also provide a list of what they regard as public places, no fewer than 131 "Iglesias y otros sitios públicos" (Churches and other public places), a number that includes the seventy monasteries and convents. Twelve of those public places are the Royal Library, City Hall, the bullring, and so on. The rest are religious establishments, 119 in a city that, although its population had grown fivefold but remained within the confines of the *cerca*, the wall that Philip IV had ordered built in 1625 and that remained standing until the 1860s and the beginning of the construction of the *ensanche*, the first expansion. The implantation of the liberal State and Mendizábal's disentailment of 1836 changed the relation of power between Church and State in ways that I cannot possibly discuss within the confines of this text, at the same time that it radically altered the city's morphological order.

Nevertheless, what had been a deep and abiding city/State asymmetry remained in place beyond the third decade of the Restoration and the slow and extremely uneven but real emergence and consolidation of a properly national economy, an evolution that was furthered by the repatriation of capital from the former colonies following the defeat of 1898 at the hands of a new imperial power, the United States, and the enormous accumulation resulting from WWI, when Spanish enterprises furnished goods of all kinds to both sides. The decisive moment when Madrid experienced a wave of modernization and began to overcome the asymmetric relation between city and State was the second decade of the century. In the approximately twenty-five years before the war, that modernizing process had a profound effect on very nearly every facet of Madrid life, beginning with something as basic as population growth. In the second and third decades of the century, there began to be a positive ratio of births to deaths, a result of the processes of modernization in basic education, housing, and health care, even if they were uneven and far less spectacular than the cinema palaces of the Gran Vía and the jazz played in American bars. But all of those phenomena taken together, along with incipient industrialization and the consolidation of a modern intelligentsia and its endeavors, such as the Junta para Ampliación de Estudios, the Residencia de Estudiantes, and a lengthy etcetera, speak to a modernizing process in which the three and a half centuries of asymmetry between city and capital began to break down. But there were limits and they were political. The State model that Cánovas had created beginning in 1875 could not contain Madrid's modernity and failed catastrophically, with fearsome consequences that I discuss in the third part of these remarks.

Until the war, the *casco antiguo*, the old city that constituted the historical center of Madrid, was to a considerable extent an interclass phenomenon typically dominated by vertical zoning, although with areas of horizontal zoning, distinctly working-class neighborhoods, especially in the southern part of the *casco*. The postwar growth and industrialization swallowed up towns in the province and turned them into industrial suburbs that received a vast wave of internal immigration in the first two decades of the dictatorship, prior to and during the exporting of workers and importing of tourists that characterized the development plans of the late 1950s through the early 1970s, until the oil crisis of 1973 cut them short. Postwar Madrid was a city that included immigrant *chabolas*, shantytowns that grew into small cities, suburban communities that played a leading role in the opposition to the dictatorship. At this point in the city's history, the asymmetrical relation of *villa* and *corte* had been replaced by a spatialization of class distinctions in which the proletariat occupied a south that, to a considerable extent but far from completely, lay beyond the city borders. In the final decades of the twentieth century and into the first decade of the twenty-first, until the Great Recession set a new and infinitely destructive limit, those communities received new waves of immigrants, especially from the Maghreb, sub-Saharan Africa, and Latin America. Vastly different people with shared objectives. The bombs of March 11, 2004, made no distinctions.

Why Sol?

The protesters who camped out in the Puerta del Sol on May 15, 2011, the day of Madrid's patron saint, San Isidro, might have chosen any number of symbolically freighted spaces such as the Plaza de Oriente, the Retiro Park, the Plaza de Castilla, and a fairly lengthy etcetera. Why Sol?

To find an answer, we need to go back to the construction of the Plaza Mayor and remind ourselves of its chief functions until the middle of the nineteenth century. When Philip II and his court arrived in Madrid in the summer of 1561, they understood that there was a paucity of space for the representation of State power, for the staging of the Hispanic monarchy's grandeur. The Alcázar was not much to look at in those years, Madrid was a city almost entirely lacking in representational spaces, and the Plaza Mayor served as the initial solution to the problem. Throughout the seventeenth century it was the public stage of both the seigneurial monarchy and the court nobility and the Counter-Reformation Church. In the Plaza Mayor, the blood elite of the Hispanic monarchy was on display. Here bulls were lanced by noble horsemen, criminals both high- and lowborn were executed, heretics were burned, and the monarchy displayed itself. Beginning in the second decade of the seventeenth century, it was Madrid's most symbolically charged space, and it remained so throughout the early modern period and until the middle of the nineteenth century.

In 1812, in the momentary absence of José I, the city government initiated what in succeeding decades was to be a nearly endless series of name changes in the Plaza Mayor, all of which have been faithfully tracked in Luis Miguel Aparisi Laporta's monumental *Toponimia madrileña* (Madrid Toponymy):

> 1812. Constitución of Cádiz. Absence of José I, Plaza de la Constitución
> 1814. Fernando VII returns to Madrid, Plaza Mayor
> 1820–1823. Trienio Liberal, Constitution of Cádiz, Plaza de la Constitución
> 1823. French invasion of 1823, return of Ferdinand VII to absolute power, Plaza Real
> 1833. Death of Ferdinand VII, Plaza de la Constitución
> 1835. Proclamation of the Estatuto Real (1834), Plaza Real
> 1840. Progresista government, Plaza de la Constitución
> 1843. Moderantismo, Plaza Mayor (Aparisi I, 716)

At this point there still was general agreement that the Plaza Mayor was the iconic space where *corte* and *villa*, State and city, met. Through all the changes, there is overwhelming evidence that no one ever called the site anything other than the Plaza Mayor. Still, the dance of the toponyms continued through the Republic of 1873, following which the Restoration finally settled on Plaza de la Constitución. Nonetheless, I have chosen to stop at 1843 because during the *moderado* period there began a shift in which the Puerta del Sol would become the center of the liberal State. Nothing in this shift involved name changes. The key was a political decision based on a territorial value that Spanish liberals shared with the eighteenth-century Bourbons and the twentieth-century fascists—centralism of a kind that in the middle of the nineteenth century was uncompromising. In 1847 the *moderado* government placed the Ministerio de la Gobernación in the Real Casa de Correos, the post office that had been built in Sol in the early years of Charles III's reign. Gobernación was not just any ministry: it was the political ministry *par excellence*, the central nervous system of the liberal State, and it occupied what would become the central point of the centralized capital city of the centralized and radialized nation under the new regime. (During the Franco dictatorship, this privileged position was enshrined as Spain's Kilometer 0.) Still, in the middle of the nineteenth century, Sol was an oblong and not terribly attractive creature.

Until the middle of the nineteenth century, Sol did not really have any strictly political significance, but beginning in the seventeenth century, it became extremely important as a popular venue because it was home to the city's most important *mentidero* (rumor mill), located on *las gradas de san Felipe*, the stairway of the Augustinian convent of San Felipe, between Calle del Correo and Calle Mayor. Before the Real Casa de Correos opened in 1768, the post office was located on Calle del Correo, a short distance from the convent, and letters containing news and rumors were prized and shared at the *mentidero*. Until the slow and very uneven emergence of a more or less periodical press in the middle of the eighteenth century, the *mentideros* were an essential aspect of news production and circulation, along with chapbook ballads and *relaciones de sucesos* (news pamphlets). The combination of mail and rumor mill endowed Sol with a purely popular dimension: an oral culture that had a critical edge to it and that, unlike the printed chapbooks and *relaciones*, was very difficult for the authorities to control.

The presence of Gobernación beginning in 1847 created a tension in Sol between popular and State power; 170 years later, that tension has not dissipated. Sol was the stage for *pronunciamientos* in the nineteenth century; the second Republic was proclaimed on the balcony of Gobernación on April 14, 1931; in our own day, it has almost inevitably been the *terminus ad quem* of countless demonstrations because it resonates with what often is nationwide tension between the State and the people. M-15 chose Sol because for a very long time it has been the central space of that tension.

After Carmena, What?

Fifty years ago and more, it was the question on everyone's mind; in what was probably its most widely circulated iteration, it furnished the title for Santiago Carrillo's pamphlet *Después de Franco, ¿qué?* Today, in Madrid, a not dissimilar question is on everyone's mind: *después de Carmena, ¿qué?* The question is particularly pressing because Carmena regards herself as a *política ocasional*, in effect an accidental politician. She has stated countless times, whenever she is asked and without being asked, that she will not be a candidate in the municipal elections that will take place in Madrid and other Spanish cities in the spring of 2019. So, what comes after Carmena?

Let me state at the outset my belief that Manuela Carmena is one of the few really good things that has happened to Madrid's city government since Pedro Rico was mayor. The Predation Party (PP), specializing in crony capitalism and the privatization of nearly everything within its grasp at ten cents to the euro, savagely misgoverned the city from the moment that José María Álvarez del Manzano assumed the mayoralty in 1991 until nearly a quarter century later, May 2015. At that point Ahora Madrid, a citizens' platform, something both more and less than a political party, won a closely contested victory with the internal support of Podemos and Izquierda Unida and the external support of the PSOE, thus depriving Esperanza Aguirre, the candidate with the plurality of votes, of that high office.

Venues matter. What happened in Madrid in the May 2015 municipal elections also happened, albeit with local variations, in other cities such as Barcelona, Valencia, Zaragoza, and Cádiz as well as in Galicia, where the *mareas* of A Coruña, Ferrol, and Santiago de Compostela won the day. Venues matter, and it is clear that in Spain today, democratic political change can be had, if it is to be had at all, at the municipal level. But because venues matter, the kinds of hard-won electoral agreements reached in the May 2015 municipal elections could not be and were not transferred to the national elections, where the interests and the protagonists presented a very different profile and the electorate responded in noticeably different ways, including massive abstentions by the Left in June 2016. The agreements reached in the run-up to May 2015 came from places, mainly bottom-up social activism, that were at a remove from national party politics, although Podemos aspired to embody both. In the case of Madrid, the ultimate source of those accords was 15-M, a veritable explosion of popular, democratic, and civic values.

At this point we need to backtrack for a moment to a historical consideration. Somewhere around the midpoint of Felipe González's second administration, call it 1987, I began—finally!—to realize that his and the PSOE's political behavior was in many ways similar to that of the two governing parties of the Restoration, Cánovas's conservatives and Sagasta's liberals. In each instance, the reason was essentially the same: the near absence of a civil society. In 1875, Cánovas, based on his political experience inside the *moderado* system of governance and outside the democratic and Republican *sexenio*, sought to eliminate from the political stage both the military on the one hand and the general run of Spaniards, particularly the city dwellers, on the other. This, in a context in which the liberal State was weak and civil society was all but nonexistent. What ensued was the Restoration *partitocracia*, a political arrangement in which, absent a civil society, the elites of the two-party system occupied that gaping void in concert with local and regional networks of political bosses. In 1901 Joaquín Costa described the real, as distinct from the formal, political system with stunning accuracy in *Oligarquía y caciquismo* (Oligarchy and Political Bossism).

The Spain of the second decade of the twentieth century bore relatively little resemblance to the Spain of 1875, and in its complexity and modernity, however relative, the new iteration could not be contained within the institutional corset that Cánovas had devised. The Restoration State failed catastrophically beginning in 1916/1917 and the failure turned very quickly into a full-blown legitimation crisis in which no political institution functioned the way that, at a purely formal level, it was intended to and there was no general agreement regarding who would govern, to what ends, and by what means. In a country whose political arc began on the Right with the Comunión Tradicionalista and ended on the Left with the CNT, what followed was an improvised military dictatorship, an attempt at Republican democracy, a civil war, and forty years of a vocationally homicidal dictatorship that was in love both with itself and with the Counter-Reformation. The dictator died in the early morning hours of November 20, 1975. The denouement of the sixty-year-long legitimation crisis is what we call the Transition.

• • •

All the political questions that the Transition had deferred, everything that the two-party system had suppressed, all that the partitocrats had usurped, came to the surface with the Great Recession of 2008, which hit Spain with hurricane force. What had been deferred and what had been suppressed and what had been partitocratized in three decades of involution can be stated in a single sentence: "No nos representan" (They do not represent us). And if they do not represent us, we have no choice but to represent ourselves. M-15 was that initial act of self-representation that turned Sol into a space of democracy because it had the effect of returning popular sovereignty momentarily to its rightful owners. Nonetheless, everyone there knew that the effect was temporary, that Sol was merely the first battleground in a struggle for citizenship and democracy that had barely begun.

Viewed from the perspective of the Great Recession and 15-M, it is not surprising that in some quarters the Transition is seen as a vast enterprise of political deceit and, worse still, one carried out by prior agreement of the protagonists. This view is one that I understand, but it is not one that I can fully share, for two compelling reasons. First, it leaves out too much, beginning with the real and inescapable relation of forces following the dictator's death. The Right didn't just win the war and the four-decade-long postwar period, it won the Transition as well, and given the relation of forces on the ground, I cannot see how it could have been otherwise. The effacement of the PCE and the ascendance of the PSOE is the fullest expression of that fundamental truth. Second, there is an element of that view of the Transition that seems to me undeniably generational, which inevitably relativizes it. Plainly not everyone in the Sol encampment was under the age of 30, but the generational component was a strong one. The young people's outlook was determined by two basic facts—they were born in democracy and they were born in Europe—and here I cannot avoid personalizing these immensely powerful historical circumstances. Toward the end of the first decade of the new century, in all of my dealings with my students in the Facultad de Ciencias Políticas y Sociales at the Universidad Complutense, what most struck me about their attitudes toward the world they lived in were those two facts. By way of contrast and leaving aside the exiles, who for obvious reasons are a special case, the protagonists of the Transition, the men and women who brought sixty years of legitimation crisis to a close, were for the most part children of war and dictatorship. When those men and women were in their late teens and twenties, democracy was a distant objective to be fought for and Europe was something akin to a rumor. During the Transition they were acutely aware that they, or at least the progressives among them, weren't achieving everything they wished; they were doing what they could and deferring the rest. This doesn't mean that the younger generation's view of the Transition lacks validity; it simply means that their view is in some measure a generational one and thus relativized, whereas their expression of that view tends to be absolute. An example: to speak of the "regime" of 1978 is to assimilate it by means of a rhetorical gesture into the regime of 1939–1975, and *this is a historic untruth of oceanic proportions.*

Let us return to Carmena and the future. As I write this, in the third week of January 2017, no reasonably sane observer would venture a guess regarding the outcome of the municipal elections that will be held in the spring of 2019. On the Right, will Esperanza Aguirre still be with us and will the PP continue both to lose votes and garner the most votes? Will a portion of the Madrid electorate finally tire of waiting for Ciudadanos to turn into the Civilized Right that supposedly it is, and if so, what will those voters do about it? On the Left, Podemos, a political formation that is celebrating its third birthday as I write this, is once again experiencing growing pains, while the PSOE, like so many other European social-democratic parties, is experiencing shrinking pains, all of it acrimoniously, much of it in public and in preparation for their respective party congresses. At the same time there is at the national level a very substantial pocket of left-of-center voters who in last June's general election turned their backs on both the PSOE and Unidos Podemos, the electoral fusion of Izquierda

Unida and Podemos. Nationally, they may add up to a couple of a million potential voters . . . or abstainers, if they believe that the Left has nothing to offer them at the national level but an electoral food fight.

None of this lends itself to predictions, but at the municipal level Ahora Madrid really does intend to be both more and less than a political party, and Carmena's aspiration for it comes down solidly on the side of *more*—that is, her repeatedly stated preference for a broader, deeper, and more inclusive citizens' platform. She expressed this view most recently in a lengthy interview in *Contexto* (99, Nov. 1, 2017), the digital journal of opinion founded by a refugee from *El País*, Miguel Mora. He and Soledad Gallego-Díaz had an extended conversation with the Mayor in which her take on this problem surfaced very quickly.

Contexto: Usted es una alcaldesa independiente apoyada por Podemos, IU, Ahora Madrid y otros grupos municipalistas. ¿Cómo es su relación con Podemos . . . ?

Carmena: Yo no he tenido ninguna relación con Podemos. Desde el primer momento dije que nosotros éramos un grupo de ciudadanos a los que no nos unía una vinculación de partidos sino una relación de ciudadanos.

Contexto: Pero para consolidar el trabajo que hayan hecho tendrá que haber alguien que quiera continuarlo. Y en principio eso sería un partido político, ¿o no?

Carmena: No, yo creo que lo novedoso de nuestro ayuntamiento es que somos conscientes de que nuestra continuidad no va a ser como la de los demás grupos políticos, nosotros no tenemos un partido.

Contexto: Esa coalición que fue Ahora Madrid, ese partido instrumental, ¿va a seguir?

Carmena: Sí o no, ya veremos, no lo sabemos.

Contexto: Si desaparece, ¿cómo van a defender lo hecho durante su mandato?

Carmena: Me parece que tiene que ser una iniciativa más de la sociedad que de nosotros mismos. Nosotros podemos poner encima de la mesa lo que estamos haciendo. . . . A mí me gustaría poder decir a los madrileños "si estáis interesados en que esto continúe, hagamos una gran coalición de ciudadanos." Las coaliciones de ciudadanos, sobre todo en el ámbito municipal, son el futuro.

Contexto: You are an independent mayor supported by Podemos, IU, Ahora Madrid, and other municipal-minded groups. What is your relationship with Podemos?

Carmena: I have had no relationship with Podemos. From the very beginning I said that we were a group of citizens joined not by party membership but by our status as citizens.

Contexto: But to consolidate what you have achieved there will have to be someone who wants to continue it. And in principle that would be a political party, wouldn't it?

Carmena: No, I think what is unique about our city government is that we are aware that our continuity will not be like that of the other political groups, we do not have a party.

Contexto: The coalition that was Ahora Madrid, that instrumental party, will it continue?

Carmena: Maybe yes, maybe no. Let's wait and see, we don't know.

Contexto: If it disappears, how will they defend what has been accomplished under your administration?

Carmena: It seems to me that the initiative has to come more from society than from us. We can put what we've been doing on the table. . . . I would like to be able to say to the *madrileños*, "If you are interested in this continuing, let's put together a great citizen coalition." Citizen coalitions, particularly on the municipal level, are the way of the future.)

Carmena may be right, citizen coalitions may be the future. There is no doubt that in some very important Spanish cities they are at present the privileged agent of democratic change and the construction of civil society. Nonetheless, I cannot help feeling in her words the tug of utopia, a harmonistic belief in spontaneity with Rousseauian overtones. Just in case, the next time I go by San Francisco el Grande, I'll light a candle.

Madrid and the
Traps of Exceptionality

Estrella de Diego and Luis Martín-Estudillo

David Hockney's trip to California, where he "discovered" swimming pools in the early 1960s, can be seen as a paradigmatic example of the power of the gaze to create exoticism from a mundane reality. Pools fascinated the artist, who had rarely encountered them in his native, rainy England. Hockney found in swimming pools a motif through which he could explore stylistic issues and a worldview. Once again, the exotic proved to be in the eyes of the beholder.

Whereas this type of invention (in the word's primitive sense of "discovery") offers an artist the possibility of casting new light on ordinary setting, exoticism has very different implications in other discourses. As scholars, we strive to be cognizant of the power of our own gaze to create exceptionalities, which are the basis of the exotic, and to realize the extent to which we need those exceptions to fit the fantasies we concoct. Exception happens, by definition, in a singular moment in time and space. Then it is subsumed under the flow of time, the movement of people and ideas, and the conventions that regulate life. At the same time, while we reject the "exceptionalist" paradigm, we should make it clear that we understand the discourse of "normality" to be just another trap: both are constructs that respond to interests and illusions. The normality/exceptionality dichotomy is another example of the type of binary thinking that still endures in our disciplines and governs much of our daily lives.

Along these lines, we could state that, for better or worse, Madrid is not "exotic"—and that, at the same time, neither is it "normal." The question here, then, would be why it looked so different to foreign visitors during different periods in history. Recent manifestations of this two-faced discourse, which presents the city within a historical dialectic of order/disorder (or normality/exception), include the 1980s Movida Madrileña and 15-M. These are presented as two periods of unusual intensity that came to define Madrid as a whole beyond the limits of the events' temporal, spatial, and sociological frameworks, according to some observers.

After all, cities are invented spaces: we use written and visual narratives to formulate them as we need them to be. In fact, all cities are texts. Texts that we read, imagine, and interpret. We perceive cities following the hegemonic narrative in which they are inscribed. Are we trapped in that narrative? Or, to put it in other words: can we escape stereotypes? The preexisting textual city may blind us to the plural narratives within each city; a scholarly perspective should take this diversity into consideration, acknowledging that a variety of narratives always share time and space. Of course, scholarly work is inevitably done from a certain point of view. There is no locus of enunciation outside of perspective—what is indispensable is to be aware of the intrinsic limitations that this perspectivism entails and the narratives that it produces.

Narratives tend to be heroic; when one has been exhausted, there arises an urgent need to replace it with another epic narrative. One may say, oversimplifying a much more intricate problem, that in the specific case of Madrid, the narrative function of *brigadistas* in some scholarly discourses about the city was substituted by that of the Movida, and, more recently, the Movida was replaced by 15-M. Fortunately, reality—the city—is much more complex than that.

Besides, those heroic narratives never truly end; they come back to haunt us. This became apparent on the occasion of the 2017 Feria Internacional del Libro de Guadalajara (Mexico). The world's largest Spanish-language literary event invited Madrid to be the guest of honor for its 2017 edition. In response to that honor, Mayor Manuela Carmena proposed that the city be represented by the 15-M spirit in an attempt to highlight the city's recent upsurge of creative energy ("Madrid llevará"). Nevertheless, a closer look at the book fair's program reveals that the everlasting ghost of the Movida is still with us. One of the main events that the Spanish organizers put together to showcase the city was the exhibition *Pongamos que hablo de Madrid* ("Let's say I'm talking about Madrid," a title taken from Joaquín Sabina's popular 1980 song that practically became a generational anthem). Well-known figurative artists from the 1980s related to the Movida (Carlos Alcolea, Luis Gordillo, Ouka Leele, Manolo Quejido, and so forth) had their own exhibit as part of the event in Mexico. The show, according to its official website, "presenta una explosión incontrolada de creación contracorriente que inundó Madrid de luz y alegría en los años 80 con una cultura que podría caracterizarse como un ejemplo singular de postmodernismo vitalista" (presents an uncontrolled explosion of against-the-grain creation that inundated Madrid with light and joy in the 1980s, with a culture that could be characterized as a singular example of postmodern vitalism).

Besides the fact that the exhibition turned again to the familiar tropes of a sun-drenched, jubilant nation as well as to the discourse of exceptionality, it is worth asking why the organizers would again evoke the Movida when the aim allegedly was to present Madrid as a city changed by 15-M. To what extent did 15-M really have an effect on the overall image of the city? Can cities be transformed by a single phenomenon of that nature, as is asserted in the first issue of the latest incarnation of *Ajoblanco*, a "pop underground" magazine previously published in the 1970s and 1980s? Just as, in the Movida-stirred city of the 1980s, it was rather hard to run into the type of fashion-victim cab driver imagined by Pedro Almodóvar and played by Guillermo Montesinos in the 1988 film *Mujeres al borde de un ataque de nervios* (*Women on the Verge of a Nervous Breakdown*), it is now similarly difficult to find unmistakable traces of 15-M spread out across the surface of Madrid.

The city is much more diverse than any of the images of it that have been manufactured for local or foreign consumption. As in all complex cultural phenomena, there is a quotient of imaginary adscription: a few taxi drivers may have dreamed of becoming Almodóvar's character, and nowadays first-time visitors to the Madrid Río area may think that their experience there is the result of 15-M's vision, whereas in fact the recreational and cultural area was the product of the grand-scale initiatives of conservative mayor Alberto Ruiz-Gallardón. It is true that Madrid Río contributes to making the capital a more participatory and inclusive place (although, for some, what it advances is the city's gentrification). The redesigned area tries to overcome the divide created by the Manzanares (a divide, again, founded more strongly on imaginary than on physical reasons, as it has always been an "arroyo aprendiz de río": a stream that is a river's apprentice, as Francisco de Quevedo called it in a celebrated ballad). But it is no less true that the ideals of democratic openness and participation in a modern city cannot be credited exclusively to any specific political party or social movement.

The history of Madrid as a sustainable, embracing place goes back to the creation of the modern city: the royal court attracted people from throughout Spain and from every echelon of society. Madrid became the nation's clearest center of opportunity, traditionally open to people from other parts of the country and, more recently, from other parts of the world, especially Africa and Latin America. This spirit of openness, which could be related to Madrid's citizens' relative lack of attachment to the place, may be one of the main elements that facilitates the commingling of people of different origins in some areas of the city.

In any case, variants of the exceptionality paradigm whose latest manifestation is 15-M, are not new either. Difference was officially promoted for external consumption from the beginning of the tourism industry in the 1920s. The continuities under the Franco regime are clear in the 1960s-era publicity campaigns from Manuel Fraga's Ministry of Information and Tourism, which were based on the slogan "Spain Is Different" (see Fuentes). Nevertheless, those campaigns did not just promote the standard exceptionality of the country: Spain's deactivated orientalism, its exoticism and sun. Even during Franco's time, there was some interest in promoting something close to what we would now call "cultural tourism." It would be interesting to map Madrid within this touristic imaginary. In this respect, one could point to the work of Dutch photographer Cas Oorthuys, whose book *This Is the Heart of Spain* appeared in 1956. Apparently, it was a widely used source of information for Dutch visitors to central Spain. Oorthuys portrayed many different faces of the city, including aspects of modern urbanism and life, with modest skyscrapers and cafés; areas still under construction, such as the surroundings of the Chamartín stadium; and picturesque scenes with livestock occupying the streets.

Notwithstanding Oorthuys's seemingly apolitical, rather than exotic, view of the city, according to the critiques of some politically engaged people, under the Franco regime the city was the center of an aberration within Western Europe. Sometimes the town was equated with the dictatorship, as if the former were a metonymy of the latter. This view tended to overlook the long siege that Madrid suffered during the war in defense of the legitimate Republican government, and the fact that it was one of the last cities to surrender to the Nationalist army. This history seems essential to understanding Franco's own relationship to the city itself and his effort to (re)present it as an emblem of loyalty to his regime. It is no exaggeration to assert that Franco hated Republican Madrid as much as Hitler hated liberal Berlin. In Hitler's case, he built a completely new city to erase the liberal past he reviled so much. Franco, a much more mediocre urbanist but just as willing to stamp his imprint on the city, erected the Arco de la Victoria (Victory Arch) near Moncloa, not far from the wartime battlefront. The arch not only emulated the classic *puertas* (gates) that once circumscribed the city; it also signaled the way to his pharaonic Valle de los Caídos (Valley of the Fallen) and reminded the university community of the regime's surveillance through its positioning right next to the most important college campus in town. Undoubtedly, during the dictatorship, progressive *madrileños* and *madrileñas* suffered repression just as many other liberal-minded citizens in other parts of Spain did—perhaps even more intensely, given the physical proximity of the dictatorship's brutal power.

Later, with the restoration of democracy, Madrid's negative differential status as the capital city of a fascist regime dissipated. Franco had attempted to transform Republican Madrid into the capital of his anachronistic "empire," but that worked only to a very limited degree. As soon as 1979, just four years after the dictator's passing, socialist Enrique Tierno Galván became mayor of Madrid with the support of the Communist Party. Professor Tierno was an uncontested elderly intellectual who was able to congregate a conflicted left around his leadership. With Tierno in power, Madrid came to be portrayed once more as a capital of exception. The Movida was the core of this new exceptionality based on freedom, joie de vivre, and cultural life in a city that demanded to be experienced nonstop under the recently reestablished democracy. Today, Manuela Carmena can be seen as a mayoral figure in the Tierno mold. The parallel between the two periods does not end with the election of the city's main official. If Tierno was iconic for the Movida, Carmena is central to the aftermath of 15-M, a movement that has become a source of inspiration for the local government's cultural policies.

That parallel between the Movida and 15-M reinforces a construct that stresses the city's supposedly exceptional character. This view also places Madrid at a unique crossroads, the juncture of North and South. From our point of view, these traits are not constitutive of an exception, but rather they are the local manifestation of global trends that define almost any large urban center. As is well known, they all display what we could term overlapping peculiarities: features that appear unique to each of those cities but that in fact manifest realities common to most of them.

Problems unfortunately shared by many cities have also had major impacts on Madrid in recent times. Air pollution has been a long-term problem, but the authorities have acted on it only recently, and not effectively enough. Serious cases of political corruption have greatly damaged the credibility of the conservative Partido Popular, which dominated local and regional politics for some two decades. The sheer volume of their criminal practices, with dozens of officials implicated and millions embezzled from public funds, and the party leaders' reluctance to acknowledge the problem and clean up their organization, are shocking. Surprisingly, they have not paid a price at the voting polls. Even so, the successive changes in Madrid's local government during the democratic period have not brought along drastic discontinuities in most policies, as is the case in most major Western capitals. As in other cities large and small, big plans have sometimes succeeded (such as the Madrid Río project, widely seen as an example of neighborhood revitalization) while at other times they have failed, sometimes to the relief of many citizens (such as the bids to host the Olympic Games).

In the meantime, Madrid has managed to exercise a strong power of attraction for initiatives that would be the envy of any world-class capital. One recent example, especially telling in relation to the present volume, is the establishment of a new institution that will serve as a hub for innovative thinking about cities. After carefully considering a number of other exciting locations in Europe and North America, the legendary architect Norman Foster chose Madrid as the home for a new foundation that bears his name. In Foster's words, his choice is "a vibrant city with strong professional and cultural links with our family and with excellent connections and possibilities . . . with a global outreach" (Foster 7). The Norman Foster Foundation has the potential to place Madrid on the map of the main "think-cities" where experts from a variety of disciplines are identifying current and future problems faced by urban centers around the globe.

The foundation opened its doors on June 1, 2017, with an event that brought together international thinkers and practitioners who are working at the forefront of areas such as architecture, urbanism, and engineering, often in integrated ways. The foundation aims to offer responses to the challenges that cities face from a multidisciplinary perspective. One of the issues that Foster stresses as part of the center's mission is the importance of combining fields that are more obviously related to sustainable urban design with others that are not often included in the discussion, most notably history and the arts. This position reveals a profound humanism inherent to Foster's holistic rethinking of shared spaces, as evidenced in his own project (in collaboration with Madrid-based architect Carlos Rubio) for the Prado Museum's Salón de Reinos. At the same time, Foster's vision does not shy away from the connection between the arts and capital—from a point of view that some may perceive as too prosaic or utilitarian, but which has nevertheless fueled myriad cultural developments over history, including many that are clearly critical of the status quo. Maybe that is why Mayor Carmena openly showed her support for this new enterprise to be located in Madrid. The underlying conviction seems to be that culture will attract capital, rather than vice versa. This initiative also opens the door to a discussion about the role of the humanities in shaping a better life for the inhabitants of cities.

In the case of a city like Madrid, whose livable and sustainable character Foster himself emphasized at the forum, good infrastructure for public transportation, an inclusive health system, and so on, is accompanied by a growing network of participatory contemporary art centers. Three cases are particularly relevant: La Casa Encendida (a private initiative of the organization now called the Fundación Montemadrid), Matadero (managed by the city), and Centro de Arte 2 de Mayo (CA2-M) in the nearby city of Móstoles (run by the regional government). La Casa Encendida, in the Lavapiés area, was founded in 2002 (before the neighborhood became fashionable) as a cultural and social center. Its activities include initiatives that range from Patti Smith performances to Spanish language classes for non-native speakers in the area to techno music concerts. Matadero, created in 2006 in the working-class area of Embajadores (also increasingly popular), is very connected to the Madrid Río area. The center, located in a former slaughterhouse of remarkable architecture, has developed a multifaceted program that emphasizes the relationship between the arts and includes an area open to citizen participation. CA2-M has been from its very beginning a catalyst for local participation and cutting-edge art exhibitions. Móstoles, situated to the south of Madrid, originated as a bedroom town, with scarce opportunity for leisure or culture. This fact is one of the reasons the regional government decided to place its art collection away from the capital city. Ever since the 2008 opening of CA2-M, the center has become a magnet for both locals and connoisseurs who come into the city from Madrid, a place where a melting pot gathers: from youngsters going to the movies to senior citizens growing vegetables in its urban garden, and a motley crew of art scenesters and students. The two public institutions were opened by conservative governments, proving that *madrileños* and *madrileñas* have had a steady interest in culture regardless of the candidate they elected to manage their city.

One could say that Madrid, an open, eclectic city—even in its architecture—where any newcomer quickly becomes a local, tends to see culture also as a meeting ground, an additional means for communication. In some of its old popular buildings, such as the *corralas* (communal housing structures with shared bathrooms), now declared an official part of the city's heritage and present mainly in Lavapiés, one can still appreciate the welcoming spirit of the city. Not many years ago, and not too far from the Reina Sofía museum, older neighbors took their chairs outside to the street to enjoy the breeze and chat—forums of their own, in which one could easily imagine that the topics of conversation would include the use and management of that area of the city. Now, similar gatherings take place in Lavapiés plaza, where migrants from Africa and Latin America join in this substratum of civic conviviality. After all, an open city like Madrid is a never-ending conversation between apparently opposite poles.

Strolling south along Madrid Río, the icon of Madrid's sustainable and inclusive future, from San Antonio de la Florida, that little chapel painted by Goya, one will eventually arrive at Matadero. This walk from the classic to the contemporary, in a space of continuities and diversity, embodies the never-ending conversation in which everybody is welcomed as a *madrileño* or *madrileña*. If during our stroll we engage with some of the conversations that assault us from unexpected corners, we may find the antidote for the preconceptions we all harbor when experiencing a city. The imagined city and the desired city can now overlap on the map.

Madrid, June 2017

WORKS CITED

Foster, Norman. "A Personal Reflection." *Norman Foster Foundation*. Madrid: Norman Foster Foundation, 2017. 5–9.

Fuentes Vega, Alicia. *Bienvenido, Mr. Turismo. Cultura visual del* boom *en España*. Madrid: Cátedra, 2017.

Gutiérrez, Bernardo, and Álvaro Minguito. "El Madrid rebelde." *Ajoblanco* 1 (June 2017)

"Madrid llevará a la Feria del Libro de Guadalajara la onda creativa del 15-M." *El Diario Vasco*. June 6, 2017.

Oorthuys, Cas. *This Is the Heart of Spain*. Photographs by Cas Oorthuys. Text by Bert Schierbeek. Oxford: Cassirer, 1956.

◆ CONTRIBUTORS

Edward Baker is an independent scholar who has taught at several American universities as well as the Facultad de Geografía e Historia and the Facultad de Ciencias Políticas y Sociales of the Universidad Complutense de Madrid. He has edited several works on Madrid themes, including Ramón de Mesonero Romanos's *Rápida ojeada sobre el estado de la capital* (1989), and, with Malcolm Compitello, a collection of critical studies, *Madrid de Fortunata a la M-40* (2003). In addition, he has written two books on Madrid literature and culture, *Materiales para escribir Madrid* (1991) and *Madrid cosmopolita: La Gran Vía, 1910–1936* (2009). In other areas of criticism and research, he has written *La lira mecánica. En torno a la prosa de Antonio Machado* (1986), *La biblioteca de don Quijote* (1997), and, along with José Álvarez Junco, Gregorio de la Fuente, and the late Carolyn Boyd, *Las historias de España. Visiones del pasado y construcción de identidad* (2013), volume 12 of the *Historia de España* coordinated by Josep Fontana and Ramón Villares. Most recently he has published a study of prewar Madrid kiosks in *Kiosk Literature: Modernity and Mass Culture* (2017), coordinated by Susan Larson and Jeffrey Zamostny. At present he is working on *Spanish Literature, the History of a Syntagma*, a study of the emergence in the late eighteenth century and the consolidation and institutionalization in the nineteenth and early twentieth centuries of Spain's national literature.

Silvia Bermúdez is professor of Iberian and Latin American studies at the University of California Santa Barbara. Her critical work and teaching focuses on Spanish cultural studies, feminism and women's studies, poetic discourses, politics, and migration studies. She is the author of *Las dinámicas del deseo: subjetividad y lenguaje en la poesía española contemporánea* (1997), *La esfinge de la escritura: La poesía ética de Blanca Varela* (2005), and *Rocking the Boat: Race and Migration in Contemporary Spanish Music* (2018). She coedited the volume *From Stateless Nations to Postnational Spain/De naciones sin estado a la España postnacional* (2002, with Antonio Cortijo Ocaña and Timothy McGovern), and *A New History of Iberian Feminisms* (2018, with Roberta Johnson).

Scott Boehm is an assistant professor of Spanish and global studies at Michigan State University, where he specializes in contemporary Spanish cinema and cultural studies. He is the author of several essays on memory such as "Privatizing Public Memory," "Por una memoria activa," and "Specters of Genocide: Mass Graves, Horror

Film and Impunity in Post-dictatorship Spain." Scott also helped launch the Spanish Civil War Memory Project at UC San Diego and collaborated with the Association for the Recovery of Historical Memory as a Fellow of the Human Rights Center at UC Berkeley. His current research focuses on the intersections of memory, crisis and popular culture.

Malcolm Alan Compitello is a professor of Spanish and head of the Department of Spanish and Portuguese at the University of Arizona, specializing in Hispanic cultural studies and cultural geography. He is the author of numerous studies on contemporary Hispanic topics. His current research focuses on the intersections of cities, culture, and capitalist accumulation in Madrid.

Estrella de Diego is professor of art history at the Universidad Complutense de Madrid. She has been a Fulbright scholar at New York University, where she has also held the King Juan Carlos I Chair of Spanish Culture and Civilization. At the University of Illinois Urbana-Champaign she was Ford Foundation Visiting Professor. In 2012, Professor de Diego was awarded the Gold Medal in Fine Arts, granted by the Spanish government in recognition of her career as a writer and researcher. She has recently been inducted into Spain's Royal Academy of Fine Arts, becoming the third woman to join the institution since it was founded in 1744. Her research focuses on gender and postcolonial studies, identity constructions, visual and cultural studies, and Spanish and Latin American art. Her latest books include *No soy yo: Autobiografía, performance y los nuevos espectadores* (2011) and *Rincones de postales: Turismo y hospitalidad* (2014).

Eli Evans is a lecturer at the University of Massachusetts Dartmouth. He holds a PhD in comparative literature from the University of California, Santa Barbara, an MFA in creative writing from the University of Arizona, and an MA in theory and criticism from the ArtCenter College of Design. He is a frequent contributor to magazines and journals such as *N+1*, *The American Reader*, and *Quimera*; has had work anthologized in *MFA vs. NYC: The Two Cultures of American Fiction;* and has translated work by Juan José Millás and Jaime Rodríguez Zavaleta for publication in English. Recently, his history of the precarious rise of the "post-neoliberal" Spanish political party Podemos was published in *Field Day Review*.

Anthony L. Geist is a professor of Spanish and comparative literature at the University of Washington and the executive director of the UW León Center. His fields of research include the poetics of the Generation of '27, post-Franco poetic production, and cultural manifestations of the Spanish Civil War. Geist is the editor-in-chief of *Poéticas: Revista de Estudios Literarios*. He is the author of twelve books and over fifty articles, including *La poética de la Generación del 27 y las revistas literarias: De la vanguardia al compromiso, They Still Draw Pictures: Children's Art in Wartime from the Spanish Civil War to Kosovo*, and *Otra cara de América: Los brigadistas y su legado de esperanza / Passing the Torch: The Abraham Lincoln Brigade and Its Legacy of Hope*. In 2016 his translation of the Peruvian poet Luis Hernández, *The School of Solitude*, was a finalist for the PEN Prize and was named one of the 100 must-reads of Latin American literature by BookRiot. Geist's current projects include a book on surrealism and the crisis of the Generation of '27 and a translation of Alberti's *Roma, peligro para caminantes*.

Susan Larson is the Charles B. Qualia Professor of Romance Languages at Texas Tech University. Her research and teaching lie at the intersection of Spanish literature, film, and cultural studies and engage with the discourses of modernity that have been at play in Spanish culture since the early twentieth century, paying special attention to the cultural implications of urban planning and architecture. Dr. Larson is the cofounder (with Benjamin Fraser) of the Palgrave-Macmillan Hispanic Urban Studies book series and senior editor of the *Arizona Journal of Hispanic Cultural Studies*. Her books include *Constructing and Resisting Modernity: Madrid 1900–1936* and the coedited collections of essays *Visualizing Spanish Modernity* (with Eva Woods) and *Kiosk Literature: Modernity and Mass Culture* (with Jeffrey Zamostny).

Alicia Luna is an award-winning screenwriter, having received a Goya and Best European Script Award for the screenplay of *Te doy mis ojos* (2004, cowriter). She has also co-written *La vida empieza hoy* (2010), winner of the Critics' Award at the Malaga Film Festival; *Pídele cuentas al rey* (1999), winner of the Audience Award at the Valladolid International Film Festival; and *Sin ti* (2006). Luna has also published two books about tools of screenwriting: *Matad al guionista* and *Nunca mientas a un idiota*. She is the founding director of the Escuela de Guión de Madrid (*www.escueladeguion.es*), where she teaches screenwriting, and also lectures at the Screenwriting Master Program at the Universidad Carlos III. Additionally, she works as a project adviser for several international development programs: Proimágenes (Colombia), Oaxaca Screen Lab (México), Lab Novas Historias (Brasil), and Bolivia Lab (Bolivia). Luna is a frequent contributor to the *Huffington Post (España)*.

Luis Martín-Estudillo is an associate professor at the University of Iowa and the managing editor of Hispanic Issues and Hispanic Issues Online. He has received two fellowship awards from the National Endowment for the Humanities. His books include *La mirada elíptica: El trasfondo barroco de la poesía española contemporánea* (2007) and *The Rise of Euroskepticism: Europe and Its Critics in Spanish Culture* (2018).

Jill Robbins is the former Chair of the Department of Spanish and Portuguese at the University of Texas at Austin and former Dean of the School of Social Sciences, Humanities and Arts at the University of California, Merced. She is the author of two published monographs, *Crossing through Chueca: Lesbian Literary Culture in Queer Madrid* (2011) and *Frames of Referents: The Postmodern Poetry of Guillermo Carnero* (1997); editor of the book *P/Herversions: Critical Studies of Ana Rossetti* (2004); coeditor with Roberta Johnson of *Rethinking Spain from Across the Seas*, a special issue of the journal *Studies in XX/XXI Century Literature* (2006); and coeditor, with Adolfo Campoy-Cubillo, of a special issue of *Transmodernity* about the Western Sahara (2015). She has published numerous articles and book chapters about poetry, film, narrative, celebrity activism, and the book industry. Her forthcoming book, *Poetry and Crisis: Cultural Politics and Citizenship in the Wake of the Madrid Bombings* (University of Toronto Press), was supported by a fellowship from the National Endowment for the Humanities.

Jonathan Snyder is an adjunct professor for the Madrid study abroad programs at ACCENT International, Boston University, and University at Albany, SUNY, specializing in Spanish literary and cultural analysis in urban contexts. He is the author of *Poetics of Opposition in Contemporary Spain: Politics and the Work of Urban Culture* and has published on cultural production (photography, film, performance, literary fanzines) in relation to La Movida, Spain's *Transición* to democracy, and recent social movements. His current research has him reading queer and anarchist fanzines in Spain since the 1990s with an interest in how these underground publications explore themes of emancipation and desire.

Rosa M. Tristán is a journalist specializing in environment issues, human development, and science. For 23 years she worked at the daily newspaper *El Mundo*, covering both local and international news, particularly the science section. In 2012 she was awarded the Doñana National Prize for Journalism for Sustainable Development. In the last 20 years she has become intimately acquainted with Africa, having traveled in 22 different countries on that continent. Currently she collaborates with different print and radio media (*Huffington Post España*, *El País*, the magazine *Ballena Blanca*, Radio Nacional, etc.). She is the communications director for the Alianza por la Solidaridad, an NGO that works in seventeen countries. She is also the communications director for the polar science project Trineo de Viento (whose founding director was the explorer Ramón Larramendi).

INDEX

VOLUMES IN THE HISPANIC ISSUES SERIES